# Never Without Consent

# Never Without Consent

James Bay Crees' Stand
Against Forcible Inclusion
into an Independent Québec

*Grand Council of the
Crees (Eeyou Astchee)*

ECW PRESS

CANADIAN CATALOGUING IN PUBLICATION DATA

Grand Council of the Crees (Eeyou Astchee).
   Never without consent : James Bay Crees stand
against forcible inclusion into an independent Québec

ISBN 1-55022-301-1

1. Cree Indians — Quebec (Province) — Government
relations. 2. Indians of North America — Canada —
Government relations — 1951–   3. Cree Indians —
Quebec (Province) — Legal status, laws, etc.
1. Title.

KE7709.G73 1996   342.714′0872   C96-990056-2

The photographs appearing in the centre section are all reproduced
courtesy of *The Nation*; except the 'Cree and Inuit paddling the Odeyak'
and the 'Cree and Inuit at Earth Day 1992' photos, which are reproduced
courtesy the Grand Council of the Crees (Eeyou Astchee).

Cover design and artwork by Al Pilon.
Imaging by ECW Type & Art, Oakville, Ontario.
Printed by Printcrafters, Inc., Winnipeg, Manitoba.

Distributed in Canada by General Distribution Services,
30 Lesmill Road, Don Mills, Ontario M3B 2T6.

Distributed in the United States by General Distribution Services,
85 River Rock Drive, Suite 202, Buffalo, New York 14207.

Published by ECW PRESS,
2120 Queen Street East, Suite 200,
Toronto, Ontario M4E 1E2.

www.ecw.ca/press

PRINTED AND BOUND IN CANADA

# Contents

# Foreword

## *An impending crisis*

Sometime in the next three years or so, the separatist government of Québec intends to hold another referendum on Québec secession from Canada.

If the "Yes" option gains a simple majority (50 per cent plus one of the vote), the Québec separatists say they will give Canada a brief period — perhaps one year — to negotiate the breakup of the country. If these negotiations fail, the Québec

KING, *THE OTTAWA CITIZEN*

9

National Assembly may proceed with a unilateral declaration of independence or "UDI."

A seceding Québec, the separatists say, would then proceed to establish its own legal system, which would have to compete for authority and legitimacy with existing legal systems under Canadian and Aboriginal law. Confusion and chaos would inevitably result.

As the government of Québec well knows, a UDI is an illegal act. It would violate the Canadian Constitution. It would also violate the fundamental Aboriginal, treaty, and international human rights of the James Bay Crees and other Aboriginal peoples in the province, including our right to self-determination. And it would violate the democratically expressed will of the James Bay Cree people — in our own Cree referendum of October 1995, over 96 per cent of Cree voters rejected being separated from Canada without our consent.

In 1992, the Crees notified the United Nations Commission on Human Rights, and informed the international community at large, that unilateral secession of Québec, imposed on the Cree without our consent in regard to Cree territory, would violate our right to self-determination under international law. Since then, we have continued to make every effort to voice our concerns and to assert our fundamental rights.

The Québec separatists say the new Québec "State" would impose its authority on Aboriginal peoples and any others who may oppose the illegal secession. Such statements sow the seeds of future conflict. Yet, the Cree people have firmly declared that we will use ballots and words, not bullets and war, to resist our forcible inclusion into a sovereign Québec.

We urge the parties to this debate to seek legal, peaceful, respectful, and just means to resolve these issues and to ensure in this context that the fundamental rights of the Aboriginal peoples in this land are not violated or denied.

We are grateful for widespread public support.

# A Message from Grand Chief Matthew Coon Come

## A Message Regarding the Rights of the Crees and Other Aboriginal Peoples in Canada

This book is about the rights of *Eeyouch*, the James Bay Crees.

At least four times — in 1670, 1870, 1898, and 1912 — Eeyou Astchee, our traditional lands and waters, have changed status.

HOGAN, *MONCTON TIMES-TRANSCRIPT*

Our land was somehow transferred between kings as gifts, or deeded between colonial companies and governments, all without our knowledge, and certainly without our consent. It has always been assumed that we, the James Bay Crees, the owners and occupants, simply passed with the land like cattle, without voice, and without the right to determine or even know what was being done with us.

Now, at the dawn of the millennium, although we live in a modern and apparently democratic state, it is being proposed that our people and our territory once again be transferred from sovereign to sovereign, this time from Canada to a newly independent state of Québec.

Although there is now a United Nations, with a Universal Declaration of Human Rights, and a vast array of international human rights instruments that should protect us, a process has been set in motion that would forcibly remove the Crees from Canada, and incorporate us and our lands in this new state.

What is our remedy against this threat to deprive us of our rights, status, and interests — to hand a whole people over — against its democratic will — to another state? What action can we, the Crees, take now to prevent this assault on democracy and human rights?

This book holds part of the answer. Herein we set out our rights as the Cree people, as one of the world's indigenous peoples, as citizens in Canada, as residents in Québec, and as a people with internationally protected human rights. This is a timely call to avoid the unjust repetition of history, and to invoke fairly and democratically the principles of equality and non-discrimination. This is the ultimate circumstance in which the Crees' right to self-determination must be invoked.

In October 1995, one week before the Québec referendum on secession, we Crees held our own referendum. We asked our people if, in the event of a *yes* vote in the Québec vote, they consented as a people to be separated from Canada. Over 96% of the Cree people voted *no*. Other Aboriginal peoples in Québec held similar referendums with similar results.

Although this book has its origins in the possible separation of Québec from Canada, its scope extends far beyond the

Québec referendum into the future of the Crees in Canada as a self-governing people. It explores our rights as a people bound to Canada by a treaty and the land itself, and it examines our right of self-determination as it pertains to our aspirations and our rights to share fairly and equally in the development of our country.

The myth persists in Québec and elsewhere in Canada, that this country consists of two founding nations or peoples, the English and the French. This fiction denies our presence, our rights and status, and our role in the history, economy, and well-being of this country.

Now, as Canada debates once more its own possible renewal or disintegration, many would prefer to conduct this debate without facing the troubling and far-reaching questions regarding our rights as an Aboriginal people. "Solutions" are being proposed that once again exclude us. And some Aboriginal peoples would also prefer to stay in the background and allow the "non-natives" to fight this out among themselves.

For the Crees this is not possible. It is our people and our own land that is being threatened, and the Crees must be heard or we may become the victims of our own silence, passed along with the land.

It will become clear when you read this book that we have been making extensive preparations to defend ourselves. We know our rights, and we can reply strongly to every one of the many false arguments and double standards that have been advanced by those who consider it in their own interest to deny our rights.

This debate will continue in Canada. In this context, there is great need to recognize and respect the rights of the Crees and other Aboriginal peoples in order to advance the well-being of its citizens. To do so will be to strengthen Canada's democracy, its respect for human rights, and its future as a country that includes Aboriginal peoples in its own vision of itself.

That has not yet happened. Perhaps the unity debate, and the examination of Cree rights and status that it brings into focus, will help to bring this about. That is certainly one of our goals, and perhaps a most important reason to read this book.

In any case, this is certain: the Crees will be here. We are not going anywhere. Nothing will be done with us, now, or in the future, without our informed consent.

Grand Chief Matthew Coon Come
Nemaska, Eeyou Astchee — November, 1997

# Eeyouch of Eeyou Astchee

## The Crees of James Bay (Québec)

We Crees of northern Québec (who call ourselves *Eeyouch*) have occupied and used the vast lands around James and Hudson Bays for several millenia. We were there thousands of years before the first Europeans set foot on this continent and have occupied and owned our lands for at least twelve, possibly twenty, times as long as Europeans have lived in Québec. The name of our vast homeland is *Eeyou Astchee*.

We *Eeyouch* have always lived in harmony with our physical environment, and over the millenia, as hunters in the northern forest, have developed, as Mr. Justice Albert Malouf of the Québec Superior Court concluded in 1973, "a unique concept of the land, making use of all its fruits and produce, including all animal life therein." He added that any interference with this way of life compromises our very existence as a people.

Presently, the *Eeyouch*, when not out on the land, live in nine communities: the four inland settlements of Nemaska, Mistissini, Oujé-Bougoumou, and Waswanipi; and the five coastal settlements of Whapmagoostui on Hudson Bay, and Waskaganish, Chisasibi, Wemindji, and Eastmain on James Bay.

The Cree Nation is an organized society and includes about 12,000 people. The Grand Council of the Crees represents us politically; it is a corporation of the Cree Nation, recognized under Canadian law, and has obtained consultative status with the United Nations Economic and Social Council.

# Introduction

*Wherein it is shown that many important questions about Québec secession are off-limits for the public and have not yet been properly considered*

We *Eeyouch* have lived in our vast territories in northern Québec for thousands of years. During these countless generations we have carefully looked after the land and all the creatures that inhabit it. Central to our values has always been the idea of sharing. As an elderly Cree told his nephew when handing down to him custody of the family land,

> You will look after this land, take care of it as a white man would his garden. It is up to you to protect, preserve, make rules where necessary and enforce good hunting practices. You will look after it as I have shown you in the past. You will also look after your people and share what you have on the land.[1]

In that advice from an elder to a young man, one finds the essence of our practices and beliefs as *Eeyouch*: our love of the land, our deep concern to protect it, our assertion of our jurisdiction and control over our traditional territories, and our spirit of sharing. Recounting this story, the younger man commented, "My uncle . . . gave me the land to look after it; he did not sell me the land or ask for anything in return." We

are proud of our stewardship of the land on which we have lived for so long.

We have always thought, too, about the future. "We are not thinking only of ourselves," said Mary Bearskin, a veteran Cree hunter in 1972, "but of all those young kids . . . that have yet to be born."[2]

Over the years we have made many agreements and accommodations with the Euro-Canadians who have come among us, accepting their presence from time to time, aspects of their religions, and sharing our territories with them according to our most cherished principles. But now comes a challenge to our treaty, to Aboriginal and other human rights, and to our deeply held relationship with our land — from a government that insists it is free to change our status without taking into account in any way our decisions on the matter. To put it in blunt terms, the separatist government of Québec intends, if necessary, to kidnap us and our territories. We have decided we won't be kidnapped. We will always insist on the principle of Cree consent.

Since its creation in 1968, the Parti Québécois (PQ) that now forms the government of Québec has been working to have the province secede from Canada and become an independent State. When elected to office in 1994, the PQ immediately set up the mechanism for a unilateral declaration of independence, commonly called a UDI, to take effect within a year of an affirmative majority vote in a provincial referendum.

This book is about the impact that such an event would have on us, the Cree people of northern Québec, the *Eeyouch*.

The Québec people have been consulted twice on this question, in 1980 and in 1995, and have twice rejected separation. On the second occasion, the margin of victory was extremely slim. The campaign brought a new leader, Lucien Bouchard, to the premiership of the province, and he immediately announced that yet another referendum would be held within two years. Later, he has appeared willing to postpone this third referendum for a few years. He now wants Québec to be independent by 2001.

We Crees, in our own referendum in 1995, voted more than 96 per cent against being separated from Canada. Yet in spite of this, the Québec government and its separatist supporters have refused to recognize that we have the same right to self-determination that they claim for themselves.

We have already brought this proposed violation of our rights to the attention of the United Nations. Our Grand Council of the Crees (of *Eeyou Astchee*) is one of only about a dozen Aboriginal organizations in the world to have obtained consultative status at the UN Economic and Social Council. In that capacity we have been active for several years in placing Aboriginal problems in Canada before international opinion, an activity that has ruffled the feathers of governments in Canada. Some separatists have gone so far as to say that in expressing our opinion to an international audience we commit an act of "treason" against Québec. (We deal with this in chapter 11.)

Our view, however, is that an enormous range of topics concerning Québec's proposed secession urgently needs to be more fully discussed within Canada, as well as further afield. The political atmosphere in Québec and other parts of Canada

19

around this subject has been muted and rather strange. We believe the ultra-cautious approach taken by so many federal and provincial leaders — usually for fear of exacerbating the situation — should be replaced by open, honest discussion of the real problems, and this book is a contribution to such discussion.

This book originated in a 1992 submission by our Cree Grand Council to the United Nations Commission on Human Rights in Geneva, an arm of the UN Economic and Social Council. The submission was based on a study by Paul Joffe, a Montréal lawyer who was asked by the Grand Council to examine Québec's possible secession in a manner consistent with Cree perspectives, policies, and positions.

Until our UN submission in 1992, it is fair to say, few non-Crees in Canada had heard much about our detailed legal, political, and social arguments in face of the threat of Québec independence. We take the view that we have firm and inalienable legal and political rights that cannot be simply shoved aside in the drive towards independence. Our position is based not only on Canadian and international law, but on our own laws, customs, and practices.

"What Aboriginal people mean when they talk about their Law," reported an Australian Royal Commission, "is a . . . worldview which is a religious, philosophic, poetic and normative explanation of how the natural, human and supernatural domains work."[3] We can accept that. And we accept too the statement in the draft *United Nations Declaration on the Rights of Indigenous Peoples* that our rights to lands, territories, and resources "derive from political, economic and social structures and from (the) cultures, spiritual traditions, histories and philosophies" of indigenous peoples.[4]

## Crees establish an international presence

Canada has always avoided discussion in the international arena of Québec's proposed secession, but our 1992 Cree submission in Geneva helped to change things dramatically. It brought political developments in Québec to the attention of the international community for almost the first time (with particular emphasis, of course, on the injustice to the Crees implied in Québec's proposed course of action).

When we Crees were faced with the 1995 referendum, we updated and expanded our 1992 submission to the UN into a 494-page book, *Sovereign Injustice: Forcible Inclusion of the James Bay Crees and Cree Territory*,⁵ which we published ourselves. That book examines in even more detail the international literature and practice about the rights of indigenous peoples, with particular emphasis on our treaty rights vis-à-vis Québec secession. We circulated *Sovereign Injustice* extensively to government decision-makers and university libraries worldwide; it attracted considerable attention across North America, earned immediate international respect for the Cree argument, and continues to make an important contribution to the debate about Québec's future.

Because of the separatists' refusal to accept the democratic will of the voters as expressed in the 1995 referendum, the issue remains unsettled. We Crees want our position to be understood by the greatest possible number of people. And so we offer this shorter, updated, and more "user-friendly" version of the case presented in *Sovereign Injustice* to the general public. (Those who want a more detailed explanation of the legal case, including more than 1,400 footnotes and hundreds of references, can consult *Sovereign Injustice*, which is in its third printing and is still available from the Grand Council of the Crees.)

This has been, and still is, an immense effort of public education for a small group of people to undertake. But already many fair-minded people are becoming aware that Québec separatists have a high-handed and arrogant attitude towards the rights of Aboriginal peoples.

Indeed, because of the rigidity of separatist attitudes, it is not too much to say that this issue could turn out to be the Achilles' heel of the Québec independence movement.

One effect of our Cree analysis has been to challenge the separatist pretence that they can secede from Canada using allegedly democratic and legal means, and do so by unilateral decision. Their real intention has thus been flushed out: they now declare that Québec can become a sovereign State by means of a unilateral declaration of independence (UDI) by the Québec National Assembly, following an affirmative majority vote by Quebecers in a provincial referendum. The sole limitation they place on this scenario is that it would happen within a year or so of Québec's making a formal offer of economic and political partnership with Canada.

According to this separatist reasoning, the territorial integrity of Canada is of no consequence, and neither are the rights of Aboriginal peoples (who are, it appears, not even to be consulted about their future). As for our traditional Cree territories, the Québec government claims that the province can separate from Canada with its present borders intact, taking our land *Eeyou Astchee* with them, ignoring our long occupation, management, and control of our huge territory, and regardless of our wishes. This unilateral policy was declared unconstitutional by Québec's Superior Court even before the 1995 referendum took place,[6] and we hope to convince readers that not only is all this clearly illegal under Canadian law, but it has no support in international law, either.

The illegality of its intentions having been thus exposed, the Québec government now argues that constitutional or legal questions are irrelevant, claiming that a simple majority vote would confer on Quebecers a "legitimate" and "democratic" right of secession. The Crees do not agree. Such a course is neither legitimate nor democratic. It places the views of Quebecers above the law and, if carried out, would seriously impinge on the fundamental rights and interests of Aboriginal peoples and non-Aboriginal groups within Québec.

## *Vital questions go unanswered*

It is astounding that so many questions vital to the future of the Crees (and central to the whole debate about secession of Québec from Canada) have been inadequately addressed, or remain completely unanswered by the proponents of Québec independence. Although the independence project is of central concern to everyone living in Canada, discussion of it has been hampered by the creation of a number of taboo subjects — areas of contention that the secessionists have succeeded in making virtually off-limits. Unfortunately, in an atmosphere of nationalist fervour, the press in Québec, like the separatist parties, has tended to equate serious questioning of the separatist agenda with a negative attitude towards Québec itself.

There is no justification for this, certainly as far as we are concerned. How could we be against the territory that Canadians call Québec? We have been here far longer than anyone else. One has only to talk to Cree people to know how we feel about our homeland. "I have true and honest feelings when I hear someone speak of the land, for I can understand them," says Annie Eagle, from our Cree community of Waswanipi. "For years I have depended upon the land as a way of life, it's kept my children from being hungry, as it kept my ancestors alive for many years." In saying that, she speaks for all Crees. Indeed, it is because of these intense feelings for *Eeyou Astchee* that we insist so firmly on discussing, in the most open and profound way possible, the future of our beloved territory. One important context for that future is this proposal to make Québec an independent country. If this were to happen unilaterally, our treaty and Aboriginal and other human rights would be violated. We cannot accept the idea of so many separatists that to discuss what is so fundamental to our way of life can be in any way inflammatory. For us, our lands, resources, and future are not taboo subjects.

This separatist defensiveness, however, has led to some peculiar incidents and a total misreading of Cree intentions. For example, when our Grand Chief Matthew Coon Come announced at a press conference the result of the Crees' 1995 referendum, a journalist asked, "Is this a declaration of war?" Similarly, when we launched *Sovereign Injustice*, someone attending the press conference described it as a "war manifesto." This suggests the extraordinary atmosphere in the province: even when we Crees pursue our aims by exercising all the instruments of democratic debate — books, studies, referendums, for example — as we have done for many years, we are attacked for being belligerent and warlike. It is strange to have to point out that books and democratic votes are the antithesis of war.

Our purpose in this book is to simplify for the reader the complexities of the law, addressing in detail some of the questions that have remained largely undiscussed in Québec and other parts of Canada. We want answers to many unaddressed questions:

1. Can the Parti Québécois government deny Aboriginal peoples their right to self-determination, which includes our right to choose to remain in Canada with our traditional territories and resources?

2. Can Crees, Inuit, and other Aboriginal peoples be forced by the PQ government to self-identify as part of a single "Québec people" for purposes of secession?

3. Do "Quebecers" have the right to self-determination under present circumstances? And if so, would this give them the right to secede from Canada under international law?

4. Even if "Quebecers" were to have the right to secede, which they do not, could they force Aboriginal peoples in Québec to become part of any new Québec State?

5. Can the PQ government credibly claim that Québec secession is based on "legitimacy" and "democracy," when it denies Aboriginal peoples the same rights that it claims for Quebecers?

6. In view of the opposition of Aboriginal peoples and others, could a secessionist Québec achieve "effective control" over all regions currently within the province, without the use of force?

7. Can the PQ government credibly claim that Canada is divisible, but the territory of a secessionist Québec would be indivisible?

8. On what valid basis could a seceding Québec claim the northern regions of the province, the traditional homeland of Crees, Inuit, and other Aboriginal peoples for thousands of years?

9. If Quebecers overwhelmingly choose to secede from Canada, is there any fair and balanced manner — other than partition — of respecting the rights, interests, and wishes of all peoples concerned?

10. Could a secessionist Québec unilaterally alter existing treaties with Aboriginal peoples, signed by Canadian and Québec governments, and approved by their legislatures, confirming a permanent federalist arrangement?

11. Could a secessionist Québec unilaterally take over existing Canadian constitutional obligations to Aboriginal peoples without agreement of the other parties?

12. Is it "democratic" for Québec to secede unilaterally from Canada simply on the basis of a 50 per cent plus one affirmative vote in a referendum?

13. While claiming legitimacy for a 50 per cent plus one vote, can the Québec government credibly deny the results of the 1995 Cree, Inuit, and Innu referendums of October 1995, in which more than 95 per cent of the voters expressed their collective will not to be separated from Canada?

14. Can the PQ government acknowledge, as it has done, that the Crees and other Aboriginals in Québec are "peoples" and "nations," yet credibly declare that their rights are subordinate to those of "Quebecers" in the secession context?

15. Is Québec's proposed independence comparable with recent secessions from the former Soviet Union, Yugoslavia, and Czechoslovakia?

These are just some of the issues that the Québec independence movement has brushed aside in its rush to separate Québec from Canada and that merit greater attention than they have received in all parts of Canada.

The answer to all these questions is "No." Yet the PQ government continues to claim that unilateral secession is based on "democracy" and "legitimacy." This claim, as we will illustrate, is misleading, discriminatory, and false.

# Continuing colonialist attitudes

The root of the Québec separatists' attitudes towards Aboriginal peoples lies in the arrogant colonial perceptions imported with the first settlers 390 years ago. Unfortunately, these attitudes have persisted right up to the present day and have caused profound alienation among Aboriginal peoples. We Crees believe that, if healing is to occur, a first priority should be the correction of these colonialist attitudes. Québec secessionists could start by abandoning their high-handed denial of the status and rights of Aboriginal peoples.

Without an enormous change of this kind, the healing process will inevitably fail. Dr. Erica-Irene Daes, a Greek diplomat, human-rights expert, and chairperson of the UN Working Group on Indigenous Populations, has said that, ". . . for healing to begin, there must be some clear recognition of the legitimacy of the victim's claims to justice. We must acknowledge the wrong that has been done. We must place responsibility where it truly belongs, on the oppressor, and not the victim."[7] We Crees agree with that.

This book is a contribution to the peaceful and, we hope, serious debate that must take place before Québec separatists contravene international, Canadian, and Aboriginal laws, as they seem determined to do. In the Cree view, the Québec programme for secession is a threat to the rule of law, democracy, and fundamental human rights.

The issues addressed here have important international dimensions that people outside Canada should be aware of. If a Québec UDI based on a simple majority vote were to ignore indigenous self-determination and break up the existing State of Canada, the precedent provided could have a profoundly negative impact on international efforts towards peace, stability, and human rights. We wish to reach, among others, those in the international community — the United Nations and its member States, political observers, human rights organizations, the formidable body of interested academics around the world — who are concerned about our Aboriginal status and rights in Québec.

In addition, of course, we address our concerns to fair-minded Canadians from coast-to-coast (including Quebecers, from many of whom we Crees have received continuing support). We are sure that Canadians everywhere wish to hold their governments accountable and to compel them to respect the rights of others.

Finally, the Québec and Canadian governments must fully respect the principle of Cree consent. We have resolved that our people and our traditional territory and resources will not be forcibly included in any seceding Québec "State." Cree self-determination cannot and will not be cast aside. Whether within or outside Canada, no new constitutional arrangements directly affecting us and our future will be possible by Québec — without our consent.

This is the essential message we Crees wish to convey.

# I

# Who and what constitute a "people"?

*Wherein it is shown that Québec separatists deny to others the same rights that they claim for themselves*

The Québec separatists want to establish that there is one people in Québec, and this people has the right to self-determination. The most important part from the perspective of Quebecers, other Canadians, and Aboriginal peoples is this: many sovereignists then claim that such a right gives them the right to secede from Canada.

To put it another way, a short syllogism has been a key part of the logic and foundation of Québec separatism: "We Quebecers are a people. All peoples have the right under international law to self-determination, that is to determine freely their political future. Therefore, we Quebecers have the right to secede from Canada."

The question "Who and what actually constitute a people?" is, therefore, of some importance as some Quebecers actually proceed, on the basis of this logic, to bring about the separation of Québec from Canada.

The separatist arguments produce a constantly moving target: when challenged, they stop talking about self-determination and claim that, in any case, they can secede by a simple declaration of their intention to do so and that this will be internationally accepted as "democratic" and "legitimate."

We Crees of James Bay challenge these assumptions for a wide range of reasons. Let's begin with the question of whether "Quebecers" constitute a "people."

Québec separatists claim that other "peoples" can be included in their independence project without voluntary consent — in other words, forcibly. Many well-informed people believe otherwise. For example, Gordon Robertson, a distinguished retired Canadian civil servant and former holder of the powerful position of secretary of the Privy Council Office, told a commission of the Québec National Assembly in 1992,

> There is no clear principle in international law, and there is no clear definition in any of the United Nations covenants — of which I am aware — that would say there is a right of self-determination by the peoples of Québec as a whole, but no right to self-determination by an Aboriginal people.[1]

The James Bay Crees, having examined this question in detail, do not deny that French Canadians constitute a distinct people (although there is confusion about exactly who is included in this distinct people). But we do deny that a Québec government can compel other distinct peoples, such as we Crees, to identify as part of the "Québec people" for purposes of secession.

Québec separatist concepts about "peoples" and their rights to self-determination are mired in confusion. It is useful to examine these concepts, and these confusions, in more detail.

## Definition of "peoples"

First, what is the definition of a "people" or of "peoples" with a right to self-determination?

There is no single internationally accepted definition of "peoples," even though UN declarations are studded with references to them.[2] The *United Nations Charter* itself, signed in

1945, refers to "peoples" in its very first article, recognizing they have the right to self-determination. So do many international human-rights instruments that have been signed in the last half century. Canada's *Constitution Act, 1982*, refers to the rights of "Aboriginal peoples of Canada" and includes in this term "Indians, Inuit and Métis."[3]

Québec has played a curious game around the question of the status of Aboriginal peoples within the province. The Québec National Assembly in 1985 passed a resolution formally recognizing Aboriginal peoples in Québec as distinct "nations," and not simply as ethnic groups.[4] This resolution was adopted by the National Assembly against the wishes of the Aboriginal peoples in the province, who did not agree with its contents. However, even this recognition is not followed in practice.

For the Québec government, Quebecers constitute a "nation" with the right to self-determination, but no such right belongs to Aboriginal nations. The eleven Aboriginal nations of Québec are often relegated by Québec legislators in the most cavalier fashion to a lower order than English-speaking and French-speaking Canadians. These are the so-called "two founding nations," which, curiously enough, exclude those peoples and nations who had already been here for thousands of years when the two "founding nations" came to this land.[5]

Nor is the separatist Parti Québécois the only political party in Québec that adheres to this double standard. In 1991 the Liberal Party government under Premier Robert Bourassa made unacceptable distinctions between "Quebecers" and "the Amerinds and Inuit" in a piece of legislation called *An Act Respecting the Process for Determining the Political and Constitutional Future of Québec*. This act's preamble said that "Quebecers" were to be "free to assume their own destiny, to determine their political status and to assure their economic, social and cultural development"; but "Amerinds and Inuit" could only "preserve and develop their specific character . . . to assure the progress of their communities."[6] There is a world of difference between a people free "to assume their own destiny" and another free only "to assure the progress of their communities." Any community in the country is free to do that.

# Are "Quebecers" a distinct "people"?

Efforts are being made in contemporary Québec society to transform the French-Canadian nation that is centred in Québec into a more pluralist Québec nation. While this is possible, it certainly does not follow that the whole population of the province comprises a single, distinct people, as the separatists claim. Here we run into a massive contradiction at the very heart of separatist doctrine.

Separatists want to take into independence the entire territory of Québec and all the people who live within it. If they are to pull this off, the notion of being "Québécois" has to be transformed to include not only French-speaking Quebecers, but the many other groups who also inhabit the province — Aboriginal peoples, anglophones, and the so-called "allophones" (those whose mother tongue is not English or French).

"It is not clear to us to whom the term 'Quebecers' refers," Ghislain Picard, vice-chief of the Assembly of First Nations, told the Québec National Assembly's committee on sovereignty in 1992. "Are French-Quebecers and First Nations within Québec part of a single people? If this is your view, it is contrary to our right to self-determination and self-identification."[7] In fact, each of the eleven Aboriginal nations in Québec self-identify as separate and distinct peoples.

Some commentators argue that Québec nationalists are ready and anxious to include non-francophones as real Quebecers.[8] Yet, as even many Quebecers themselves point out, it is common for highly placed nationalists to keep talking in the old, exclusive way.[9] Revealing examples of this crop up frequently. For example, Bloc Québécois[10] MP Phillippe Paré suggested in 1995 that only "old-stock Quebecers" should be allowed to vote in the next referendum on Québec's future.[11] The poet and singer Raymond Lévesque told a National Assembly committee that immigrants should be denied a vote because the issue of independence concerns only the founding (francophone) people of Québec.[12] One Québec jurist even suggested that anglophones might be accorded the right to vote in a referendum, but with different coloured ballots so that they might be distinguished from francophone voters.[13] And everyone is painfully aware that, in his infamous referendum-night speech in October 1995, former Premier Jacques Parizeau used the word "nous," over and over, referring only to French-speaking "old-stock" Quebecers.

From time to time nationalist parties distance themselves from such xenophobic views, but there is much francophone-centred thinking in their own documents and statements that minimize other peoples' status and rights. For example, a Bloc Québécois policy book, edited by the present Premier of Québec, Lucien Bouchard, refers to Canada as containing many nations, including Aboriginal nations, but on another page says that Québec is "one people, one history, one territory."[14] How does he reconcile such disturbingly conflicting views?

Likewise, in an article published a few months before the 1995 referendum in the American journal *Foreign Affairs*, Parizeau referred to the "eleven native nations of Québec."[15] Yet in the same article when he posed the question of how many nations live in Canada, his answer was brusque and unmistakeable: "obviously two." This was no aberration, but very much part of his thinking, as Canadians understood in the 1995 referendum-night speech (referred to above) that sent shocks up and down the land: he blamed the defeat of the separatist option on "money and the ethnic vote." The outcry was intense. He resigned next day.

The Parti Québécois programme of 1994 is quite clear about which Quebecers they have in mind when they propose independence:

Canadians of the seventeenth century, French-Canadians of the eighteenth century and now Québécois, rarely has one seen a people search so long for its identity and yet assume its essence with such persistence. This people is born in America and claims to be of America. It has always been of the French language and has constantly wished to reinforce the base of its culture and the foundation of its solidarity. Francophones of

33

America, it is in this way that Quebecers wish today to register on the list of peoples who shape the global civilization.[16]

To add emphasis, the same programme says that only the Québec government has legitimacy in the eyes of the Québec people and that, "without the French language, the Québec nation would no longer exist." To this, Québec Premier Bouchard added his unmistakeable stamp when he told a receptive student audience in 1997:

> I will remind Quebecers that . . . we are not diluted in the Canadian people. We are not better than the others but we are not like the others. We are not in the Canadian people. . . . There is one Québec people which is distinct by its history, its territory, its official language, which exists, which has aspirations and which has given birth to the sovereignty movement over the past twenty-five years.[17]

These attitudes do not attract many non-francophone adherents to the secessionist camp. Non-francophone Quebecers tend to be wary of the separatists' intentions towards them, for obvious reasons.

In contrast to these views, political columnist Lysiane Gagnon of Montréal's *La Presse* writes that "the base of the independence movement is the idea of a French-Canadian nation concentrated in Québec," the nation being defined as a collectivity with a common history, territory, and will to live together. She comments on the separatist claim that their nationalism is territorial and includes Quebecers of all origins: "The reasoning is politically correct . . . but it does not correspond to the reality. . . ."[18]

Nevertheless, Québec politicians persistently act as if the people who live in Québec are a monolithic whole. For example, the draft report of the National Assembly's Committee on Sovereignty (1991) claimed, "Quebecers have become aware that they form a people, a distinct national collectivity. There is a broad consensus on the composition of the Québec people: a Quebecer is anyone who is domiciled in Québec."[19] For the purposes of self-determination or of separation, this conclusion is not accepted by Crees and many others who live in Québec.

In fact, from the Cree point of view, this insistence on forcing everyone into the single collectivity of a purported "Québec people" appears to be nothing more than a cover for a massive land-grab — the land in question being that of our Cree traditional lands, *Eeyou Astchee*, and other Aboriginal territories in Québec.

## The importance of "common will"

It is not the intention here to deny that the Québec population constitutes a people, since it is up to Quebecers to define themselves. However, one must consider what some separatists leave out of their calculations regarding the question of "common will." In international law the common will of a "people" is essential, and central, to the idea of self-determination.[20] A "people" can, of course, be made up of different ethnic, linguistic, or religious groups, but only if there is a common will among all these groups to live together as a people.

Fernand Dumont, a Laval University sociologist and well-known poet and philosopher, described the situation eloquently in a 1995 book:

> History has shaped a French nation in America; by what sudden decision do you think one can change it to a Québec nation? To define the nation by territorial borders, is to affirm that the state identifies with the nation; a construction of political tacticians that is wholly verbal and perfectly artificial. . . . In any case, anglophones and Aboriginal peoples will not be duped; they will see without difficulty that we wish simply to adopt to our profit a logic that we condemn when it works to our disadvantage. . . . If our fellow English citizens in

Québec do not wish to belong to our nation, if many allophones are loath to the idea, if Aboriginal peoples refuse, can I include them through the magic of vocabulary?[21]

Jean-Pierre Derriennic, a Laval University political scientist and frequent commentator on secession issues, writes:

> It is odious to refuse to others a right that one accords to oneself. If the Québécois have the right to decide that they are a people distinct from the Canadian people, the Amerindians, the Gaspesians, the inhabitants of the west of Montréal or others have an equivalent right. They can decide that they are peoples distinct from the Québec people or that they are not peoples distinct from the Canadian people. . . . It would be totally paradoxical that the right of one group to change its political status entails the right for them to impose on others a change that the latter do not want.[22]

Alain Dubuc, editorial writer of *La Presse*, stated the matter very clearly in October 1994:

> The rigidity of the sovereignists is indefensible on a strict level of logic. They refuse Indians the right to separation which they claim, affirm the integrity of Québec territory while denying that of Canada, affirm that their referendum will be decisive but not that of the Aboriginal peoples. There is here an incoherent double standard which could lead the government to stinging defeats, especially in regard to the Crees, whose case is very solid.[23]

From this it is clear that the Québec separatists are espousing a territorial nationalism that they hope will assure them sovereignty over the whole territory they claim; to the extent that it is a stratagem denying the status and rights of other peoples and ensuring domination by French-speaking Quebecers, it is also an ethnic nationalism. A logician writing in a British publication says that to equate a people (in this case the French-Canadian people) with a State (in this case the geographical territory of Québec) is to confuse categories: "A people is a kind of collectivity, or group of human beings; a State is a kind of governing and administering apparatus."[24]

We Crees agree wholly with the statement by a judge of the International Court of Justice who, in a case about the Western Sahara in 1975, said, "It is for the people to determine the destiny of the territory, and not the territory to determine the destiny of the people." The Court ruled that self-determination can be realized only through "a free and genuine expression of the will of the peoples concerned."[25]

Richard A. Falk, professor of international law at Princeton University, and an internationally known writer on legal issues, told the National Assembly Committee on Sovereignty in 1992: "The territory of Québec, as such, has no right to self-determination. This right inheres in a people, really in the peoples, that live in the territory, and these peoples alone can exercise that right. It cannot be exercised on their behalf."[26]

Yet this is exactly what Québec secessionists are trying to do. Some jurists argue that a "people" must be large enough to be able to form a viable State and that this should be a condition limiting their right to self-determination.[27] But this has been flatly rejected even by the Québec National Assembly's own legal study of the impacts of separation.[28] The numerical smallness of a group entitled to self-determination may serve to limit its practical choices, but cannot nullify its right.[29]

## Cree rights should prevail

The Cree conclusion from all this is that the Québec National Assembly cannot unilaterally decree that a single Québec people will exercise their vote on Québec's collective future. Even Daniel Turp, legal adviser to the separatist Bloc Québécois and since 1997 a federal member of Parliament, told the National

Assembly, "We must ask [the Aboriginal peoples] how they wish to be identified. It is their business, it is their right to self-determination that comes into play here."[30] In the same vein, *Le Devoir* editorial writer Jean-Robert Sansfaçon affirmed that Aboriginal peoples are not Canadians or Quebecers, like others. He said our status as first inhabitants of this country confers rights which require the negotiation of "a new covenant of co-existence."[31]

There is one last point: the right of self-identification of indigenous peoples is, as is now being affirmed under various international instruments, a fundamental aspect of our rights.[32] "Indigenous groups are unquestionably 'peoples' in every political, social, cultural and ethnological meaning of this term," writes Erica-Irene Daes:

> They have their own specific languages, laws, values and traditions; their own long histories as distinct societies and nations; and a unique economic, religious and spiritual relationship with the territories in which they have lived. It is neither logical nor scientific to treat them as the same 'peoples' as their neighbours, who obviously have different languages, histories and cultures.[33]

That passage, explaining the draft *United Nations Declaration on the Rights of Indigenous Peoples*, serves as an excellent description of the contemporary Crees of James Bay, the *Eeyouch* of *Eeyou Astchee*.

As long ago as 1796, the French Declaration of Rights stated: "Each people is independent and sovereign, whatever the number of individuals who compose it and the extent of the territory it occupies. This sovereignty is inalienable." And 121 years later President Woodrow Wilson declared what the Crees believe today: "No people must be forced under a sovereignty under which it does not wish to live."[34]

Our view is that James Bay Crees cannot be compelled to be part of some single Québec people, or peuple Québécois, for purposes of Québec self-determination or secession.

Forcing the Crees' into such a definition of a single Québec people in this way has no basis in law, and seriously detracts from the Parti Québécois' claims to "legitimacy" and "democracy."

This all also brings into serious question a fundamental separatist tenet, namely that there is indeed a single Québec people for the purposes of separation from Canada. The consequences of these and other questions are explored in the following chapters of this book. They will be of great importance to all who live in this land in coming months.

# 2

# Does self-determination include the right to secede?

*Wherein it is shown that under international law secession is considered the last resort of a severely oppressed people (which francophone Quebecers are not)*

According to international legal authorities, the right to self-determination does not include the right to secede from an existing State, unless that State is tyrannical or oppressive towards its inhabitants (or some part of its inhabitants).

It is hard to conclude, notwithstanding the ongoing claims of separatist leaders, that Canada is not oppressive towards Quebecers, and, therefore, that Quebecers do not have the right to secede, at least on these grounds alone.

The concept of self-determination moved to the forefront of public discourse during the Second World War when the Nazi regime of Germany appeared to be overrunning the world. To emphasize the principles of democracy, as against those of tyranny, self-determination was given authority and status in the Atlantic Charter in 1941. The idea then made its way into the founding charter of the United Nations in 1945. At that time everyone was concerned to establish that the war had been fought for freedom everywhere, that a new world would arise from the ashes of the war in which "respect . . . for the self-determination of peoples"[1] would be a central principle.

..HAS THE RIGHT TO SELF-DETERMINATION...

..HAS THE RIGHT TO SHUT DA G＊＊ UP AND DO AS TOLD BY Ⓐ....

TAB, CALGARY

At first the right to self-determination was meant to apply only to people living in colonies and other nonself-governing territories.[2] Applied to such peoples, and only to them, the concept was intended to include a right to secede from a tyrannical or oppressive nation.[3]

Self-determination as an idea has evolved considerably since then. This evolution began almost immediately and has continued to our own day, when it has become a central concept in the draft *United Nations Declaration on the Rights of Indigenous Peoples* that has been proposed for adoption by the General Assembly sometime during this decade.

By 1960, fifteen years after the UN was founded, the General Assembly had adopted unanimously a resolution about independence for colonized peoples, using words which have echoed down to our own times through nearly four decades: "All peoples have the right to self-determination; by virtue of that right they freely determine their political status and freely pursue their economic, social and cultural development."[4]

These words have been adopted, unchanged, in most international covenants signed since then.

The 1960 resolution was considered by most experts in international law to cover only nonself-governing peoples or colonies, not peoples in States that were already independent, such as Canada. These limits have expanded as public opinion around the world has become more sensitive to issues of human rights, and the right to self-determination has become recognized as a universal human right.[5]

On 31 October 1996 in Geneva, the government of Canada formally declared its position on the right of peoples to self-determination:

> ... the question of self-determination is central to the [draft *United Nations Declaration on the Rights of Indigenous Peoples*]. It is a right which is fundamental to the international community. ... As a state party to the UN Charter and the Covenants, Canada is therefore legally and morally committed to the observance and protection of this right. We recognize that this right applies equally to all collectivities, indigenous and non-indigenous, which qualify as peoples under international law.[6]

## The Canadian government's evolving position

Although the government of Canada is a signatory to numerous human-rights instruments recognizing the right of peoples to self-determination, Canada and other nations have been cautious in the past about affirming this right in respect to indigenous peoples. But as noted earlier, Canada has recently adopted a more balanced and fair position, consistent with its international and constitutional obligations.

Late in 1996, the Canadian government accepted for the first time a right of self-determination for all collectivities who qualify as "peoples" under international law. This includes indigenous peoples. Though the news of this change did not make much of a splash in Canada, it was a truly dramatic event for Aboriginal peoples, because we have been insisting for years that we have the right to self-determination. The new Canadian policy was announced in Geneva during discussion of the draft *United Nations Declaration on the Rights of Indigenous Peoples.*[7] Canada's change of heart was warmly welcomed by our Cree representative at the United Nations, Ted Moses.

The Canadian government statement conceded that the right to self-determination is central to the developing draft declaration and formally declared that, as a party to the *United Nations Charter*, Canada is legally and morally committed to observing and protecting this right.

There were many problems with Canada's former attitude. For example, if, as seems likely, Canada opposed the use of the term "peoples" specifically to deny Aboriginal peoples their right of self-determination, this is a form of discrimination prohibited under the *International Convention on the Elimination of All Forms of Racial Discrimination*, to which Canada is a party.[8] (It is worth remarking that during the years that the government was taking a regressive stand in Geneva against Aboriginal self-determination, the governing Progressive Conservative party at its annual meeting recognized "the right of the men and women of Québec to self-determination," and then-Canadian Prime Minister Brian Mulroney described it as "no big deal."[9] For his government, self-determination was good enough for Quebecers, apparently, but not for the Crees.)

In 1970 the UN General Assembly, in a document usually referred to as the *Declaration on Friendly Relations and Cooperation between States*, warned against any action that would "dismember or impair" the territory or political unity of independent States. This declaration was an attempt to strike a balance between the principles of equal rights and self-determination of peoples, on the one hand, and the territorial integrity and national unity of States, on the other. The Declaration provided that only a government that represents the whole people of its territory without distinction as to race, creed, or colour can invoke the principles of national unity and territorial integrity to prevail over a claim for external self-determination (which might, in exceptional circumstances, include secession by part of the nation).[10]

When announcing its recent change of policy, Canada referred to the 1970 Declaration and admitted that the notion of self-determination is expanding to groups living within existing States, but only if it "respects the territorial integrity of States." In his response, Moses said the test is not simply whether a State is sovereign or democratic, but whether it conducts itself in compliance with the principle of equal rights and self-determination of peoples. "We find Canada's statement an encouraging and positive development, reflecting the continued evolution of the understanding of our rights as indigenous peoples," he said. In speaking for the Crees, he obviously had in mind the attitudes of Québec separatists.

Many governments come to mind that discriminate against their own citizens (Iraq, for example, in relation to the Kurds; South Africa in its apartheid days; the military regime of Burma, now called Myanmar, suppressing political expression for tribal peoples). Under international law, governments like these might have to yield to a claim for secession by some of their citizens because of their oppressive or discriminatory actions. But even against immoral governments, many legal experts believe that secession is acceptable only as a last resort in face of severe discrimination and other forms of oppression. In other words, aside from colonized peoples, international law is reluctant to recognize a right, or an act, of secession.

Nevertheless, it is obvious that in some countries a peaceful life cannot be maintained without changes in boundaries. And although international law does not sanction insurrection, there is support for the idea that a people deprived of representative government, or subject to gross discrimination or other serious human-rights violations, is entitled to "external self-determination," including, in extreme cases, secession.

We Crees agree with the many international jurists who hold that self-determination is now a universally accepted human right and that the right of secession arises only in exceptional circumstances.

# Separatists deny our rights

Still, the separatist leaders of the Parti Québécois and Bloc Québécois are unequivocal: they say repeatedly that Aboriginal peoples in Québec have no right to self-determination. For example, Lucien Bouchard, now premier of Québec, in May 1994 when he was leader of the Bloc Québécois in the federal House of Commons, said: "The natives of Québec don't have a right of self-determination. It doesn't belong to them."[11]

That statement is clear enough, certainly, but is it correct? Not all sovereignists agree. Daniel Turp, when legal advisor to the Bloc Québécois, told the Québec National Assembly in 1991 that in his opinion Aboriginal peoples in Québec have "a right to self-determination at the same level as Québec."[12] Later Turp appears to have been muzzled on this issue by Bouchard, then leader of the BQ. (This incident is described in more detail in chapter 11.) The separatists, however, are finding it increasingly difficult to skate around this fundamental question of how they can claim a right for themselves that they deny others.

A host of Canadian authorities not only recognize the right of Canada's Aboriginal peoples to self-determination, but urge that this right should be acknowledged. "It is our assessment," wrote the Aboriginal Justice Inquiry of Manitoba in 1991, "that Aboriginal rights to self-determination must be acknowledged openly and freely by all levels of government. . . ."

University of Toronto law professor and Aboriginal rights expert Patrick Macklem emphasizes that ". . . aboriginal nations have an 'inherent' right to self-determination and self-government, and that this inherent right must find both practical and constitutional recognition by the Canadian state."[13]

Jack Woodward, a British Columbia lawyer and author in Aboriginal law, suggests Canada may have made a commitment to recognize the right for self-determination of the Aboriginal peoples when it signed the international covenants on human rights that we discussed in chapter 1.[14] We believe Canada's recent change of policy was necessary in order for it to be consistent with Canada's international obligations undertaken many years ago.

Many Quebecers have also shown that they disagree with Bouchard. La Commission des droits de la personne du Québec has recommended that the right to self-determination and the political autonomy of the Aboriginal nations "must be explicit in the fundamental laws of Canada and the provinces."[15] And a Québec group called Groupe de Réflexion sur les Institutions et la Citoyenneté has expressed the strong conviction that

> the equality of the right of Aboriginal peoples and the Québec people must be established. Their respective right to self-determination, to freely choose their political status and to assure as freely their economic, social and cultural development must be equally affirmed with conviction and without reservation.[16]

Similar support has been expressed by editorialists, political scientists, and even by some politicians.[17]

Let us repeat: we Crees have never been and are not secessionists. There is no Cree independence movement, and we are not looking to secede in the present context. Actually, we are seeking to retain and strengthen our links with Canada and Québec. We do, however, reserve our right to secede if we are forced into a secessionist Québec.

In that case, we demand that the principle of self-determination will be equally applied to Aboriginal peoples in Québec without discrimination. This aspect of equal treatment without discrimination is of central concern. Legal scholar Russell Barsh, now of the University of Lethbridge and a long-time legal representative of Aboriginal groups to United Nations bodies, has written that indigenous peoples should not have lesser rights than non-indigenous peoples alongside whom they live, simply "by virtue of their indigenousness."[18] And other jurists agree that, in the words of one of them, "so lofty a principle as self-determination [cannot be applied] in a racially discriminatory manner: yes for whites in Québec, no for indigenous peoples throughout Canada."[19]

46

In fact, the blatant double standard applied by Québec separatists in claiming rights for themselves that they deny Aboriginal peoples has already drawn severely disapproving notice internationally. For example, Rachel Guglielmo, an elections officer with the Organization for Security and Cooperation in Europe, recently wrote: ". . . nationalist Québécois leaders are drawn into implicitly racist arguments to explain why French-speaking residents of Québec have the right to self-determination and secession, while other arguably equally distinct peoples within Québec do not."[20] There can be no double standard in recognizing the rights of Aboriginal peoples to self-determination, and the Crees are widely supported in this conclusion.

A particularly hypocritical and self-serving argument made by Québec separatists is that if the Cree right to self-determination is recognized (in the context of Québec secession) it would open a door through which all Aboriginal peoples in Canada would march, claiming the right to secede. David Cliche, now a minister in the Bouchard government of Québec, said in 1994 that "if the Crees in Québec go their own way, the next will be the natives in British Columbia, and then the Ojibway in northern Ontario, and eventually every native nation on three continents."[21] Bernard Landry, now deputy-premier of Québec, made the same absurd claim in almost identical words, on a nation-wide CBC forum in February 1995.[22]

This is simply scaremongering. The right to self-determination is not synonymous with the right to secede. In our Cree referendum of 1995 we chose not to be separated from Canada, but to maintain our relationship with it. It defies logic that we can now be accused of wanting to break up the country. Landry and Cliche were given a sharp and unequivocal answer by Grand Chief Matthew Coon Come. He told a gathering of the Canadian Club in Toronto a few weeks later:

> It should be clear to everyone by now that we are not separatists. You have never heard about a Cree independence movement, because there is no Cree independence movement. We most certainly have grievances

against the government of Canada. Our relationship is in need of profound reform. But we are not separatists.[23]

## The Crees' right to choose

In the context of a possible Québec secession, we Crees stand squarely on the principle that the status and rights of our people and territory cannot be changed without our consent.

We believe we have the right to choose our own future. Many authorities support our freedom to choose, but perhaps the action of the European Parliament in a 1994 resolution on indigenous peoples indicates how widely accepted it has become. The resolution acknowledges that indigenous peoples have "the right to determine their own destiny by choosing their institutions, their political status and the status of their territory."[24]

Québec separatists keep changing their minds about the basis for their claim to secession. In the early nineties the Québec National Assembly hired five international legal experts to examine aspects of Québec sovereignty. Their report is examined in detail in chapter 14, but here it is sufficient to note that in their opinion the right to self-determination cannot be relied upon by Quebecers as justification for secession.[25] When they realized this, the Québec separatists who had commissioned the study quickly changed their tactics. (Here again we have the constantly moving target!) As we have shown in the previous chapter, they ceased to claim the right to self-determination as sufficient reason for seceding from Canada. (They did not, however, cease their attack on Aboriginal peoples, continuing to claim that the whole country might fragment if Aboriginal self-determination is recognized.)

It is typical of the confusion of the separatist thinkers that in April 1997 they once again returned to asserting their right to self-determination as a basis for secession (keep that target moving!). A Québec Cabinet decision reiterated "that the Québec people is free and able to assume its destiny and its

48

development and it is up to it to determine alone and democratically its political status."[26] Some separatists disagreed.
Turp, for instance, said during the 1997 federal election campaign that Québec secession has evolved from being based on
self-determination into "a very political gesture of a government of Québec."[27]

However confusing the constantly changing separatist attitude towards self-determination may be, there is no doubt that
the recent Canadian change of policy is positive for Aboriginal
peoples. Canada's reluctance in the past to recognize explicitly
this Aboriginal right suggested to many Aboriginal peoples that,
if they were taken out of Canada against their wishes, there
might be no protest from the Canadian government.

Zebedee Nungak, president of the Québec Inuit's Makivik
Corporation, has graphically described the absurdities that
resulted for Aboriginal peoples from denial of their right to
self-determination in past eras. In a speech to the Centre for
Canadian Studies at Johns Hopkins University in December
1996, he said his great-grandfather, whose name was Patsauraaluk, had been born a Rupertslander (in the days when
Rupert's Land was governed by the Hudson's Bay Company),
but woke up one morning in 1870 "as a newly minted citizen
of a jurisdiction called the Northwest Territories" (Rupert's
Land having been sold to Canada). Forty-two years later the
same Patsauraaluk woke up on 1 April 1912 to find himself a
newly minted citizen of the province of Québec, because the
territory had been handed over to the province. "Another
political earthquake," said Nungak, "man-made, that determined the status of my people and my ancestors, who had
absolutely no influence on how that status was determined."

He added, "We have an intractable objection to being ban-
died about once again, against our will, by processes in which
we have absolutely no input . . . the governing authorities
treating us as jurisdictional playthings, and dragging us against
our will, hijacking us, kidnapping us against our will, into a
destination not of our own choosing.

"I have determined by observation," he continued, "that the
rationale for people who embrace Québec independence as an

issue is because their lives seem to be very gloomy and miserable. It is living misery for them in Canada. They are surrounded permanently by humiliation, belittlement, and unfulfilling down-troddenness that Canada, whatever it may do, will never satisfy. And so, I believe, in many ways, we ought to give them a country they may call their own, but restrict it in size to what their ancestors called New France, and do not force other peoples against their will to a political destination that is to us not constructive at all."[28]

Such reasoning infuriates many separatists, turning against them as it does their own spurious argument that life in Canada is unbearable for real Quebecers.

The conclusion must be that the unilateral secession of Québec from Canada would be a fundamental breach in Aboriginal relationships with non-Aboriginal society. Everything would be thrown open. Faced with a Québec attempt to become independent, we would have to exercise our right to choose. We have emphasized many times that secession is of no interest to us, unless we are forcibly deprived of our right not to be separated from Canada, or if a secessionist Québec triggers the disintegration of the federation.

All of this depends on the Québec push for separation, so it is time to consider the secessionist case in more detail. In particular, is unilateral secession justifiable in terms of national and international law?

# 3

# Is Québec
# secession legal?

*Wherein it is shown that separatists realize their*
*project is illegal, but decide to pursue it anyway*

Challenges mounted by Québec lawyer Guy Bertrand, to the
separatist referendum plans in 1995, led to some extraordinary
and dishonest manoeuvring by the Parti Québécois government in the months leading up to the referendum.

The upshot of it all was that the PQ government knew what
it was proposing was illegal, but tried to mislead the electorate
into believing it was legal, or, in any case, that the law did not
matter.

Here is what the PQ government did: in 1994 Québec Premier
Jacques Parizeau introduced a draft bill into the Québec
National Assembly called *An Act Respecting the Sovereignty of
Québec.*[1] This bill purported to bind the National Assembly to
proclaim that "Québec is a sovereign country" within a year or
less following an affirmative vote in a referendum.

Bertrand was one of the founders of the Parti Québécois in
1968 and, at one point, was a candidate for the leadership of
the party, but in more recent years he has abandoned the
separatist option and has become a newborn federalist. It is fair
to say that he was widely denigrated in the Québec media for
his change of opinion. Nevertheless, he decided to challenge in
Québec Superior Court the legality under the Canadian Constitution of Québec's proposed binding referendum.[2] He did

not seek to block Quebecers from voting in a consultative referendum, but to prevent the holding of a referendum whose result could be taken by the PQ government as a binding mandate to establish an independent State.

In the Québec media his action was widely denounced as quixotic. Nevertheless, his challenge was sufficiently pointed that it wrecked the separatist plans. Parizeau, evidently realizing that what he was proposing could never withstand a court challenge, did not even table his draft bill in the National Assembly.

Instead, in an effort to outflank Bertrand, in September 1995 the Premier tabled a different bill (since known as Bill 1), called *An Act Respecting the Future of Québec*.[3] This bill made no reference to a referendum and did not purport to bind the government or legislature to proclaim a UDI following an affirmative vote.

The day after Bill 1 was tabled, Mr. Justice Robert Lesage of Québec Superior Court delivered his verdict on Bertrand's case, and it was a clear rejection of the Québec government's argument. Lesage declared that the process described in the draft bill, which Bertrand had objected to, was indeed "manifestly illegal" and "constitutes a serious threat to the rights and freedoms . . . that are guaranteed by the Canadian Charter. . . ." He said the bill sought to confer on the National Assembly "the power to proclaim that Québec become a sovereign country without having to follow" the formula for amending the Canadian constitution.

Lesage expressed his "astonishment" that the Québec government made no submissions except to ask the court to dismiss Bertrand's motion, on the grounds that the whole proceeding was "outside the jurisdiction of the courts." The government argued that Bertrand was "soliciting the Court's interference in the exercise of the . . . functioning of the National Assembly," apparently in violation of the Assembly's fundamental privileges. But Lesage dismissed this argument on the grounds that the government, and not the National Assembly, was the respondent. He said it was "manifest" that the Québec government was giving itself "a mandate that the Constitution of Canada does not confer on it." This he described as "a repudiation" of the Constitution and a break in the continuity of the legal order.

"The government is going to very great lengths to get its way," wrote the judge. "Using its political authority and public monies, it is seeking to overthrow the constitutional order. The plaintiff (Bertrand) is opposed to this process. The tension that he and other citizens are experiencing can only increase day by day. The threat is a serious one. Similar considerations apply in the case of public order. The harm is irreparable."

Lesage did not move, however, to prevent the proposed referendum, noting that neither the offical opposition in Québec nor the federal government intended to block the referendum, and he preferred that citizens be given the chance to express themselves.[4]

The fact that their UDI strategy was illegal did not persuade the separatist authorities to abandon it; rather they simply announced that they would no longer respect the law. They have since said that, in relation to secession, Canadian law does not apply to the province of Québec (although they are willing to observe other aspects of Canadian law that please them). The principle here seems to be that they believe they can pick and choose which parts of the law they are bound by. They react similarly to the Lesage judgement: although the Québec government had denied the court's jurisdiction, they now said they were quite pleased since they interpreted Lesage's refusal to award an injunction against the coming referendum as a measure of approval of the government's strategy.

Following the referendum, Bertrand revised his case to fit the new facts and returned to Québec Superior Court to face a Québec government motion that his suit be dismissed.[5] Québec challenged the jurisdiction of the court on a number of grounds, saying, variously: that Bertrand's suit interfered with Parliamentary privilege; that the debate was "purely political" and not susceptible to legal decision; that the government's actions were authorized under international law; that the case had become hypothetical because the referendum bill had died on the order paper and consequently there was no case to answer;

and that the French version of the *Constitution Act, 1982,* had not been officially adopted.

The new judge, Mr. Justice Robert Pidgeon, however, did not agree.[6] He did not accept any of the five grounds put forward by Québec for denying the court's jurisdiction, referring the matter back to the judge of first instance for consideration on the merits. In discussing the situation under international law, Judge Pidgeon quoted Professors Henri Brun and Guy Tremblay to the effect that "the Aboriginal peoples of Canada would have better justification to invoke the principles of self-determination than would the people of Québec."[7] Having once again lost in court, the Québec government lawyers, as they had done in Lesage's court, walked out. Once again, Bertrand triumphed.

## Apathetic federal response

That, of course, is not the end of the story. Many individual Canadians, as well as Aboriginal peoples, were dismayed at the complacent and passive reaction of the federal government to these two powerful legal decisions: Canada's government did not take the opportunity offered to rise to the defence of the nation, but seemed more concerned to distance itself from Bertrand.

This continuing complacency of the federal government has encouraged among some Canadians an attitude that fundamentally this whole question is not serious, that when push comes to shove Quebecers will not go ahead with the independence project. In fact, many Canadians assume that through all these years Quebecers have been using the threat of separation simply as a lever to pry more powers for the province out of the federal government.

The close result of the referendum of 30 October 1995, when only a handful of votes stood between the two options, woke up Canadians to the fact that separatist brinkmanship had been carried to the edge of the abyss. Across the country not only

Aboriginal peoples but ordinary Canadian citizens began to develop alternative strategies (which came to be known as Plan B)[8] for standing up to the separatists in Québec and laying down conditions for any future discussions about secession. Under this pressure the federal government finally recognized the need for clarity, and on 30 September 1996 federal Minister of Justice Allan Rock asked the Supreme Court of Canada for a ruling on Québec's right under the Canadian Constitution and international law to secede from Canada. The government posed three questions:

- Under the Canadian Constitution can the National Assembly, legislature, or government of Québec effect the secession of Québec from Canada unilaterally?

- Does international law give the National Assembly, legislature, or government of Québec the right to effect the secession of Québec from Canada unilaterally? In this regard, is there a right of self-determination under international law that would give the National Assembly, legislature, or government of Québec the right to effect the secession of Québec from Canada unilaterally?

- In the event of a conflict between domestic and international law on the right of the National Assembly, legislature, or government of Québec to effect the secession of Québec from Canada, unilaterally, which would take precedence in Canada?[9]

The response of the PQ government was prompt, angry, and predictable. The move to sovereignty is "a political question" that should not be decided by the courts, the separatist leaders said. "The rule of law should never push into the background the will and legitimacy of the Québec people . . . ," said the Bloc Québécois, repeating the assertion that "the Québec people" somehow stand above and beyond the rule of law. "The [Canadian] constitution has been imposed on Québec," said Québec Premier Lucien Bouchard. "It's completely irrelevant and unacceptable to go there (to the Supreme Court)."[10]

More recently two other PQ ministers, Bernard Landry and

Jacques Brassard, have gone so far as to say that not only is Canadian law irrelevant, but so are the international courts. In other words, the separatists have got to this point: they will do what they want, no matter what anyone else says. But from the Cree point of view, how can Canadian and international law be irrelevant to the secession issue? How can this be the case especially when the legal rights of Aboriginal peoples are involved?

Canada's leading constitutional expert, Professor Peter Hogg, of Osgoode Hall Law School at York University, has commented sharply on the Québec government's cavalier attitude to the rule of law. In a speech to an Ottawa conference held by the Canadian Bar Association, he said the idea "that neither Canadian nor international law can stand against the will of a majority of the people of Québec" leads to the conclusion that "no court has any jurisdiction over the process of Québec's access to sovereignty." He described this as "an amazing theory," the more astonishing in that it was pronounced by the provincial Attorney-General, who said that "the only judge and the only jury that can decide the future of the people of Québec are Quebecers themselves."[11]

In their justifications for the separatist option, the reasoning of separatist jurists is remarkable for its lack of rigour or logic. Daniel Turp, a law professor before becoming a Member of Parliament for the Bloc Québécois, has co-produced a draft constitution for a sovereign Québec,[12] in which he has no hesitation in declaring this constitution to be "the supreme law of Québec," a position he apparently does not find contradictory to his party's insistence that Quebecers are above the Constitution of Canada.[13] In a section called "The Rights, Freedoms and Responsibilities of Collectivities," Turp says the existing rights of Aboriginal peoples would be "guaranteed"[14] in a secessionist Québec, a position he is able to advocate at the same time as his party denies that Aboriginal peoples have the right to self-determination.[15] And in the first article of his draft constitution he says that "Québec is the State of all its citizens" and that Quebecers would have "the right to resist whoever would overthrow the democratic regime."[16]

This certainly sounds as if meant to clear the way for the use of force against Aboriginal peoples and others who might resist being forcibly included in the Québec "collectivity."

Turp's "constitution" is, of course, merely a personal document, but his line of thinking encapsulates that of the separatist movement.

## So which law has precedence?

Professor Brun, of Laval University in Québec City (who is usually treated in Québec media as a neutral expert, but was, in fact, a legal adviser to the PQ government during the Bertrand cases), concedes that a unilateral declaration of independence is illegal under the Canadian Constitution. Nearly two years before Rock's reference of the matter to the Supreme Court, Brun told *La Presse* that "Canadian constitutional law does not contemplate the secession of a province. The Supreme Court would have no choice."[17]

But he added that this is "irrelevant" since international law prevails over Canadian domestic law. Brun's opinion, however, is far from the majority opinion among jurists. There is, of course, an assumption that Parliament does not intend to breach international law and also a recognized principle that Canadian law should be interpreted consistently, as far as possible, with international law.[18] But aside from colonized peoples, international law does not oblige States to recognize the demands of secessionist groups beyond protecting human rights, being fully representative, and not discriminating on such grounds as race, creed, or colour.[19] Canada observes these rights in its behaviour towards francophones and other Quebecers.

Even Professor Brun does not argue that international law recognizes the legal right for Quebecers or the province of Québec to secede, but only that Québec can become independent if it can establish "effective control" over its territory and thus gain international recognition. He told *La Presse* that on the day after an affirmative referendum vote for independence "it is essentially the effectivity of matters which will be at play."[20] And what would matter most would be recognition of an independent Québec by the superpowers and the UN.

It is a most implausible scenario that on the day after a referendum Québec will have established "effective control" over the whole of its claimed territory, or have attained international recognition by the UN or other States. As described in more detail in chapter 4, "effective control" can take years to achieve, is usually only achieved in the absence of agreement through the use of force, and without "effective control" international recognition of a secessionist Québec "State" is most unlikely. If a PQ government ever proclaims a UDI and tries to forcibly include Aboriginal territories, one should not be too quick to assume that "effective control" will be achieved by the separatists over Cree and other Aboriginal traditional territories.

It is wishful thinking by Québec separatists to dismiss the Supreme Court of Canada as irrelevant. Canadian constitutional law would continue to apply in Québec until the seceding "State" was able to demonstrate control of the whole territory it claims. Malcolm Shaw, one of the five experts hired to examine these questions by the Québec National Assembly, makes this clear: ". . . apart from recognized colonial situations there is no right of self-determination applicable to independent States that would justify resort to secession. There is, of course, no international legal duty to refrain from secession attempts: the situation remains subject to the domestic law."[21] He adds that only when such a secession has proven successful do the concepts of recognition and the appropriate criteria of statehood become relevant. Further, McGill University professor of constitutional law Stephen Scott has advised the National Assembly that the provinces are created by the Constitution which attributes to them their powers, and they have no power outside that Constitution.[22]

The conclusion must be that no province has the right to secede under the Canadian Constitution, and in addition there is no right to secede under international law that Quebecers could rely on.[23] There is no conflict between the two laws in the case of the province of Québec's proposed secession, but, even if there were, domestic law would prevail.

## Is there a "constitutional convention" on the right to secede?

The separatists argue that the federal and provincial governments of Canada and the Aboriginal peoples have already politically conceded Quebecers' right to secede. This idea rests on what we believe are faulty interpretations of fairly recent events.

Some Québec jurists argue that Canadians tacitly admitted Québec's alleged right to secede when they did not reject it at the first opportunity.[24] The events they cite begin with the 1980 referendum on sovereignty association. The federal and provincial governments could have, they say, rejected the whole idea of Québec sovereignty then, but did not. Similarly, they say, Canada did not take the opportunity offered in 1990 when the Québec National Assembly established the Belanger-Campeau Commission to consider Québec's political and constitutional future,[25] or in 1991 when an act outlined the process for a proposed 1992 referendum on sovereignty (which was never held).[26] They say that Quebecers' "right" to secede was also acknowledged when the federal Progressive Conservative party affirmed that Quebecers have the right to self-determination[27] and has since been conceded many times in statements made by Canadian politicians suggesting that Québec can determine its own future.

This question of the alleged tacit acceptance by Canadian government leaders (and Aboriginal peoples) of Quebecers' right to go it alone has been commented on by many authorities. For example, the author A. Cassese, in his book on self-determination of peoples, published in England, observes:

> While it seems highly questionable that such a constitutional convention has evolved, it should be admitted

59

that at the political level a kind of tacit acceptance of the possibility for Québec to secede seems to have emerged in large sections of the Canadian population. This political feeling, however, does not appear to be reflected in any legal change at the constitutional level.[28]

In any case, we James Bay Crees do not accept that it is legitimate for Québec to determine unilaterally the future of Aboriginal peoples and our territories, or that our Aboriginal right to self-determination can be denied by any such unwritten "convention." We *Eeyouch* would not be bound by any such "convention," even if it did exist.

Furthermore, we believe that this separatist reasoning is faulty. The Supreme Court has laid down criteria for establishment of such an unwritten "convention."[29] One of the Supreme Court's most important requirements is that the parties involved must feel themselves bound by the unwritten rule. That is, quite decidedly, not the case in Québec; certainly we Crees do not feel so bound.

The argument is faulty in other ways: the 1980 referendum, for example, merely sought a mandate to negotiate sovereignty association with Canada. If anything, the nature of the question then put to Quebecers suggests that Québec secession must be subject to negotiation and can occur only on mutually acceptable terms. The referendum was simply consultative, not binding, even on the Québec government, and it is a very strange idea that other governments and people in Canada can be said to have agreed to be bound by it, because of their previous silence on the issue.

The same applies to the 1995 referendum. The PQ government dropped its 1994 draft bill which would have made the referendum binding on the National Assembly; thus, like the 1980 referendum, the 1995 referendum was not binding on the Québec government. That being so, how in heaven's name could other levels of government, in and outside Québec, possibly be bound by some unwritten, unexpressed "convention"? That defies common sense.

Any government has the right to hold a consultative referendum on any subject,[30] but the result of that referendum certainly cannot be held to be binding on other parties, unless they express their agreement to be so bound.[31] In any case, actions by the federal government and federal Progressive Conservative party cannot bind provinces or the Aboriginal peoples, in relation to Québec self-determination. Nor can their inaction.

If an unwritten "convention" existed, as is claimed by some Québec jurists, what would be its limits? Not even separatists claim that the division of the federal debt or partition of assets can be undertaken unilaterally by Québec. And certainly there is no agreement that an independent Québec could take out of that federation all of the territories now within the provincial boundaries. On this issue, as on many others, it surely cannot be argued that all the actors involved have agreed on the same rules, with the same limits.

This whole notion that Canadians and Aboriginal peoples have silently agreed to Québec secession is untenable. After all, the so-called "convention" being proposed is based on passive acquiescence and not on any action taken by those who are supposed to be bound by it. It is inconceivable that such a "convention" could unilaterally sever the historic nation-to-nation relations that Aboriginal peoples have with the Crown in right of Canada, including with the province of Québec. To argue that such a thing could happen would be to say that this relationship could be changed without the consent of either Canada or the Aboriginal peoples. To name one important element for the Crees, the unilateral secession of Québec from Canada would fundamentally change the James Bay and Northern Québec Agreement of 1975, and this certainly cannot be done without the consent of the *Eeyouch*.

# The dire need for clarification

In summary, there is an urgent need for clarification of the basis for the Québec government's claim that the province can unilaterally declare independence. The Crees are not prepared to simply sit here and be rolled over by a rampant Québec nationalism. The situation at the time of writing includes the following facts:

- Constitutional lawyers are in broad consensus that an amendment to the Canadian Constitution would be required for the province of Québec to secede legally.[32]

- Under both Canadian and international law, "the consent of the Aboriginal peoples," as one author has written, "is necessary for any modification of the political and constitutional status of Québec, to the extent that their rights are affected,"[33] which they certainly would be by a unilateral declaration of Québec independence.

- Most experts are agreed that Quebecers cannot base their claim to secession on the principle of self-determination under international law.[34] Michel Venne, now an editor of *Le Devoir*, writes: "The Parti Québécois no longer refers in its propaganda to this right of self-determination. It proposes a process that takes its popular legitimacy from the referendum."[35]

- The separatists of the PQ government assert the idea of a unilateral declaration of independence because they have no legal right to secede under either international or Canadian law.

- The primary basis for their claim now rests on achieving "effective control" of the whole of present-day Québec.

- Québec's "effective control" over Aboriginal lands will likely be challenged by those Aboriginal peoples, who, like other communities and individuals in Québec, do not want to be forcibly included in an independent Québec State.

- So long as Aboriginal peoples and others oppose their inclusion in a secessionist State, the sole avenue open to an independent Québec to establish "effective control" and demonstrate it to the world would appear to be the use of force.

- To give this series of unilateral actions their proper name, they would be acts of insurrection and revolution.

At the moment, it seems, people in Canada, including Québec, are not fully aware of the possibility of State-sanctioned violence against the Crees and others implied by the PQ strategy of "effective control." (It is a favourite tactic, everywhere in the world, of those in authority who take arbitrary actions against their people, to accuse those who are defending themselves of creating or encouraging violence.)

We will now turn to examining the explosive concept of "effective control," and the force that we anticipate — and fear — would be needed to impose it.

# 4

# The big sleeper of secession: Québec's explosive strategy of "effective control"

*Wherein it is shown that the international community will require proof that an independent Québec will be unable to deliver*

The Québec government claims that international law sanctions the unilateral secession of Québec from an existing state.

Like many other of the separatist leaders' claims, this is not correct. International law demands that to accede to statehood an entity must first demonstrate "effective control" over the territory it claims. The separatists are now relying on this. But this principle of "effective control" is not some kind of passive, anodyne idea that clicks into place whenever some group feels like setting up its own State. Far from it: rather, it is an attempt by international law to deal with illegal and revolutionary acts, a sort of last-ditch effort, as one authority has stated, to accommodate legal concepts to the hard facts that may arise from successful illegal actions.[1]

The very notion of "effective control" implies conflict, confrontation, and, in the end, violence, or the use of some kind of force. And those who rely on this doctrine are not usually genteel, law-abiding groups: more often than not when this issue has arisen elsewhere in the world, they have been squalid, sometimes brutal, dictators, who have not shrunk from imposing their will on others, no matter what the cost to their victims.

Quebecers and other Canadians should be under no illusions: the unilateral seccession of the province of Québec from Canada would be provocative and potentially dangerous for everyone concerned. The Canadian government has taken a long time to get around to recognizing this danger, hoping that somehow the problem would go away, or be solved peacefully by some sort of harmonious agreement. But, as outlined in the last chapter, Allan Rock, Canada's former Minister of Justice and Attorney-General, finally admitted the danger publicly, and in September 1996 explicitly stated so when announcing the federal government's Reference of the Québec secession issue to the Supreme Court of Canada.

"The idea of a unilateral declaration of independence makes no sense no matter how it is considered," Rock wrote. "The issue is not a mere legal nicety. It is also of enormous practical significance. Any government that suggests it would throw Québec and all of Canada into the confusion of a UDI is being profoundly irresponsible. It is a formula for chaos."

The Grand Council of the Crees agrees. The Grand Council has intervened in this federal Reference, and in our factum of April 1997 we state the facts as we see them:

> The unilateral secession of Québec, by its very nature, is extremely provocative. It is inextricably connected to potential violation of the rights of Aboriginal peoples, unnecessary conflict, and struggle for "effective control" of territory and jurisdiction. In this way, unilateral secession is bound to lead to chaos, force and violence, and, inevitably, to a breakdown of the rule of law.[2]

# Basic criteria for international recognition

A newly independent nation should fulfil several criteria before it can expect international recognition by other States. In practical terms, the establishment of "effective control" over the claimed territory is perhaps the criterion that is inherently the most dangerous and destabilizing. Other criteria include significant majority support, solidarity and consent within the society, and a demonstrated respect for the human rights of the whole population within the territory claimed.

In at least two glaring respects, an independent Québec would not fulfil these criteria, first, because the separatist government lacks the necessary consent within its society for its proposed independence, as is demonstrated by the Aboriginal referendums already referred to of October 1995; and second, because the very act of unilateral secession would violate the treaty, Aboriginal, and other human rights of Aboriginal peoples living within the claimed territory. The basic criteria for statehood were established in 1934 by an international agreement, known as the Montevideo Convention.[3] This agreement provides that a State must possess four qualifications: a permanent population, a defined territory, a government, and the capacity to enter into relations with other States. Further, to be recognized, a State must have a government "in general control of its territory, to the exclusion of other entities. . . ."[4]

A State created by insurrection (such as would be an independent Québec) may become the foundation of a new and legitimate legal order, "if demonstrably successful." But to be considered successful the breakaway government of a new State must be judged to have established "effective control" over the territory it claims to govern and to have done so "over a sufficiently long period."[5] These are the rules by which an insurrectionist Québec government's seizure of power would be judged by the international community.

It is not clear how many Canadians, including Quebecers, are aware that what the separatists are proposing by a unilateral declaration of independence is, in reality, an insurrection (described by the *Oxford Shorter Dictionary* as "an armed rising, or revolt"), or coup d'état ("a change in the government carried out violently or illegally by the ruling power"), or even a revolution ("a complete overthrow of the established government in any State by those who were previously subject to it, or a forcible substitution of a new form of government").

Québec separatists strenuously object to the use of such terms, but there is no doubt that those who are now espousing UDI, such as the current Québec government, do seek to replace, without lawful authority, the existing constitutional order. York University law professor Patrick Monahan says Québec's proposed UDI would be "a revolutionary change . . . that would be accomplished wholly outside the existing rules of the constitutional order, involving a break in legal continuity, and establishment of a new . . . order based on a new legal foundation."[6] The process has been described by Guy Bertrand, the lawyer who has challenged its legality, as "a parliamentary coup d'état."[7]

In an attempt to assure people that ordinary life would continue as before, Premier Jacques Parizeau's 1995 draft *Act Respecting the Future of Québec* provides that all acts of the Canadian Parliament will be incorporated into Québec law on the day Québec becomes a sovereign State, and a rival judicial system would replace that of Canada.[8] This suggests that people in Canada would be caught between two legal systems. But as law professors have pointed out, the courts must support the federal principle of Canada until such time as the secession has clearly succeeded.[9] If this were to arise, it suggests a very fundamental conflict that could easily lead to violence, as we discuss in more detail in the next chapter.

## Limitations to "effective control"

The most prominent case of a UDI in the modern world — indeed, the occasion on which the initials UDI were first used

— occurred in 1965 when the colony of Southern Rhodesia (now the independent country of Zimbabwe), at that time ruled by a white supremacist government under Ian Smith, declared itself independent because it was unable to negotiate an agreed independence with the British government, which realized Smith had no mandate from the majority of Rhodesia's citizens.

Smith's government did establish "effective control" over its territory. But the international community did not grant recognition to Smith's rogue republic because this seizure of independence violated the right of self-determination of most of Rhodesia's citizens. This, then, was a case in which the United Nations considered the violation of rights to be so grave that it overrode considerations of effectiveness.[10] Therefore, the Rhodesian case established that, even if a seceding government establishes "effective control" over the territory it claims, the international community is not obliged to recognize it.

This is another PQ misconception that they have not yet come to terms with. Since the Rhodesian case, a movement attempting to secede from an existing nation has an even stronger obligation than before to respect the rights of self-determination of its populations.[11] To say in advance, as the Québec separatists say, that they will treat Aboriginal peoples well in an independent Québec, does not meet the problem. What is at issue is that we Crees and other Aboriginal peoples cannot be included in any new State without our consent. The key issue is the denial of our right to self-determination.

Furthermore, a seceding Québec has no particular "right" to establish "effective control" over Aboriginal territories against the wishes of the people inhabiting them. We Aboriginal peoples ourselves may establish or claim to have "effective control" over our territories, if we so wish. Even the Québec National Assembly's five experts in their 1992 report concluded that Aboriginal peoples in Québec have access to this principle on the same terms as the Québec government. In their words, "one or several Aboriginal peoples" could "impose the effective existence of a State" within a determined territory, and such a State could acquire a legal existence, "provided the test of 'effectiveness' were met."[12]

From our point of view, everything, therefore, depends on Aboriginal consent: the Québec government cannot claim to be acting in a legitimate or democratic manner if it fails to respect this principle. It is really quite simple and straightforward: to act without Aboriginal consent would deny our right to self-determination.[13] On the other hand, if a seceding country can obtain the consent of its peoples, the international community will react favourably, as it did when it accorded such rapid recognition to the successor States of the former Soviet Union, *after the two sides agreed to go their own ways*.[14]

In the absence of a negotiated agreement, efforts by an entity such as the PQ government of Québec to establish "effective control" might turn out to be far from peaceful. For example, Canada might challenge by peaceful means the actions of secessionist forces, or groups within Canada might assert their right to self-determination and oppose their forcible inclusion in any seceding Québec State. For instance, so long as the question of the territories ceded to Québec by Canada in 1898 and 1912 (which comprise two-thirds of the province of Québec) remain unresolved, it would hardly be possible for Québec to depend on the rule of "effective control." So there is no guarantee that even over the long term an independent Québec would be able to establish "effective control" over all of its claimed territory. We examine the case of these territories and the borders of Québec in detail in chapters 6 and 7.

## *Either force or mutual consent*

Two months before the 1995 referendum, Laval University political scientist Jean-Pierre Derriennic warned Quebecers, in an article in the nationalist newspaper *Le Devoir*, that secession is not a right enjoyed by Quebecers: it is either realized by force or by mutual consent.[15] He has also pointed out that if the Québec government ceases to govern by law, "some people within the province will continue to respect federal laws and some will act outside of any law."[16] This is more than a remote possibility if the separatists should choose to go ahead unilaterally, as they appear determined to do. Their 1995 Bill 1 provided for replacement of the present judges, laws, Supreme Court, and so on in the seceding Québec, thereby setting up two legal systems that residents of Québec would have to choose between.

Rock was not exaggerating when he described this as a recipe for chaos. To demonstrate "effective control," any new Québec State would have to exclude the application of Canadian law from its territory, to create a legal order flowing from its own laws and decisions, and do so, as we have pointed out, for a "sufficiently long time" to make it stick.[17]

Aboriginal peoples, and possibly the federal government, are likely to challenge the secessionist government's control over all or some part of its claimed territory. From all this it is obvious that a UDI by Québec would have far-reaching consequences for everyone in the province, including the Aboriginal peoples. Indeed, such action would violate fundamental rights, jeopardize separatist hopes for international recognition, and confront Quebecers with all the disadvantages of international isolation. In addition, were a rogue government of the kind now proposed to be deprived of the privileges and immunities afforded by international law, there would be a big domestic effect within a seceding Québec.

To confront all the resistance that would be created by a unilateral declaration of independence, the use of force within Québec by a secessionist government seems disturbingly possible and is a scenario that must be seriously evaluated. This is what we do in the following chapter.

# 5

# The strong possibility of violence

*Wherein it is shown that secessionists are already preparing to use force to compel Aboriginal peoples into an independent Québec*

The James Bay Crees abhor any use of force or resort to violence. We believe that the dispute about Québec secession should be resolved peacefully, based on recognition of, and respect for, the equal rights of peoples.

"We have never and never will use violence," says Cree Grand Chief Matthew Coon Come. "We ask ourselves, however, in the face of the potential breakup of Canada, who is it that is really threatening these things?"[1]

Every State uses force to impose certain controls. Many States also use violence against people who are trying to see to it that their rights and the fundamental laws of humanity are respected. But usually those in authority who are using violence illegitimately against their own people do not admit what they are doing. They tend to obfuscate the question of who is really responsible for their violence.

A classic example (very, very different from Québec) was the State violence perpetrated by the apartheid government of South Africa against the black majority: although all forms of political expression had been denied the South African people for many years, that government tried to portray itself as simply defending law and order against terrorism, a position that was rejected by the international community, which imposed sanctions against the South African government.

In Québec, separatists are already preparing to blame others for any State-sanctioned violence that a seceding Québec may use against its populations. For example, former Premier Jacques Parizeau's view is quite simple: the boundaries cannot be changed without the consent of Québec, and to attempt to change them would be an act of aggression against Québec. "Before sovereignty, it is not possible," he said in 1977. "After sovereignty, it is too late. It would be considered an aggression."[2]

We are already familiar with this technique. As we explain in the Introduction, in spite of the fact that for twenty-five years

AISLIN, *THE MONTREAL GAZETTE*

we have used all the instruments of democracy — the courts, speeches, letters to the editor, peaceful demonstrations, canoe trips, and newspaper advertisements — to press our case, we Crees have been described as warlike and hostile. When we waged our fight in the courts against the Great Whale hydro-electric project in the early 1990s, we were accused of waging "judicial guerrilla warfare." More recently, a Québec journalist asked Grand Chief Coon Come a most telling question on the day he announced the results of the Crees' own referendum on Québec secession, a few days before the Québec referendum of October 1995. No sooner had Chief Coon Come finished announcing that the Crees had voted over 96 per cent not to be separated from Canada without our consent, a very long and stunned silence was broken with the following inquiry: "Mr. Coon Come: is this a declaration of war?" It is hard to believe that ballots could be mistaken for bullets in this way.

Unfortunately, the use of force and acts of violence could be a by-product of a unilateral declaration of independence by Québec.[3] As the Aboriginal lawyer Mary Ellen Turpel-Lafond, of the University of Saskatchewan, warns: "Just because Canada is a peaceful country doesn't mean you can't have a civil war. If you can have an armed conflict over a small burial ground (such as in the Oka crisis in 1990), then what can you have if you're talking about an entire territory?"[4]

"If natives in northern Québec refuse to recognize the authority of the new Québec State," writes Toronto law professor Patrick Monahan, "Québec will be unable to lay claim to that territory unless it can, through the exercise of force if required, demonstrate that it has effective control over it."[5]

Internationally, there is certainly no shortage of causes for which people are prepared to fight wars: in 1993 thirty-eight different States were engaged in armed conflict.[6] In a secessionist Québec, it is more than possible that the separatist leaders, faced with people who wanted to continue to respect federal law, could perceive force as the only means open to them to ensure the success of their revolution. In international terms, this is not a particularly rare scenario.

Force has been used or threatened in many recent attempts

at secession from existing States.[7] It is not exaggerating to say that advocacy to break loose from a State usually breeds, or is accompanied by, disorder and violence.[8] This has even been noted recently in Québec when the narrow defeat of the 1995 referendum and the subsequent embrace by the Parti Québécois of unilateral action to enforce secession quickly gave rise to a small movement of nationalists advocating violence against anglophones in Québec, and vice versa. This in turn was followed by an increase in minor acts of violence, such as insulting graffiti, stones thrown through windows, and the like.

Members of the National Assembly of Québec, and other separatists, have made no bones about their willingness to enforce their authority on dissenting populations in their projected independent Québec, and have clearly thought a lot about the role of the army in their proposed revolution. In December 1991, Parti Québécois leader Parizeau made front page news when he declared that, as Premier of Québec, he would count on the army to ensure peace in the period following a declaration of independence.[9] (In fact, after the 1995 referendum it became known that Marc Jacob, a Bloc Québécois member of the federal parliament, had circularized francophone members of the Canadian army, asking them to transfer their allegiance to the proposed new State of Québec.)

To make sure that no one should mistake the intention of the new nation, in 1994 Jacques Brassard, who is now a Québec government minister, specifically declared that an independent Québec would resort to force to defend its territory and enforce its laws. Brassard said that this would be needed "particularly against Aboriginal peoples and other dissident groups."[10] This was no idle, tossed-off remark. Separatists have a clear idea about which groups they might have to suppress with armed force. As early as 1992, Jocelyn Coulon, a *Le Devoir* journalist specializing in military matters, talked about this to the Québec National Assembly's Committee on Sovereignty.[11] The armed force of a sovereign Québec would have multiple missions, he said. These missions would include "assuring control of the territory from the Ungava Bay to the Eastern Townships, passing by the Temiscaming to the Gaspé." This would be necessary, he said, "because there are some people who . . . even suggest that Québec can be dismembered."

Appearing before the same committee, Albert Legault, a Laval University professor, was even more specific: he said that with military installations at Valcartier and Montréal a secessionist Québec should be able to equip itself with the means to respond to Aboriginal crises. Québec would be in difficulties, he said, if it had to face two or three Okas simultaneously.[12] C. Maciocia, a member of the National Assembly, asked Legault if it would be realistic to suppose that the Canadian army might intervene "if certain Aboriginal nations . . . do not agree to respect the democratic process and . . . decide . . . to create a certain disorder. . . ."[13]

This kind of thinking suggests that proponents of Québec secession are already contemplating the use of force against Aboriginal peoples and are preparing the ground for it by use of the classic accusation that dissidents "do not respect democratic process." Canadians perhaps are not fully aware of the immense challenge this will pose to Canada's generally peaceful ways. As University of Toronto political scientist Peter Russell has commented wryly, "Violence could supplant tedium as the central feature of our constitutional politics." He added, more seriously, that violence would most likely be used "to force ethnic minorities, especially Aboriginal peoples, to be part of a sovereign Québec."[14]

Both the federal government and the Crees have repudiated the use of force. The Québec government has been challenged to do so, but has not done so clearly.

## Force has been used before

The use of force against Aboriginal peoples is not a new phenomenon for Québec governments. The most notorious example is the 1990 crisis at Kanehsetake (Oka), on the banks of the Ottawa River, northwest of Montréal, where Mohawks blockaded a road leading to some land that has great significance for them and that the local municipality wanted to use for a nine-hole extension to a golf course. The Sûreté de Québec initiated a raid which went so badly that the provincial government requested help from the Canadian Army. The siege that followed lasted several months and became an international news event. The conflict appeared to turn many francophone Quebecers against Mohawks and other Aboriginal peoples.

At the time of the so-called Oka crisis, the Mohawks and Crees raised the behaviour of the Canadian government at a session of the UN Sub-Commission on Prevention of Discrimination and Protection of Minorities, which was sitting in Geneva. As a result of this initiative Danilo Turk, chair of the Sub-Commission, asked the Canadian government to make a daily report on developments at Oka not only to his Sub-Commission, but also to the Undersecretary-General for Human Rights and to the Secretary-General of the UN himself. Canada did this, and a year later Turk said he believed that this UN surveillance had been a key factor in preventing bloodshed. The fact is that in the modern world national governments are vulnerable to international judgement, and we Crees, among other Aboriginal nations, through our representatives at UN bodies, have used this vulnerability very effectively in recent years.

Five years later coroner Guy Gilbert concluded that, while none of the parties was without responsibility, a substantial part of the blame must lie with the Québec police who initiated the raid without justification.[15]

Years before, in 1977, when the separatist Parti Québécois was first in power, the government sent riot police to Kuujjuaq (formerly Fort Chimo) in northern Québec, after Inuit demonstrated against Québec's proposed *Charter of the French Language*, which would force them to use French.[16] The Inuit objected that Québec was violating their right to choose the language they wished to use in community and regional affairs. Ironically, by that language charter Québec was taking steps to become unilingual by establishing French as the sole official language in the province, yet was demanding that Aboriginal people whose second language was English become trilingual. The Inuit and Crees said the language bill contravened the terms of the James Bay and Northern Québec Agreement which the Québec National Assembly had recently approved.[17]

The government's insensitivity towards the needs of the Aboriginal people was roundly denounced at the time. "It is ironic," stated an editorial in *The Montréal Star*, "that a government . . . committed to the preservation of a language and culture which it claims are endangered, should be so insensitive to the needs of another people, whose culture and language are genuinely in jeopardy. Compared with the problems confronting the Inuit, the problems confronting French-speaking Québec are minuscule. Where . . . they might have expected understanding, the Inuit . . . are . . . treated instead to the riot squad."[18] And a group of three academics, including Daniel Turp, who is now a Member of Parliament for the separatist Bloc Québécois, denounced the government's attitude as "incomprehensible and frankly unacceptable" and said the government was placing itself "in a colonialist situation towards the Aboriginal peoples of Québec, instead of negotiating with them on a footing of equality." In the same paper, the three said the government should recognize that it is "not the Aboriginal people who occupy OUR territory, but rather we who are attempting to occupy THEIRS." They said that to impose "our own rules of the game" on Aboriginal peoples was to act in a manner that was "unspeakably" imperialist and colonialist.[19]

Eventually, changes were negotiated in Québec's Charter of the French Language (since known as Bill 101) to recognize at least some language rights of Crees, Inuit, and Naskapi and to include certain exemptions in the language legislation, but French remains the only official language in Québec.

Some years later, a separatist PQ government again exposed its contempt for Aboriginal peoples when, during a dispute about salmon fishing, a massive police raid was mounted, far out of proportion to any conceivable need, on the Mikmaq community of Listuguj (Restigouche), seizing nets and fish and arresting many people.

If massive force can be used by a separatist government simply to quash an Inuit protest over language, or settle a fishing dispute, it requires no great leap of imagination to realize what might happen following a declaration of Québec independence, in which the stakes would be so much higher.

PQ leaders have not changed their mind about their intention to use force if they consider it needed. Québec Minister of Intergovernmental Affairs Jacques Brassard returned to the charge early in 1997, when he said that Québec would have to be prepared for any possible federal intervention in the province's referendum process, including the use of the army.[20] Having put the blame on Canada in advance, he added the next day that a secessionist Québec government would use all the power at its disposal to stop areas like the West Island of Montréal, the Eastern Townships, or the Outaouais (the Ottawa Valley), from remaining part of Canada. "There is no question of permitting any village or part of a city or county to assert a claim to such a right," he told reporters. "The population of Beaconsfield (a Montréal suburb) is not a people, no more than the population of the Outaouais." He added that Aboriginal peoples have no right to secede from Québec, either. "In international law that right to self-determination or autonomy that we recognize for native peoples doesn't go as far as the right to secession," he said.

"The government of Québec will exercise its effective authority over all its territory," he said. "That includes the parts of the territory where the majority of the population would have voted No at the moment of the referendum. . . .

"If they don't respect the laws of Québec, the State will simply see to it that the laws are respected. . . . A modern State possesses the means to ensure that laws voted democratically . . . are respected." He refused to say exactly what he meant by "effective authority," but recalled his 1994 statement: "Québec will have to exercise its effective authority, that means obviously that the government has the means to maintain public order. That means laws, the courts and the police forces, which are also the institutions, the instruments, of the State."[21]

The following day his counterpart minister in the federal government, Stéphane Dion, said Brassard's remarks were "incredible," and a day later he called on Bouchard to clarify Brassard's "grave" comments.[22]

"Will Bouchard react?" Dion asked. "Will he tell us, 'Of course we won't use force, we'll persuade people to stay in an independent Québec, we have good arguments to convince them'? Or will he say, 'Not an inch, our territory is sacred, and they (populations who want to stay in Canada) have no rights'? What's his answer?"

Dion said the federal government had stated its willingness to let Québec secede if a clear majority on a clear question wanted independence. "We don't want to keep people against their will," he said, "but we don't want populations to be annexed against their will by secession either."[23]

Bouchard's response was equivocal at best, but certainly did not answer the key question concerning violence or the use of force. Bouchard simply described Dion as a "provocateur" who "doesn't exist for me."[24]

## Contrary to international law

The UN General Assembly, in defining aggression, has affirmed that it is "the duty of States not to use armed force to deprive peoples of their right to self-determination, freedom and independence, or to disrupt territorial integrity."[25] For this resolution "State" is defined in a manner that would include a secessionist Québec.[26] A secessionist Québec that used force to prevent an Aboriginal people from choosing to remain in Canada would be acting contrary to international law, so it is not surprising that some Québec authors have pointed out the high price a sovereign Québec would pay internationally if it tried to suppress internal conflicts by the use of violence.[27]

Moreover, Judge Ammoun at the International Court of Justice has declared that the use of force in this way to frustrate the right of self-determination should be considered an act of aggression,[28] forbidden by the 1970 *Declaration on Principles of International Law Concerning Friendly Relations and Cooperation Among States in Accordance with the Charter of the United Nations*. In 1991 the Council of the European Community came to the same conclusion. With the aspiring new States of Eastern Europe and the Soviet Union in mind, the Council declared that it would "not recognize entities which are the result of aggression."[29]

Two other now widely accepted tenets of international law are also relevant to the Québec secessionist scenario: to use force to suppress self-determination is an act of aggression and is now clearly unacceptable, but to oppose such acts of aggression by using force is to act in self-defence, and any outside help given to such self-defence would be justifiable under the *United Nations Charter*.[30]

Of course, if Canada chose to assist Aboriginal peoples who were under attack by a secessionist Québec government, this would not constitute "outside help." In fact, in such circumstances the Canadian government would simply be taking action to fulfil its constitutional obligations towards Aboriginal peoples.

High-level support for this contention was given in a remarkable speech delivered in Montréal late in 1996 by Marc Lalonde, who for many years was one of the most powerful members of the long-running Trudeau government of Canada, through the seventies and early eighties. He said:

> . . . in the north (of Québec) there are regions occupied by Aboriginal peoples who, by 96 per cent, have voted in favour of maintaining their status within Canada. Their territory represents at least half of the Québec territory. They occupy this territory for at least 10,000 years, and no one can claim that they do not have their language and culture. In the case of Québec secession, no federal government, even if it wished to, could abandon them as to their future. The whole of the Canadian population, as well as international public opinion, would compel the Canadian government to ensure respect for the rights of Aboriginal peoples.[31]

For these and other reasons, we Crees believe that we cannot legitimately be denied our right to choose to remain in Canada by acts of force used against us by a secessionist Québec government. We take the position that such a violation of our fundamental rights would give rise to our own right to secede from a secessionist Québec.[32]

# What can Canada do?

The Crees reiterate that force must have no place in any struggle about "effective control." However, legal experts suggest that action by Canada to protect its Constitution, laws, and territory would constitute "legitimate self-defence." McGill University constitutional law professor Stephen Scott has indicated as much to the Québec National Assembly,[33] and Patrick Monahan, of Osgoode Hall Law School, Toronto, has said that military action by Canada to defend the country's physical integrity "would not be prohibited under international law" and would be permitted under the National Defence Act.[34]

One Québec commentator, José Woehrling, agrees that Canada would be within its constitutional and legal rights to oppose secession "with weapons," and international organizations would not intervene unless the conflict became internationalized.[35] Constitutional expert Peter Hogg has written that "as long as the federal government asserted its continuing authority over Québec in areas of federal jurisdiction, it would be difficult for the court to characterize the secession as successful."[36]

There are many actions short of military intervention that Canada could take in the face of a UDI. For example, Canada could:

- Initiate challenges in Canadian courts to emphasize the unconstitutional, illegal, and illegitimate nature of the PQ government's unilateral declaration of independence and any legislation or actions that might flow from it.

- Declare that Québec remains a part of Canada, thereby discouraging international recognition of a secessionist Québec by other States.

- Discuss with other major States to ensure that no international recognition is given to a secessionist Québec "State."

- Continue to recognize legitimate representatives of the Québec population, including members of the House of Commons and Senate, under the Parliament of Canada Act.

- Continue to recognize Aboriginal peoples in Québec as nationals and citizens of their own respective nations and of Canada (if they so desire).

- Continue (if not increase) application of federal as well as Aboriginal laws, in at least some regions of the province of Québec.

- Collect income and other taxes from the Québec population.

- Maintain Canadian airports and seaports, as well as customs and border officials at U.S.-Canada border crossings in Québec.

- Continue to work constructively with Aboriginal peoples to maintain and strengthen the presence of the federal government in their territories.

- Implement and renegotiate existing treaties with Aboriginal peoples in northern Québec, and reinforce and confirm the federal framework that they contain.

It is obvious from this list that the maintenance of Canada's legal obligations to Aboriginal peoples should be a major element of any Canadian attempt to oppose the dismemberment of Canada by a seceding Québec. This recognition by Canada of its responsibility to Aboriginal peoples will be important if recourse to force by a seceding Québec is to be avoided.

Of course, we Crees recognize that we are a numerically small and vulnerable people. Our only protection is the continued adherence of Canadian society to the rule of law. For these reasons, we believe no fundamental alteration in the constitutional status of Canada should be permitted through unilateral action by Québec.

The wise words of jurist M. van Walt van Praag are worth remembering: "The potential for explosive disintegration lurks in all States where people's human rights, including the right to self-determination, are denied."[37]

We take no pleasure in this discussion. In the event that a government of Québec decided to use force against us, it would be a very sad day. Our traditional lands, *Eeyou Astchee*, have never seen conflict. The use of violence or force is against our most fundamentally held beliefs. So, we ask all who are concerned to call upon the government of Québec to declare that it, too, will not use force under these circumstances, particularly not to deny the Cree people their right to determine democratically their future in this context.

# 6

---

# Borders: what happens following a UDI?

*Wherein secessionists dream of magically renouncing*
*Canadian laws and embracing them at the same time*

---

The traditional territory of the James Bay Crees covers some
400,000 square miles (an area almost twice as large as France).
It is often regarded by southerners as a harsh and inhospitable

DUSAN PETRICIS, *TORONTO STAR*

place. For us it is a bountiful garden. Our family traplines cover all of its valleys, slopes, river basins, and shorelines. We have travelled, walked, canoed, and named its every corner. We have raised our young, hunted for our keep, and buried our dead in its ranges for thousands of years. Some of our traditional gathering places have become permanent Cree settlements, but our presence is everywhere.

Most of this territory did not form part of the province of Québec at the time of confederation in 1867. Only in 1898 and 1912 did the government of Canada annex the northern two-thirds of today's Québec to the province, including most of the Cree and Inuit traditional territories.

No matter what governments thought they were doing with our lands, we Crees and other Aboriginal peoples occupied, governed, used, protected, and managed our traditional territories for thousands of years, and we continue to do so, in a spirit of sharing. It is not generally known that our Cree and Inuit territories extend beyond the provincial boundaries of Québec, and include offshore islands and waters surrounding the northern parts of the province. Similarly, the historical territories of other Aboriginal peoples, such as the Algonquins, Mikmaqs, Abenaki and Innu (Montagnais), and Naskapi, also extend beyond the boundaries of Québec. Confronted with the threat of Québec secession, naturally we are concerned about what is going to happen. "Whatever befalls the earth," said Chief Seattle, "befalls the sons of the earth."[1]

The probable future conflict over this territory is a central element in the determination of Québec separatists to deny the rights of Aboriginal peoples: from the separatist point of view Québec needs these territories and resources. This is exactly the need that motivated the original European colonists as they invaded the homelands of Aboriginal peoples throughout North and South America. Let us, therefore, give these separatist policies and attitudes their proper name: this is the same old colonialism that has brought so much misery and injustice to the original peoples of Canada and elsewhere.

Now we face the prospect of a possible Québec secession. The Québec government seems to believe there is a guarantee that a sovereign Québec would maintain its present borders. But Aboriginal peoples in Québec could well opt to stay in Canada, with our territories, so that belief is far from certain; a sovereign Québec could well turn out to be substantially diminished or otherwise altered.

Even if Québec's secession were successful, the new entity would keep only those parts of the present province over which it managed to impose and maintain "effective control," as we saw in chapter 5. In some parts of the province that may never happen. The fact is, in the indeterminate period following a UDI — which could last for months and even years — a secessionist Québec would lose the guaranteed protection given to its administrative boundaries by the Constitution Acts of 1871 and 1982.


# Canada guarantees
# provincial boundaries

The Canadian Constitution provides that any change in a province's boundaries requires the consent of the provincial legislature. By declaring unilateral independence, however, and thus renouncing the Canadian Constitution, Québec would have renounced this constitutional protection. As law professor Patrick Monahan, of Toronto, has commented: "[Québec] could not pick and choose among parts of the Constitution, ignoring those provisions with which it disagreed while seeking to rely on others that operated in its favour."[2] Nevertheless, the present separatist leaders, in one of their more irrational flights of fancy, claim that they can do just that.

Until a secessionist Québec is recognized as an independent State, its present borders could not in any sense be regarded as legally intact. Former Canadian Cabinet minister Marc Lalonde, in the speech quoted in the previous chapter, made this so clear that surely no one in Québec can any longer be in doubt about it. He said:

. . . a declaration of secession by the Québec National Assembly would constitute a totally illegal act, whether under domestic law or under international law. In such a case, the State of Québec would reject the rule of law and would cease to be a State of law. . . . it should be emphasized that one would then be swimming in total illegality and that in such a situation it is a free-for-all. There would no longer be a rule that holds, save for that of the strongest. The Canadian Constitution guarantees the integrity of the boundaries of the provinces as long as those are subject to this Constitution. However, from the moment the National Assembly opts for secession, there is no longer this rule of the game, since this same Assembly would declare that it is no longer bound by this Constitution. The elementary logical conclusion is that the thundering declarations of Mr. Bouchard and others will change absolutely nothing. The conclusion is inescapable: if the boundaries of Canada are not sacred, why would those of Québec be?[3]

Separatist politicians keep repeating like a mantra (as if saying makes it so) that the territory of Québec is indivisible, its borders sacrosanct, and this is guaranteed by international law. For example, Jacques Parizeau, when he was leader of the Québec opposition, in 1994 assured the readers of *La Presse* that the situation concerning boundaries "could not be more clear."[4] And in 1995 the Commission nationale sur l'avenir du Québec, appointed by Parizeau's government and made up mostly of secessionists, stated that Québec's territory is guaranteed under international law when Québec becomes sovereign, but gave no substantiation whatsoever for this opinion. (Nor did it bother itself with the question of at what point international law would consider that Québec had become sovereign.)[5]

David Cliche, now a PQ Cabinet minister, neatly ignores the indeterminate period after a UDI when he says, "All the legal opinions we have . . . say that if Québec becomes sovereign and is recognized as such by its peers, the territory of a sovereign

Québec will be the one that we know presently in the province of Québec."[6]

All this is merely wishful thinking. Again, Cliche ignores a huge question: what is the status of a secessionist Québec in the days, weeks, months, or possibly years, before its existence as a sovereign State is recognized internationally (if at all)? Might not the borders be changed by Canada during that period? Perhaps it is no wonder that Cliche has been able to get away with not being challenged publicly on this: as we've shown in the Introduction to this book, under the separatist regime in Québec, some questions have been made taboo, beyond discussion, and these boundary questions are among them.

One might almost say that there's been a conspiracy of silence on them by both the Québec and Canadian governments. Under pressure of public opinion, this situation has somewhat improved following the narrow federalist victory in the referendum. For example, Québec political science professor Stéphane Dion was appointed to the federal Cabinet and quickly raised for the first time, at this level, the possibility that Québec, like Canada, might be partitioned. He adopted the position also taken by many Canadians, experts and ordinary citizens alike, that, if Canada is divisible, then evidently Québec must be, too. Curiously, this statement of an evident fact aroused a chorus of incredulity and resentment among many Québec nationalists.

The Grand Council of the Crees, in our 1996 intervention in the federal government's Reference to the Supreme Court, has asserted that "no secession can be effected by the (Québec) National Assembly, the legislature or government of Québec that would include the James Bay Cree People or Cree traditional territory, without the consent of the [Cree People]," and Québec "cannot validly invoke notions of legitimacy and democracy" if the proposed secession "would deny the legitimate and democratic expression of the will of the James Bay Cree People, or otherwise unilaterally alter its Aboriginal, treaty, and other rights guaranteed in the Constitution of Canada."

We Crees believe it would be simply unthinkable for a Canadian government to accept a Québec declaration of independence as a fait accompli. Try to imagine the scenario: the inhabitants of a huge part of Canada declare that they wish to remain in Canada in spite of an illegal seizure of power by a revolutionary group of secessionists; nevertheless, the Canadian government calmly agrees to wave them and their territories goodbye. On the face of it, the idea is incredible. And yet, this is precisely one of the many uncertainties arising from the current separatist strategy and the so-far muted Canadian response to it.

All of these uncertainties, we believe, should be comprehensively discussed and placed before the peoples and governments of Canada in advance of any future referendum. Indeed, they should have been discussed before the 1995 referendum, but were not. Consequently neither the Canadian government nor the Canadian people were really prepared for the eventuality of Québec separation.

The federal government's vagueness as to how it would handle a Québec UDI has now given rise to many active individuals and groups across Canada (including in Québec) who have demanded that the issues be addressed head-on. They have been given good cause for their concern. The early days of the 1997 federal election were dominated by the revelation by Parizeau, former Québec Premier, that if there had been an affirmative vote in the 1995 referendum he was prepared to proclaim a unilateral declaration of Québec independence, possibly within days.[7] Parizeau denied that he had such intentions, but the actual words used in his introduction to a book of his speeches were clearly open to the interpretation given them.[8]

# Borders: no subject for government complacency

The Canadian government has been extremely complacent about this issue of borders. Take, for example, Canada's attitude when in October 1996 an all-party British parliamentary human-rights group began an inquiry into the situation facing

Québec Aboriginal peoples in the event of Québec secession. This inquiry involved the human-rights committee appointed by some two-hundred members of the House of Lords, but the Canadian government joined with the separatist Québec government in declining to cooperate. "These are matters to be dealt with in Canada by Canadians," said Harry Adams, press secretary at the Canadian High Commission in London.[9] Québec's minister of Aboriginal affairs, Guy Chevrette, dismissed the British inquiry by saying, "British parliamentarians can study whatever they want. It won't matter: the territory of Québec is indivisible." Canada's reluctance to have these issues aired internationally prompted one Québec observer, McGill University professor Robert Lecker, to conclude: "Both the federal and provincial governments seem to want the controversial business of territorial integrity kept out of international view." Yet, he pointed out, if Québec does separate, these are the very questions that foreign countries will inevitably have to examine.[10] Perhaps for that reason, the Canadian and Québec governments, though expressing noncooperation in public, did in fact (it has since become known) privately cooperate by providing documents and information to the British inquiry.

In contrast to the complacency of the governments, Quebecers themselves are extremely worried about their borders. A group that monitored the regional hearings held by the Québec government in advance of the 1995 referendum reported that most citizens who raised the subject of borders linked it to the claims of Aboriginal peoples. The monitoring group, the Council for Canadian Unity, found that sovereignists sitting on the regional commissions were "evasive" in the face of such questions. "A fact which merits being underlined is the absence of precise response on the part of members of the commissions, and, above all, members of the (Québec) government," commented the group.[11]

The separatist reasoning about their "sacrosanct" borders rests entirely on the Canadian Constitution's provision that "the limits" of a province may be changed only with the consent of the provincial legislature.[12] They therefore claim that so long as they remain a province, their borders are "guaranteed" (which is true). But they make an extraordinary leap of logic when they add that the moment they declare independence, this guarantee applies to the "limits" of the new country.

This curious argument ignores the fact that Québec's UDI would be, as stated by Justice Robert Lesage of Québec Superior Court, "a repudiation of the Constitution of Canada."[13] The separatists are trying to have their cake and eat it, too.

In its 1994 draft *Act Respecting the Sovereignty of Québec*, the Québec National Assembly tried to deal with this problem. To ensure continuity of law, they provided that "laws passed by the Parliament of Canada" would immediately be incorporated as the laws of a secessionist Québec.[14] However, to adopt some Canadian laws in this way is merely an attempt by the seceding province to mirror in its own legal system some of the same laws that exist in Canada. It would not maintain Canadian constitutional protection. The fact is almost everyone who has examined this question now realizes that there will be a long period of "judicial insecurity," as the jurists call it, should conflict arise between the legal systems of Canada and a seceding Québec.[15]

A UDI would substantially weaken the position of Quebecers. "If Québec was attempting to ignore the Constitution and secede unilaterally, it could not be heard to complain that the borders of the new State differed from those permitted under the existing Canadian Constitution," comments Professor Monahan.[16]

It is not a remote possibility that Québec could lose large territories to the Northwest Territories, as Zebedee Nungak made clear in his Washington speech late in 1996. He reminded his audience that the Inuit who are now in Québec once were in the Northwest Territories, whose Inuit inhabitants by 1999 will be living in, and masters of, a new territory known as Nunavut. These people, he said, are "our cousins and aunts and uncles," and the changes occurring among them have taken place "without any convoluted, agonizing, political wailing and gnashing of teeth." He added, "Our natural thought is, as we look at Nunavut, 'This is where we came from, before we were carved up, politically, and handed to Québec in 1912.' " He spoke of their many daily ties and relationships, and said,

"[These] are a natural extension of what we are. Those relations, we have determined, cannot be cut simply by a pair of scissors called Québec sovereignty."[17] At Nungak's initiative, Québec Inuit have discussed with the Inuit of Nunavut the idea that they might join in one constitutional region, which would be outside Québec, although there is far from unanimity over the proposal.

Clearly, it is possible that the boundaries of Québec might be altered immediately following Québec's UDI to safeguard any or all of the following interests:

- The treaties and treaty rights of Aboriginal peoples under the James Bay and Northern Québec Agreement (affecting Crees and Inuit) and the Northeastern Québec Agreement (affecting Innu).

- The federal Crown's fiduciary and constitutional responsibilities in favour of the Crees and other Aboriginal peoples in Québec.

- Canada might have to protect its territorial integrity, by ensuring geographical continuity from large parts of northern Québec to the Atlantic provinces.

- Aboriginal rights and Canadian jurisdiction would have to be safeguarded against secessionist claims in the extensive offshore areas surrounding northern Québec, so as to continue federal administration of these essential areas.

- Canadian economic, environmental, and security interests in the offshore areas, as well as possibly in northern Québec, would need to be protected.

- Canada would have to ensure under international law that certain parts of the current province of Québec would not be under the "effective control" of any secessionist government.

This could happen before the seceding province had obtained "effective control" of its territory. Much will depend on what the federal government, Aboriginal peoples, and others do. The more extreme the steps taken by a secessionist Québec the more necessary it might become to alter Québec's existing borders following a UDI.

# The doctrine on which separatists rely

In talking about the "sacrosanct" nature of Québec's boundaries, separatists are also relying on a principle known as *uti possidetis,* a concept that, as one jurist describes, is often defined in a circular fashion: "one first defines a State, and then says that it possesses the territory that it happens to occupy."[18] In its full meaning this principle seems to be "as you possess, so you may possess."[19]

*Uti possidetis* is exactly what Québec separatists are arguing today. They have defined their new, independent Québec and, then, have simply claimed that it will possess the territory Québec province now occupies, conveniently ignoring or denying the right to self-determination of Aboriginal peoples whose traditional territories extend beyond the administrative boundaries of the province of Québec. The principle derives from Roman law and has been used frequently, by agreement, "for convenience and expediency,"[20] as one jurist has described it, to settle boundary disputes, first in Latin America, later in Africa and Asia. There are, however, strong differences of opinion as to how this principle is applied and in what circumstances it is justifiable.

Often *uti possidetis* has been used in circumstances of decolonization, always by agreement and mutual consent, motivated by the desire of the colonial power and the wish of both sides to avoid use of force and to preserve the boundaries established under the colonial regime. An observation made by Ian Brownlie, a well-known author on international law, is extremely important: the principle of *uti possidetis* is not mandatory or compulsory, and the States concerned are free to adopt other principles as the basis for a settlement.[21]

For example, in a dispute between Chile and Argentina, the arbitration court did not apply the principle, even though it had been agreed to by both parties, because there were conflicting claims (as there would be in a secessionist Québec).[22] It is of particular interest to the Crees that, in a frontier dispute between Burkina Faso and Mali in central Africa, the International Court of Justice ruled in 1986 that the principle of *uti possidetis* contradicts the principle of self-determination and implied that self-determination is transcendent.[23] This is supported by a 1977 statement by the Secretary-General of the Organization of American States that *uti possidetis* "does not constitute a sacrosanct principle, but may instead be overruled or revised, especially in the light of the right to self-determination."[24] The use of the word "sacrosanct" raises echoes of the repeated statements, by Lucien Bouchard and other separatist leaders, that Québec's borders are "sacrosanct" and that Aboriginal peoples within Québec do not have the right to self-determination. Not so, according to international legal authorities. In addition, the principle can be set aside for "considerations of justice and equity."[25]

One of the arguments used to justify *uti possidetis* is that it promotes stability. But this is not necessarily so,[26] as can be seen from the many border disputes in Africa, where the principle was generally applied on the breakup of the colonial empires. Finally, the international community has never recognized *uti possidetis* as an institution of international law. Rather, in international law, occupation and effective control are regarded as the basis for sovereignty.[27]

University of Texas law professor Steven Ratner has recently commented directly on the strong claim of the Crees to their lands in northern Québec, in the event of a secession which they opposed:

> A new claimant State ought not to be able to "take its indigenous peoples with it" from the old State by assuming its size and shape are determined by prior internal borders. An example arises in the case of the lands in Québec inhabited by the Cree Indians. Their rights under international law affect not only the underlying lawfulness of Québec's attempts at secession, but the contours of an independent Québec as well. To assume that Québec must encompass all these lands, even if the indigenous peoples indicate another preference, would ignore their special claim to land and extend, to a new State, antiquated notions of territorial sovereignty.[28]

94

And Professor Peter Hogg, leading constitutional lawyer of York University, adds emphasis to what the situation would be following a UDI:

> If the James Bay Crees and the Inuit of Nunavik continue to oppose the secession of Québec, then, in the event of a secession, the province would have to be partitioned, leaving the northern part in Canada. There is no rule of constitutional law or international law that stipulates that an independent Québec would keep the same boundaries as it had as a province.[29]

## Self-determination has precedence over uti possidetis

Judge Luchaire of the International Court of Justice, in the previously mentioned dispute between Burkina Faso and Mali, has established that the right to self-determination "does not necessarily lead to the independence of a State with the same frontiers as a former colony." He adds, ". . . [it] may evidently lead certain . . . parts of the former colony to a different option from that followed by the other parts."[30]

Although Québec is not a colony, Judge Luchaire's emphasis on the right to self-determination appears to have some relevance to the current situation in Québec, where we as Aboriginal peoples are asserting our right to self-determination in order to choose (if we wish) to remain in Canada.

All of these citations lead to one conclusion: if the right to self-determination can prevail over the *uti possidetis* principle even in a colonial context, then it can hardly be argued that it would not do so in the context of modern-day Québec. The conclusion must be that to apply *uti possidetis* in northern Québec would be unjust and inappropriate, because we indigenous peoples are asserting our right to self-determination, and because our claims in that region are stronger and more compelling than those of French-speaking and other Quebecers.

The recognition and demarcation of indigenous territories has become a matter of international significance. Even Daniel Turp, separatist law professor and MP, admits that the question of indigenous territory "could cause problems (for a secessionist Québec) from the standpoint of international law." Speaking of the possible wish of Québec Aboriginal peoples to remain within Canada, he wrote in 1992, "The territorial borders of the secessionist native nations would have to be determined, and the divergent views on the very existence of a territory belonging to a native nation, as well as on its boundaries, would have to be reconciled."[31] There is no doubt that the modern right of self-determination, as it has developed in international law, transcends the question of boundaries that may have been established — as in northern Québec — without consultation with the people most deeply affected, the inhabitants. A proper interpretation of self-determination must take into account what one American jurist has described as "the multiple patterns of human association and interdependency."[32] We Crees and other Aboriginal peoples of Québec certainly have "multiple patterns of human association and interdependency" that are critical to our way of life and that simply cannot be dismissed by the Québec government on the basis of misguided adherence to absolute rules concerning boundaries.

We Crees of James Bay seek to exercise self-determination in this spirit, through self-government in a Canadian context. We want to do so in a manner that fosters our relationships with other Crees and other peoples, Aboriginal and non-Aboriginal, within Canada, including Québec. And we want to do so in such a way as to enable our historical relationship with the federal Crown to continue and evolve.

No legal rule (even if it was applicable under the present circumstances, which we dispute) concerning boundaries could possibly force us to abandon our long-standing historical relationships, to accept the denial of our right to self-determination, or to accept that our pattern of existence be limited to the present borders of a province we did not create and that may be transformed against our express wishes into those of an independent Québec.

# 7

# Borders: two-thirds of Québec at issue

*Wherein it is shown that the territory of Québec when independent might be only a shadow of its former self*

We Crees, our Inuit neighbours, and other indigenous peoples have used and occupied our traditional territories in what is now northern Québec for thousands of years. Yet, four times — in 1670, 1870, 1898, and 1912 — our lands were claimed, bought, sold, and transferred from one authority to another, and the Aboriginal peoples who lived there were virtually ignored.

"In 1670, King Charles of England gave to the Hudson's Bay Company all the land that sheds water into Hudson's Bay," says Grand Chief of the Crees of Québec Matthew Coon Come. "He named this Rupert's Land after his cousin Rupert. Nobody told or asked us, the real owners of these lands, who included *Eeyouch*, our people the Crees.

"In 1870 another Royal colonial grant was made. This time Rupert's Land was granted to Canada, a country that was just three years old. Again no one spoke to us or told us. Then again in 1898 and 1912, Rupert's Land was transferred once more, this time by [the Canadian] Parliament to a number of provinces including Québec. Again nobody thought to inform, let alone consult, us."[1]

All of this happened in spite of the fact that, as a report undertaken by Court of Appeal Justice A.C. Hamilton and commissioned by the Canadian government concludes, "no European government or monarch had the right or authority to claim or grant lands . . . they did not lawfully possess."[2] There had been no wars of conquest by which the European powers had acquired these lands. They were not obtained by discovery or occupation, because they were already the domain of Aboriginal peoples. They were certainly not *terra nullius*, "land belonging to no one," and thus open to occupation by the first newcomer who came along. Rather, they were owned, fully occupied, and governed by various Aboriginal nations.

Yet without any justification whatsoever, the King of England claimed all of this huge territory in 1670 and gave it to the Hudson's Bay Company, which sold it to the Canadian government, which in turn annexed it to the province of Québec. The Crees, Inuit, and other peoples who lived there were simply tranferred like so many cattle along with our land, without our knowledge or consent.

In 1867, when Canada was established, Québec was only one-third of its present size. The northern territories were administered by the Hudson's Bay Company, and when this land was transferred to the new Dominion of Canada in 1870, it was entirely subject to federal control.[3] The actual surrender of Rupert's Land by the Company went this way: the Hudson's Bay Company signed a deed of surrender on 19 November 1869. This ended 199 years of Company rule over about 40 per cent of what is now Canada. An Order-in-Council was signed by Queen Victoria on 23 June 1870, transferring the territory to Canada. The government of Canada paid £300,000 to the Company. The following month an Imperial Order-in-Council decreed that Rupert's Land was now part of Canada. The Canadian Parliament, in an Address to the Queen, made a commitment to "settle the claims of the Indian tribes" in conformity with "the equitable principles which have uniformly governed the British Crown in its dealings with the aborigines."[4] More specifically Canada pledged that "it will be our duty to make adequate provision for the protection of the Indian tribes whose interest and well-being are involved in the transfer."

The first boundary extension in favour of the province of Québec, north to the Eastmain River, was made in 1898. It took into Québec an area of land along the Ontario border about the size of the State of Minnesota and an area in the east that was later (in 1927) included in Labrador. This 1898 territory today includes six of the nine Cree communities in northern Québec. The second boundary extension, in 1912, took in all of the remaining part of the Ungava Peninsula north of the 1898 border which was not part of Labrador. Today three Cree and fifteen Inuit villages and their traditional territories are in this area, whose name was changed from Ungava to New Québec.

When legislation was passed by the federal Parliament and the Québec legislature to give effect to the 1912 boundary extension, certain conditions were attached. These were very specific:

- That the province of Québec "will recognize the rights of the Indian inhabitants in the territory . . . to the same extent, and will obtain surrenders of such rights in the same manner, as the Government of Canada has heretofore done." Québec shall "bear and satisfy all charges and expenditures" arising out of such surrenders.

- That no such surrender shall be made or obtained except with the approval of the (Canadian) Governor in Council.

- That the trusteeship[5] of the Indians and the management of any lands "now or hereafter reserved for their use," shall remain in the Government of Canada subject to the control of Parliament.

The territorial rights of the James Bay Crees would probably have continued to be ignored had not the Québec government in 1971 initiated the James Bay hydroelectric project right in the middle of traditional *Eeyouch* territory. Only in 1974-75, after extensive litigation, did Québec open negotiations to meet the province's obligations undertaken sixty-two years before.

There may never have been any negotiations had it not been for a 1973 decision of the Supreme Court of Canada, in what is known as the Calder case, in which Nisga'a Indians from northern British Columbia claimed recognition of their Aboriginal rights in their land. The judges' verdicts split three to three on the issue of whether such rights exist or not, but that decision prompted a reassessment of Aboriginal rights by the government of Canada.

No such reassessment was undertaken by the province of Québec, which, throughout the negotiations with the Crees and Inuit in the 1970s, insisted that there were no native rights and no obligations to meet. The lack of an appropriate response by the federal government to this outlandish position adopted by the Québec government violated the constitutional commitment to deal equitably with First Nations that was made by the Canadian Parliament in 1867 and 1869, and it also violated the government of Québec's commitment made in 1912.

Seventeen years later the Supreme Court commented in another case that ". . . the James Bay development by Québec Hydro was originally initiated without regard to the rights of the Indians who lived there, even though these were expressly protected by a constitutional instrument. . . . It took a number of judicial decisions and notably the *Calder* case in this court, to prompt a reassessment of the position being taken by the government."[6] As we shall see in chapter 9, nearly a quarter of a century after the negotiations of the early 1970s, Québec government lawyers in 1996 were still in Canadian courts denying that any Aboriginal land rights have ever existed in their province.


## *In violation of basic principles*


This whole story of the treatment of our Aboriginal lands in northern Québec is one of flagrant violation of our rights and of the basic principles and standards that bound the governments of the time. Parliamentary papers from the early part of this century indicate that the accepted standard even at that time was to transfer territory to a province only if the inhabitants agreed. This standard seems to have been applied, at least to some extent, in Manitoba and Saskatchewan, which also received part of Rupert's Land, but it was totally ignored in Québec.

In 1905 a committee of the Privy Council of Canada, speaking of Manitoba, indicated that to force people into a union that is repugnant to them would be an act "requiring strong grounds for its justification." The Privy Council recalled that Sir Wilfrid Laurier had expressly promised that people would not be forced into a union with Manitoba against their wishes, and added, "Here we have the explicit declaration of the Prime Minister that if the people of this territory do not consent . . . the parliament of Canada ought not to make the grant against their wishes."[7] In 1906, the government of Saskatchewan endorsed this same principle, describing it as a "duty" of the federal government.[8] Similar statements are recorded in 1911 and 1912. The federal responsibility to Aboriginal peoples was of the highest order, because of the trusteeship duty owed towards Aboriginal peoples by the Crown (later transferred to the Canadian government).

In Québec, nothing was done either to inform or to seek the consent of Aboriginal peoples about the Ungava transfer. In fact, on 27 April 1909 the Premier of Québec, Lomer Gouin, tabled a resolution in the Québec Assembly which stated baldly that Ungava "geographically forms part of the province of Québec, and it is in the interest of such territory as well as in that of the province, that it be annexed" to the province of Québec.[9]

This mindset has persisted up to our own time. In 1979, just before Québec's first referendum on sovereignty, the Parti Québécois (then ruling the province) put out an official publication loaded with fanciful and imaginative accounts of how Québec got its hands on the natural resources in the province. They wrote: "Québec's resources are permanent. We do not owe them to a political system, or to specific circumstances. They are a gift of nature, which has favoured us more than others in this respect by allowing us to play a more important economic role, thanks to our resources."[10] In fact, however, the huge resources of the northern two-thirds of the province were not given by nature to the Québec government: far from it, they were the result of a Canadian political deal that gave the province expanded law-making powers without the knowledge or consent of the Aboriginal peoples in the area and at our expense. What was done at that time would certainly not meet the requirements of international law today concerning the need to obtain the consent of the Aboriginal peoples.

Things have been changing dramatically. In international law there is growing legal opinion that failure to obtain the consent of the inhabitants of a region for which cession is contemplated is a violation of their right to self-determination.[11]

This idea, actually, is not that new; it has simply taken time to become a generally accepted principle of international practice. Eighteenth-century French philosopher Jean-Jacques Rousseau, whose writings so influenced the French and American Revolutions, commented on the issue directly and succinctly. "It is making fools of people," he wrote, "to tell them seriously that one can at one's pleasure transfer people from master to master, like herds of cattle, without consulting their interests or their wishes."[12] More than one hundred years later U.S. President Woodrow Wilson emphasized how fundamental it is to obtain people's consent in the context of self-determination and transfer of territory. "The settlement of every question, whether of territory, of sovereignty, of economic arrangement, or of political relationship, [must be] upon the basis of the free acceptance of that settlement by the people immediately concerned . . ." he wrote in 1918.[13]

In 1975 the International Court of Justice came to the same conclusion, insisting, in a case about the Western Sahara, on respect for "the right of the population . . . to determine their future political status by their own freely expressed will."[14] Similarly, the practice of the United Nations General Assembly confirms that the ultimate sovereignty over territory resides with the indigenous people to such a degree that a genuine assessment of their consent, as one writer has put it, "has become a virtual requirement of legal transfers of territorial title."[15]

# Some novel ideas

Québec jurists, politicians, commentators, and journalists have resorted to defensive arguments, which are sustainable neither in fact nor in law, about the transfer of the northern territories. Their purpose is to claim that an independent Québec would have the right to retain the northern territories that it obtained as a province of Canada. In their attempts to establish this they have come up with some novel ideas.

Professor Henri Brun, for instance, who made an extensive study of Québec's boundaries a quarter of a century ago, argues that Canada received Rupert's Land in 1870 from Britain in a capacity not representing the federal government, but as somehow representing the interests of the four existing provinces (Ontario, Québec, New Brunswick, and Nova Scotia).[16] This, a pretty far-out idea, is not supported by the facts. In fact, the opposite is the case, and Québec jurists must know this.

The Rupert's Land and North-Western Territory Order, under which the 1870 transfer was made, explicitly refers to the Canadian government and Parliament, as well as to their obligation to Aboriginal peoples. This reflects the human-rights position of the British Parliament of that period. In the late eighteenth and early nineteenth centuries, the British Empire had brought English settlers into contact with Aboriginal peoples in many parts of the world, and a strong movement had grown in Britain to advocate and insist upon the protection of these peoples wherever British power was imposed. A Select Committee on Aborigines was established by the British House of Commons, and in 1837 it recommended that protection of Aborigines was a duty "peculiarly belonging and appropriate to the Executive Department Government . . . either in this country or by the Governors of the respective Colonies." The Select Committee added, "This is not a trust which could conveniently be confided to the local Legislatures . . . ,"[17] by which, undoubtedly, they meant such bodies as provincial Parliaments or legislatures in Canada. So much for Professor Brun's argument.

When the land transfers were made, Britain gave the central authority in Canada, the federal government, the power to safeguard Aboriginal peoples and their lands from prejudicial actions by the provinces. Parliamentary papers of that time show that, when the boundaries of Québec, Ontario, and Manitoba were extended in 1912, this was done solely to enable the provinces to develop better *as provinces* and thereby further unify the Canadian federation. The provinces concerned had no preexisting rights in these territories, none at all. The reasons for the provincial boundary extensions were pan-Canadian. For example, Prime Minister Laurier wanted the provinces to have equal access to Hudson's Bay, and Manitoba was extended "to preserve geographical symmetry" within Canada,[18] which was held to be "essential for confederation."[19]

Thus the sole basis of the extension of provincial jurisdiction over Ungava was Québec's status as a province. Continuation of that status was an implied condition of the transfer. Québec did not buy the Ungava. It was voluntarily transferred by Canada along with certain powers. Canada retained the remaining powers. Thus jurisdiction was held jointly.

Many contemporary jurists and commentators support this view. For example, Professor Stephen Scott, of McGill University, says that "an independent Québec has no valid historical or legal claim to the northern part of the present province. The immense territories . . . were . . . under English sovereignty long before the cession of New France in 1763, and (had) no connection with New France. These territories were added to Québec to be governed as part of a Canadian province."[20] Similarly, a 1991 editorial in Canada's national newspaper, the *Globe and Mail*, said that ". . . the district of Ungava was ceded to Québec by acts of Parliament, as part of Canada. It was not meant as a going away present."[21]

# Imposing Québec's "territorial integrity"

Over the last four hundred years the Crees have experienced a melancholy history of colonialist controls imposed on them and their lands with no pretence of democratic validation. Though we are now living in a world that is better informed than ever before about principles of consent, justice, and democratic legitimacy, it seems that the Crees must yet again confront colonialist attitudes: the Parti Québécois government now claims that the "territorial integrity" of Québec is "unassailable," regardless of the rights of Aboriginal peoples.

"There is no way that any Quebecer would accept that a square inch of that territory be extracted from Québec," said current Premier Lucien Bouchard, in 1994.[22]

And David Cliche, who formerly worked for the Grand Council of the Crees in Great Whale River, and who for many years has been the separatist politician most closely identified with Aboriginal matters, has said as recently as February 1995, ". . . the freedom to walk away from an independent Québec. . . . That's where we don't agree. . . . We can never accept the idea that Aboriginal lands can be taken out of Québec."[23] The province of Québec, apparently, can walk away from Canada, but no one, absolutely no one, can walk away from the province of Québec. Or so they say.

Many people have commented on this double standard. Professor Scott told the Québec National Assembly Committee on Sovereignty, "I cannot accept this kind of reasoning, be it on the level of constitutional law . . . international law, or even . . . of simple morality. . . . [To] suggest that Québec is indivisible suggests . . . that Canada is as well. . . . [To] suggest that Canada is divisible suggests that Québec is also."[24]

More than a year before the 1995 referendum, Michel Venne, a reporter for *Le Devoir*, the nationalist newspaper in Montréal, wrote that "the Indian chiefs of Québec . . . reject the concept of the integrity of Québec and affirm . . . the right to choose whom [they wish] to associate with. . . . They emphasize that . . . any amendment to the constitutional or political framework requires [their] consent."[25] Conferences held late in 1994 by First Nations in Québec and the Nunavik (Inuit) Leaders each declared that changes in their status require their consent.[26]

Separatists deny Aboriginal rights, exaggerate their claims to territory, and proclaim shameless double standards, for reasons that were perhaps explained by Jack Aubry, an Ottawa *Citizen* reporter, who wrote in May 1994, "The stakes over Québec's territorial integrity are high. Without its North, an independent Québec, with its emphasis on hydro development, would have difficulty remaining viable."[27]

We Crees reject the so-called "principle" that places Québec's "territorial integrity" above our right as Aboriginal peoples to choose our own future. We know that if ever Québec does attempt to seize independence by an illegal process, this question of "territorial integrity" is likely to become a flashpoint. With that in mind, the Grand Council of the Crees has already, in 1992, formally submitted our objections to the United Nations Commission on Human Rights. Many reasons are cited by the Grand Council:

• Québec has no historic claims or preexisting rights in the northern territories. We have such claims going back thousands of years.

• Crees will not validate prejudicial and unfair colonial actions by Canada and Québec. Cree traditional territory became part of the province of Québec without Cree knowledge and consent. This violated national and international norms and has had far-reaching adverse consequences, leading to the current Québec claim on Cree territory. These prejudicial actions have not yet been equitably addressed.

• The most urgent issue is to guarantee the integrity of the traditional Cree and other Aboriginal territories. The Crees and other indigenous peoples are threatened repeatedly by Québec and other governments with dispossession, denial of title, unwanted development projects, environmental degradation, and other unacceptable actions. These actions severely undermine the continuing development of the Crees and other First Nations.

- The alleged paramountcy of the "principle" of Québec "territorial integrity" seriously detracts from any principle of equal rights of peoples. If applied it would entrench the concept of superior title, rights, and status by Québec over indigenous peoples and their territories. Far from resulting in equality, this would perpetuate colonial dominance and racial discrimination against Aboriginal peoples. Instead, Québec should explore the possibility of genuine cooperation and equality with Aboriginal peoples.

- This so-called "principle" of the "territorial integrity" of Québec is used in an effort to sever Aboriginal peoples from our traditional territories and natural environment. The separatist Québec government has repeatedly ignored Cree rights, values, priorities, and concerns, with its hydroelectric and other developments in Cree traditional territory. Only through enormous Cree effort and a year-long campaign was the Great Whale hydroelectric project indefinitely postponed.[28]

- The territorial integrity of a secessionist Québec would be in doubt unless and until "effective control" over its territory were clearly established. But even if Québec were recognized as an independent State, there is no rule in international law that the "principle" of the "territorial integrity" of States is always paramount over other principles such as the right to self-determination. The creation of an independent Québec without the informed consent of the Crees would be a fundamental violation of Cree rights, and that alone would invalidate Québec's claims to "territorial integrity."

- Although the Québec government demands that Aboriginal peoples should recognize that their rights are inferior to Québec's "territorial integrity," a secessionist Québec would never agree to a similar concession vis-à-vis Canada, that is, to recognize the supremacy of the territorial integrity of Canada over the rights of Quebecers. Far from it: when applied to

Canada, the Québec government seeks to minimize the significance of territorial integrity.

- If Aboriginal peoples were to concede the principle of Québec "territorial integrity" we would likely be faced with having our traditional territories automatically included in any secession by Québec from Canada, without our consent. This could severely undermine our right of self-determination and restrict, if not totally deny, our potential options. In this regard, we may recall Bouchard's statement that Aboriginal nations do not have the right to self-determination.

- Based on existing constitutional provisions, Parliament and the government of Canada have fiduciary responsibilities to protect Aboriginal territories should they be threatened with forcible inclusion in a new Québec "State." This constitutional responsibility would be reinforced by the fact that there is no existing legal right demanding respect for the "territorial integrity" of a seceding Québec. Rather, in the event of a unilateral declaration of a UDI by the PQ government or the National Assembly, legally speaking, it would be the territorial integrity of Canada that would merit respect.

As Professor Tony Hall, of the University of Lethbridge, writes, "By supporting the right of First Nations in Québec to assert their own territorial integrity, the federal government would in turn be advancing the territorial integrity of Canada."[29]

Even the first separatist Premier of Québec, René Lévesque, said northern Québec was our country. He told the Québec National Assembly, ". . . if one takes into account several centuries of history . . . it was their country and . . . it is this country that we share now."[30] The idea of the sacred or sacrosanct nature of Québec's boundaries was also given short shrift by Barry Came, a journalist who looked into the matter for *Maclean's* magazine of Toronto in 1995: "[It is] . . . faintly absurd," he wrote. "To the natives (who have inhabited the place continuously since the last ice age ended 10,000 years ago), the current provincial frontiers are arbitrary lines on a map, drawn by European newcomers who paid scant attention to the well-established territories of many native populations."[31]

Chief Billy Diamond, one of the negotiators of the 1975 treaty, has summed it up well: "We Cree people live in and govern our territory in the north. . . . As long as we continue to be Cree people and feel that attachment to our land and resources, no piece of paper nor legal scheme can change that."[32] In short, as our Cree representative told the United Nations Commission on Human Rights, it is unacceptable to say that our Aboriginal rights are subject to the so-called principle of Québec's "territorial integrity." What is important for us is to secure recognition of our own right to self-determination and ensure the integrity of our traditional territories that remain so highly vulnerable to the actions of others.

Unfortunately, following the 1995 referendum, the attitude of the Québec government has hardened towards Aboriginal rights. It would be good to be able to report that enlightenment has struck the government, but it does not appear to have happened. Perhaps this hardening of attitude has arisen from desperation born of the growing realization that Aboriginal rights could sink the secessionist hopes for an independent nation. Whatever the reason, the separatist Québec government's lack of sympathy with Aboriginal peoples has now been taken to such a point that in 1996 the government sent its lawyers to the Supreme Court of Canada to argue for colonialist doctrines that were outrageous when first imported to Canada with the first arrival of Europeans and are scarcely believable when advocated nearly four hundred years later. This case, which nakedly exposes the separatist movement's pretensions to democracy and legitimacy, is dealt with in chapter 9.

# Summary: a history of arrogance towards the Crees

As can be judged from the foregoing, the attitude of both the federal and Québec governments towards the claims of the James Bay Crees has over many years been harsh, unsympathetic, and unyielding. Right up to the present day the Québec government, with the support of some Québec academics, has insisted that there are no Native rights and no obligations to meet; and in their rush to independence they pay scant attention to our long-held Cree rights in relation to traditional territories. We know, however, that our rights are central to any discussion of the borders of a secessionist Québec.

The federal government, for its part, has failed to respond to Québec's denial of Aboriginal rights. For many decades Canada's apathy and indifference permitted Québec to avoid its constitutional commitments which were undertaken by the Canadian Parliament in 1867 and 1869, to deal equitably with First Nations.[33]

It is worth noting the actual words used in the *Québec Boundaries Extension Act, 1912*, when our traditional territories were annexed to the province of Québec: "That the trusteeship of the Indians in the said Territory, and the management of any lands now or hereafter reserved for their use, shall remain in the Government of Canada subject to the control of Parliament." Although this section was repealed by legislation passed in 1976–77 to give effect to the James Bay and Northern Québec Agreement, this repeal did not abolish the federal fiduciary responsibility towards the Aboriginal people of James Bay and our lands, because the 1912 act did not create that responsibility. In legal language the 1912 act simply declared a preexisting fiduciary duty, and this fiduciary duty continues. The statute repealing that provision states that "Parliament and the Government of Canada recognize and affirm a special responsibility for the said Crees and Inuit."[34]

Some jurists have argued that the historical grievances of the Crees are irrelevant to the future disposition of our northern lands.[35] Yet the injustices suffered by *Eeyouch* began with the arrival of the first Europeans among us and have continued to the present day. These injustices make a formidable list:

- Canada and Québec should have determined the wishes of the *Eeyouch* and others before changing boundaries, in 1870, 1898, and 1912, but they did not.

- Canada should have insisted that Québec fulfil its 1912 obligation to recognize the rights of Aboriginal peoples in the former Rupert's Land, but it did not.

- In 1971 Canada and Québec vigorously and repeatedly denied that we *Eeyouch* had any land and resource rights in our traditional territory, and we were forced into court in defence of our way of life.

- At that time, Canada and Québec compelled the *Eeyouch* and Inuit to negotiate the James Bay and Northern Québec Agreement under unconscionable conditions (dealt with in detail in the next chapter).

- At that time, the Canadian government totally abdicated its constitutional and fiduciary responsibility to protect Aboriginal rights and territories, by adopting a position of what it called "alert neutrality" towards Québec's unconscionable actions.

- Today, in confronting Québec's possible secession, Canada should be defending and supporting Cree rights in Québec, but is not. Québec should recognize these rights, but on the contrary, against all legal precedent, denies them.

Thus, this sad history of betrayal and double-dealing continues to the present day. The separatist leaders Jacques Parizeau, Lucien Bouchard, and others react with strong indignation to any suggestion that the northern territories could be removed from an independent Québec. They become indignant, too, if the authority of Québec over natural resources is even questioned. We *Eeyouch* are still being deprived of resource rights in our traditional territory.

It is not pleasant for us to admit that the injustices suffered by the *Eeyouch* continue.

# 8

# The James Bay and Northern Québec Agreement: a treaty denied

*Wherein governments have to be dragged kicking
and screaming to court in an effort to force them to
obey the law*

In 1975 Crees and Inuit signed the James Bay and Northern Québec Agreement (JBNQA) with the federal and Québec governments. We believe this agreement has since been misused by these governments. Yet whatever our reservations about it, our rights in the agreement are recognized and protected under Canada's Constitution in the same way as a treaty, and the courts have ruled that the agreement cannot be changed without the consent of all parties.

That includes us, as the two governments discovered to their cost when they tried to do an end-run around us in their effort to force the Great Whale hydroelectric project through in the early 1990s.

The agreement was signed on the assumption of a continuing and permanent federalist framework. The secession of Québec from Canada would create a most fundamental change in this treaty, and in itself would be a violation of our rights.

Separatists say the JBNQA is irrelevant to the question of Québec secession. We do not agree. It is not only relevant, but is an issue of central importance to the future of Québec and Canada. Let us consider this agreement in more detail, its pros and cons, and the controversial circumstances (extremely onerous for its Aboriginal signatories) in which it was signed.

At first we *Eeyouch* had some hopes for the JBNQA, believing it to be a social contract concerning our future, a document that would continue to evolve with changing circumstances. From the beginning, however, Québec has interpreted the agreement "as a carte blanche to pursue hydro-electric development," to quote Dietrich Soyez, a German geographer.[1]

Indeed, both governments have interpreted the agreement in a manner so careless of Cree values and interests that Grand Chief Matthew Coon Come has described it as "a shameful reminder of Canada's duplicity and ingratitude. . . . infamous as Canada's first modern broken treaty."[2]

The reason that the agreement has not worked for the Crees is that it did not, as we had hoped, give us real control over what is happening in our traditional territories, and our consent is not sought before projects are undertaken. The agreement promises protection for Cree rights and way of life, but most of the many boards, commissions, and other governmental bodies established under it were merely advisory and have not functioned properly. Unfortunately, the two governments, instead of honestly using this structure to provide Crees with control over our destiny, have used it to bypass Aboriginal values, priorities, and aspirations and to push hydroelectric, mining, forestry, and other industrial projects at the expense of the Cree economy, way of life, and culture.

Internationally, it is now recognized that indigenous peoples should be closely involved in planning all activities that impact on our territories, and our consent should be obtained for future projects, even by regional and local governments.[3]

We Crees now find ourselves confronted with staggering double standards. Secessionists argue that Québec needs greater powers to ensure its future, but in almost the same breath they say we Crees have no right to self-determination.

On the one hand they say we have autonomy under the agreement; on the other, that all Cree rights have been extinguished.[4] Extinguishment of Indian rights, titles, and interests has been Canadian government policy for centuries. But this policy has been described by Chief Billy Diamond as "an anachronistic antique from the days of colonialism and attempted conquest," and he is not alone in believing that the policy is "illegitimate, immoral and has no effect on our fundamental rights."[5]

Québec separatists repeatedly claim that the JBNQA is a model of fairness and generosity,[6] but it is clear what they have in mind: their main interest is to assert that we Crees and Inuit have surrendered our right to self-determination and, therefore, to the northern lands.

PQ minister Jacques Brassard has left no doubt about the separatist attitude: "In this agreement, in return for receiving a certain number of things: money, very certainly, but also other things, including a certain governmental autonomy, the Crees renounce . . . their rights to the northern territory of Québec," he told the National Assembly's Committee on Sovereignty in 1991.[7] When he heard Brassard say that, André Patry, of the Université de Montréal, who has at various times been a law professor at all three of Québec's major French-language universities and an international advisor to the government of Québec, responded immediately. By Brassard's logic, he said, the Crees would no longer be an Aboriginal people:

> An Aboriginal person . . . maintains with nature a quasi-mystical relationship. There is no question of sovereignty nor of ownership, these terms do not exist in the native languages. [Theirs] . . . is a concept of management . . . of responsibility: to respect nature and follow its destiny. If they abandon all these rights, they are no longer Aboriginal peoples.[8]

# The unconscionable behaviour
# of governments

The 1975 agreement arose in response to the many threats posed to the Crees by the Québec government's 1971 decision to build a huge hydroelectric project right in the middle of our traditional territories. Aboriginal people were not even advised of what the government had in mind, but had to read about it in the newspapers. When the Québec government lawyers got to court in 1972 (dragged there unwillingly by the Crees and Inuit), they argued that the Aboriginal case was "absurd," that the Crees and Inuit did not have, and never had, any rights of any kind, that, in fact, there was no case to answer.[9]

The Québec government's attitude was brutal. The project was announced and preliminary work begun without any environmental or social assessment of any kind. Only engineers counted. Little biological information about the territory was available, even to the Euro-Canadian scientific system. And the government exhibited a profound contempt for our Cree and Inuit knowledge about the biology of the land and animals with which our people have lived so intimately for so many centuries. The Aboriginal knowledge, of course, is far more profound for this territory than that of science, whose accumulated knowledge at that time had merely scratched the surface of a territory on which non-Aboriginal peoples had made little impact.

Those Crees with the most profound knowledge, our elders, had no doubt about the effects the project would have on the land, the animals, and, thus, themselves. "There will never be enough money to pay for the damage that has been done," said Chisasibi hunter Job Bearskin, in 1972. "I'd rather think about the land, and think about the children. What will they have when that land is destroyed? The money means nothing."

"When the dams are built, where will the animals go? The caribou won't know which way to go," said hunter Samson Nahacappo. And Charlie Gunner, of Mistissini, said, "If you set fire to the land, the land remains, and life returns to it. If you set fire to a piece of paper, like a dollar bill, it burns away to the end, and nothing is left."

Isaiah Awashish, of Mistissini, a man whose entire life had been lived, as we Crees say, "in the bush," told a meeting held to discuss a government offer in 1974, "The money we have been offered is really nothing. The land is the most important thing of all. It is what everyone here has survived on, and we cannot sell it. We cannot exchange money for our land. That way cannot be. In ten years the money, maybe, will all be gone."[10]

The engineers and their political sponsors, however, had no real concern about any of these things. When it first announced the scheme in 1971, the Québec government proposed to change completely the runoff patterns of three rivers running into James Bay, used by millions of migrating birds in the spring and fall, without even considering the impact this would have on the lands and waters (and, of course, the birds, animals, and people) of the Bay. This was not only the height of irresponsibility, but it revealed a staggering arrogance, both towards the workings of nature and towards Aboriginal peoples whose way of life depends on the very lands and waters that were to be so drastically modified. No respect or consideration whatsoever was given by either government to Cree territorial rights. It was more than half a century since Québec had been under the strict condition to deal with the land rights of Crees, Inuit, and other Aboriginal groups. On that basis, no resources should have been extracted from these territories until the Aboriginal rights had first been dealt with. But nothing had been done. And during those fifty years the federal government had acquiesced in Québec's negligence.

Now that the matter had become one of survival for the Crees, the federal Indian Affairs department continued to sit on its hands in complete violation of Canada's trusteeship responsibility to ensure that Indians were fairly dealt with. Only after litigation was initiated by the *Eeyouch* did Québec and the federal government decide to negotiate with us.

When the Crees did get to court, Justice Albert Malouf of Québec Superior Court found, after a six-month hearing, that any disruption of the Cree way of life "compromises their very existence as a people."[11] Nearly twenty years later, Justice Paul Rouleau of the federal court came to a similar conclusion. This time what was at issue was the Great Whale hydroelectric proposal, slated to begin in 1991 in continuation of the massive James Bay project. Construction had been going on along La Grande and other rivers continuously for twenty years. The many dams that had been built and the huge reservoirs behind them had already completely disrupted enormous areas of our Cree hunting grounds. By the time of the 1991 case, the Québec and Canadian governments were legally obliged by the 1975 agreement to undertake environmental and social assessments of the project. Both governments refused to do so. This time we Crees were better prepared. We knew what to expect; the apprehensions expressed by our elders twenty years before had proven to be more than justified. This time our leaders went to battle with the white man's political structure. They now had the chance to tell the decision-making bodies the Cree viewpoint. For example, Robbie Dick, Cree Chief in Great Whale River (Whapmagoostui), testified before the National Energy Board:

> My people don't think the land can be replaced by anything. Once it is lost, it is lost. . . . It is impossible for my people to even think of the idea that the land they use will not be there. They cannot conceive that this can happen. If it happens, we will lose part of our life. Because our land is our life. . . . The river is going to be totally lost up to the first rapids. . . . Once the river disappears, part of our culture disappears with it.

At the same hearing, the veteran hunter John Petagumskum indicated in a remarkable passage the intimate Cree relationship with the animals (something that had been totally ignored by decision-makers twenty years before):

> We hold the highest respect for the freshwater seal; because although it was hard to hunt, it saved the lives of entire families at times past when famine struck.

When all else was not available, by miracle a hunter killed a freshwater seal. It was as if the Creator planned it this way. . . . There was, and still is, a belief that one has to show respect for the game that was given to him by the Creator for his very subsistence. . . .

His estimate of the probable impact of the Great Whale project was as devastating as that of the elders when first confronted by hydroelectric construction in the early 1970s, and equally moving:

[The project] will no doubt be devastating to the Crees. . . . It will impact on the land, and the animals, fish and birds that live in the river valleys and around the lakes. . . . Disease will strike all those animals, because new things will be in the water. . . . This disease will eventually affect other game, one after another, because they live on each other, and the water. It will eventually affect humans, because we eat this food. We have no other land, and this project is on the rivers and lakes where all things live. . . . The animals all need each other, and with the passing of the animals, the Crees of Whapmagoostui will lose their way of life.[12]

This profound understanding of the intimate relationship between all living things, expressed here by Petagumskum, lies at the heart of the Cree view of life and is something that is seldom, if ever, taken into account by engineers, accountants, and politicians as they dream up their massive projects.

This time our Cree Regional Authority went to court in an effort to force the governments to respect the agreement they had solemnly signed in 1975 and had written into their own laws. Astonishingly, both governments argued that the signatures of their leaders and the approval of their legislatures did not create legally binding obligations in favour of Aboriginal peoples. This is typical of the specious and duplicitous arguments we Crees have repeatedly faced when we have tried to get governments to observe their own laws.

Fortunately, the two governments were handed a humiliating backhander by the courts. Justice Rouleau described some of the government arguments as "ludicrous." He said the Québec and Canadian governments had tried to change the agreement without the participation of the Crees, one of the signatories, and that this could not be done. He wrote, "This agreement was signed in good faith for the protection of the Cree and Inuit peoples, not to deprive them of their rights and territories without due consideration. . . . I feel a profound sense of duty to respond favourably. Any contrary determination would once again provoke, within the native groups, a sense of victimization by white society and its institutions."[13]

Justice Rouleau's decision in our favour was upheld by the Federal Court of Appeal, so that eventually (entirely because of the Cree court battle) the two governments were forced to undertake an environmental and social assessment of the impact of the Great Whale hydroelectric project. This study delayed the start of the project for some years. When it was finished, the study was so unfavourable to the project that, on the day after it was received by the Québec government, Premier Jacques Parizeau postponed the Great Whale project indefinitely.

## An oppressive negotiation

This foot-dragging reluctance of the governments to respect the law is, of course, nothing new. It merely echoes their behaviour in the 1970s, when the JBNQA was signed. The Crees and Inuit were forced to sign the 1975 agreement after a long negotiation in which we were placed under extreme duress and were opposed by powerful and wealthy entities that did not hesitate to threaten and bully us. For the twenty years since then, the governments have used the 1975 agreement to favour hydroelectric and other resource exploitation and suppress Cree rights. All this has seriously eroded Cree confidence in the JBNQA. And it has also made Crees understand how we are likely to be treated within an independent Québec, should it ever come into existence.

The following section should give readers some idea of what went on during negotiation of the JBNQA:

**Extreme duress:** The hydroelectric project was being built on La Grande River, against Cree wishes, while the negotiations were going on. So, confronted with the imminent destruction of the rivers and the flooding of vast areas of land, we really had no choice but to try for the best deal we could get. "We saw the need to limit the damages, seek remedial works and have certain fundamental rights recognized. . . . We really had no other choice," wrote Chief Diamond, one of the major Cree negotiators, twenty years later.[14] Government negotiators arrived at the table with surrender and extinguishment of rights as conditions which were not subject to discussion or debate. "Canada made it clear," wrote Chief Diamond, "that if we did not proceed with the agreement process, unilateral legislation would have been imposed on us."[15]

The Grand Council of the Crees, in November 1993, described to the Royal Commission on Aboriginal Peoples the duress under which our leaders negotiated:

- Our rights to our lands, waters, and way of life were being taken from us while we negotiated. The Federal Government was threatening to cut off funds we depended upon to defend our rights. All governments were using false and illegitimate arguments, including that we had no Aboriginal rights or title. We were told we were squatters. Thus the agreement was negotiated under conditions of fundamental error, if governments truly believed what they told us, or of fraud if they did not.

- The social position of our people was desperate, and programs we depended on were being cut and frozen while negotiations were underway.

- We were obliged to negotiate against the might of three development corporations and two governments.

- We were forced to accept structures, institutions, and principles that did not reflect Cree law, culture, or beliefs but, rather, those of the dominant societies.

- The federal government failed to assert its fiduciary obligation to protect our rights and interests, instead maintaining a morally and legally bankrupt position of what it called "alert neutrality."

- We knew that by the time we could reach the Supreme Court of Canada the project would be completed, and the balance of convenience would have swung against us.[16]

The duress we were under was described at the time by Joe Clark, then Leader of the Opposition in the federal Parliament and, later, Prime Minister of Canada. He said in 1976,

> [They] . . . were negotiating under the gun of a deadline to which they had to adhere. If they did not adhere, they and their people would suffer serious consequences. . . . [The] process . . . has had the effect of forcing upon Native people in a distant part of this land agreements which in all reasonable likelihood they would not have accepted had they been able to negotiate free of the constraints that were placed upon them.[17]

Professor Peter Cumming, of Osgoode Hall, York University, author of one of the first comprehensive legal studies of Native rights in Canada,[18] agrees. He wrote in 1979:

> The James Bay settlement is simply a forced purchase, an offer "that could not be refused," in the sense that no other offer would be made. Construction . . . went on throughout the negotiations. All provincial parties supported the hydroelectric

scheme. . . . The federal government was not prepared, and indeed was politically unable, to exert any pressure upon the Québec government. It was the provincial government that negotiated this settlement.[19]

Wrote Paul Joffe and Mary Ellen Turpel, ". . . it would be most difficult to avoid the conclusion that the Aboriginal parties . . . were repeatedly subjected to inappropriate, unlawful coercion or duress. . . . These actions were incompatible with the fiduciary obligations of both governments and substantially affected the fundamental terms of the 'agreement' reached."[20]

**False premises:** The Québec government from the beginning vigorously maintained that the Crees and Inuit had no rights[21] and that the obligation in the *Québec Boundaries Extension Act, 1912*, to "recognize the rights of Indian inhabitants in the territory," did not apply to the Crees and Inuit. These were false premises, as was confirmed when Aboriginal rights were recognized and affirmed in Canada's *Constitution Act, 1982*, just seven years after the signing of the agreement.[22] Had this happened earlier, the governments could not have denied existence of Aboriginal rights within Québec. Nevertheless, these were the assumptions under which the Aboriginal parties were compelled to negotiate.

**Erroneous information:** Throughout, the Québec government relied on a study of the "territorial integrity" of Québec made in 1971 by the Dorion Commission, which pronounced on Aboriginal rights in Québec without ever consulting Aboriginal peoples themselves.[23] Dorion himself later admitted he had no expertise in questions of Aboriginal territorial rights.[24] The research for Dorion's Commission was carried out in part by Professor Henri Brun, of Laval University,[25] whose view was that Aboriginal rights (if they exist at all) are limited to some hunting, fishing, and trapping. The Québec lawyers entered the court case in 1972 with these assumptions about Aboriginal rights. In light of Supreme Court of Canada decisions, this is a completely anachronistic view of Aboriginal rights, yet, even after taking a beating in the court case, the Québec negotiators continued to rely on the outdated assumptions of the Dorion Commission. By 1991 (twenty years too late, alas!) even Brun admitted (rather grudgingly) that "the territorial rights of Aboriginal peoples have always existed. They have been recognized for a relatively short time, for the past twenty years. . . ."[26]

It is outrageous that the Québec government based its negotiating position in the 1970s on the unreliable, erroneous, and prejudicial findings of the Dorion Commission, and of course this seriously affected the ability of the Crees and Inuit to negotiate a fair agreement in 1975.

**Land selection criteria violated basic rights:** The Québec government unjustly imposed criteria for land selection that excluded all Cree and Inuit traditional lands with mineral potential. This denied the Crees "the inherent right . . . to enjoy and utilize fully and freely their natural wealth and resources," which is a right of peoples recognized by the *International Covenant on Civil and Political Rights* and ratified by Canada. This was a major violation of the Aboriginal right to economic self-determination and, to this day, perpetuates a situation of economic dependency among the Crees. No other land-claims agreement in Canada has so severely limited selection of lands with resource potential. For example, the Inuit land-claims agreement covering the eastern Arctic, signed on 25 May 1993, provided Inuit beneficiaries with, in addition to financial compensation, ownership of 136,000 square miles (about 18 per cent of their traditional territory), of which some 14,000 square miles will include mineral, oil, and gas rights.[27] But under the JBNQA (so often described as equitable and generous) the governments purport that the Crees and Inuit do not have ownership of any land, but merely have management rights over less than two per cent of their traditional territory, with no mineral rights.

Professor Douglas Sanders, of the University of British Columbia, comments that "a denial of indigenous rights to lands and resources can only be supported by invoking doctrines of racism and colonialism."[28] These land selection criteria imposed by the Québec government were contrary to Canadian and international standards, have still not been redressed after twenty years, and are a black mark on the history of Québec.

**Corporate involvement in land claims:** The Crees and Inuit faced not only the federal and Québec governments, but also Hydro-Québec, Société d'énergie de la Baie James, and Société de développement de la Baie James. Nowhere else in Canada have Aboriginal peoples been compelled to negotiate land claims with development corporations as well as federal and provincial governments. Generally, Québec's harsh positions were dictated by the three corporations. They could reasonably have been consulted about technical modifications to the hydro project, but it went far beyond that, and they were fully involved in all aspects of the land-claims negotiation. This severely affected the protections the Aboriginal parties were able to negotiate, especially for environment, lands, and resources.

**Rights of Aboriginal third parties extinguished:** The government of Québec insisted that the land rights of certain Aboriginal peoples in northern Québec be extinguished, even though these peoples were not party to the agreement.[29] These included the Inuit of Belcher Islands, the Inuit of Labrador, the Innu of Québec and Labrador, the eastern Crees of Mocreebec in eastern Ontario, and the Algonquins. Although such unilateral extinguishment appears to be invalid and unconstitutional, this serious violation of fundamental human rights has never been redressed. The Naskapi sought to avoid the consequences of this draconian measure by quickly negotiating the Northeastern Québec agreement in 1978. As a result, they have suffered hardships similar to those experienced by the Crees.

**Abdication of federal responsibility:** Although legally responsible for the Aboriginal people in the Rupert's Land territories, the federal government casually permitted the many above-named transgressions to occur in spite of the extreme prejudice caused to the Aboriginal parties in the negotiations. The federal government not only shirked its responsibility to defend indigenous peoples and their lands, it didn't even defend other areas of federal jurisdiction such as migratory birds, fisheries, and navigable waters. All it did was provide a loan (since repaid) to pay for the Aboriginal legal action. (In fact, the government used this loan to put pressure on Crees by threatening to limit the funding of the later negotiations.)[30]

**Threats to withdraw essential services:** The Québec government included in the agreement, in what could almost be described as a gloating tone, a description of how the Crees and Inuit had been forced to surrender some of their fundamental rights in exchange for essential services that are provided for everyone in Canada as a matter of course. This was included in a section called "Philosophy of the agreement," written by John Ciaccia, the Québec Premier's main representative at the negotiating table. He wrote,

> The inhabitants of Québec's North, like everybody else, have to have schools, they have to be able to depend on health services, they have to have the security of justice and a system of law enforcement. The agreement responds to those needs, and provides the structures through which they can be met. There will be local school boards, police units, fire brigades, municipal courts, public utilities, roads, and sanitation services. . . . These are all

steps that would have to be taken, these are all services that would have to be provided and developed anyway, regardless of whether or not there was a James Bay project.

The obligation of governments to provide all peoples in Canada with essential services is now enshrined in Section 36 of the *Constitution Act, 1982*. The cynicism of Ciaccia's "philosophy" is extraordinary and illustrates the unjust nature of so much in an agreement that the Crees had no choice but to sign, however unwillingly.

Again, Leader of the Opposition Joe Clark described this disgraceful negotiation in forceful terms at the time. He said the government of Canada had abandoned its responsibility:

> We owe more to the native people of Canada; we owe more to the concept of social justice; we owe more to any minority which could be the next victim of a government that is prepared to abandon its responsibilities in the name of alert neutrality. For that reason . . . my colleagues and I cannot accept the process which has led to the agreement which is enshrined in the bill before us today.[31]

Taking all these factors into account, the Honorable A.C. Hamilton, former Associate Justice of the Manitoba Court of Queen's Bench, commented in 1995,

> . . . Aboriginal peoples believe they have not been dealt with fairly in the treaties that have been signed in recent years. Many feel the modern treaties have only been signed . . . because they had to sign. Many signed because they needed the funding and other benefits for their impoverished people. . . . If one or more of the parties sign an agreement reluctantly or under some indirect pressure and does not really accept all of its terms, the technical certainty

thought to have been achieved through surrender
may be fleeting and illusory.[32]

The trouble with the James Bay and Northern Québec
Agreement could not be more accurately stated, and that
by a distinguished jurist and former judge.

## Denial of Cree self-determination

In the nine years after the agreement was signed, the Crees tried
to negotiate greater control over their lives and territory, and
the Cree-Naskapi Act, which came into force in 1984, was the
result.[33] The agreement and the act should have provided rights
of self-government over the vast traditional territories of the
Crees and Naskapi. However, the act covered only what are
known as Category IA lands. These are somewhat analogous to
reserves in other parts of Canada, but Québec was so reluctant
to permit any federal jurisdiction within Québec that only some
1,200 square miles of land were left in Cree control outside of
provincial jurisdiction. These lands comprise less than two per
cent of our Cree traditional lands.

In fact, we had already been robbed of our traditional lands,
because the Québec government had created on Cree territory
(once again, of course, entirely without consulting the Crees)
a massive "municipality" to be administered by a huge, non-
elected superagency called the Société de développement de la
Baie James (SDBJ). This agency was given a large measure of
control over everything that lived, breathed, and died in an
enormous territory bigger than France.

Even the small areas established as Cree lands under the
agreement were divided into two categories. The so-called
Category IB lands, which cover only 844 square miles, remain
under provincial jurisdiction, and in them the Crees have been
compelled to accept "public corporations" that conform to
Québec practice, rather than Cree practice and beliefs. Through
such actions the Cree nation was denied the right to determine

freely its own institutions, although this is one of the rights specified in the United Nation's draft *Declaration on the Rights of Indigenous Peoples.*

Twenty years later Chief Diamond described this agreement as "a massive land-theft."[34] The Crees have been disenfranchised rather than empowered, confirming the comment of an international jurist that "unless [indigenous peoples] are able to retain control over their land and territories, their survival as identifiable, distinct societies and cultures is seriously endangered."[35]

Not only did the JBNQA contravene Canadian norms, it also failed to meet both existing and emerging international standards, described more fully in chapter 14. A specific set of standards is laid down in the International Labour Organization's *Indigenous and Tribal Peoples Convention, 1989,* which came into force on 5 September 1991, when ratifications were registered by two member States, Norway and Mexico. (An interesting point here is that throughout the negotiation of this convention, Canada played a larger role than any other State in watering down the guarantees provided by the convention, arguing that this was necessary in order to get the maximum number of ratifications by nations. Ironically, however, Canada itself has not yet ratified the convention.)

There are a multitude of ways in which Québec (and Canadian) practice still does not meet the requirements of this and other international instruments that cover civil, political, and other human rights, and the way the JBNQA has worked out illustrates this only too clearly. As interpreted by the Québec and federal governments, the JBNQA does not, for the most part, respect the recognized right of Aboriginal peoples to retain our own customs, laws, and institutions (for example, Cree customary adoptions are not recognized under Québec and Canadian law). Nor does it properly safeguard the Crees' internationally recognized right to benefit from resources on traditional territories; or recognize the Cree right to decide our own priorities for development; or ensure the Crees the effective right to participate in formulating, implementing, and evaluating proposals, plans, and programmes that affect us; or provide for

## the Nation
Volume 2, No. 23 • November 3, 1995
*every two weeks*

# 96.3% No
# 3.7% Yes

$2.00 **Free** IN THE JAMES BAY TERRITORY     SERVING THE JAMES BAY CREE NATIONS SINCE 1993

Cree Nation self-determination: Grand Chief Matthew Coon Come
casts the first ballot in the Cree Special Referendum of 26 October 1995

Cree Nation continuity: young child and proud mother at Cree "walking out" ceremony

Future Cree Nation leaders

Aboriginal rights at home and abroad  *Top:*  Cree Nation Ambassador
Dr. Ted Moses defending aboriginal peoples' rights at the United Nations
*Bottom:*  Cree Nation legislative assembly in Eeyou Astchee

Cree Nation leadership *Top:* Chief Matthew Mukash addresses a gathering in the Cree community of Whapmagoostui *Bottom:* Chief Billy Diamond and others at a community meeting in Waskaganish

Cree Nation democracy: participants in a community gathering discuss Cree rights

On the land in Eeyou Astchee: freighter canoes on the Maquato River

Sustenance from the land: elder women preparing freshly caught country food

On the land in Eeyou Astchee
*Top:* Preparing moose hide
*Bottom:* A hunter on the shores of James Bay

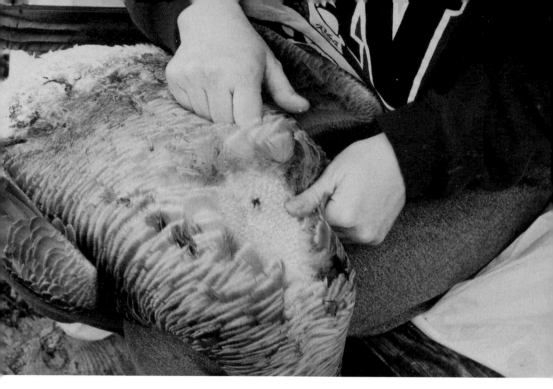

The bounty of Eeyou Astchee
*Top:* Plucking a Canada goose; everything is used
*Bottom:* Slow roasting and smoking of succulent geese

Misuse and abuse of the land: a gigantic causeway at one of the dozens of dam sites at La Grande built without any environmental and social impact assessment

Misuse and abuse of the land: hydro-electric mega-project powerlines from La Grande, illuminated as though on fire, begin their journey to southern Quebec and the United States

Cree Nation protest: Cree and Inuit take their protest against the proposed Great Whale Hydro-Electric Project to New York, paddling the "Odeyak" on the Hudson River

Cree Nation international outreach: Cree and Inuit
on the stage at Times Square — Earth Day 1992

Misuse and abuse of the land: multinational timber corporations'
clear-cutting on Eeyou Astchee, undertaken (without any environmental
impact assessment) according to Quebec government forestry plans

Premier Lucien Bouchard goes north
*Top:* The opening of a lumber mill in Eeyou Astchee in the summer of 1997
*Bottom:* Cree protesters at the opening

effective Cree cooperation in environmental and social impact assessment, for which social, spiritual, cultural, and environmental impacts are supposed to be taken into account (it even took us years of conflict and millions of dollars to get the federal and Québec governments to agree on the advisory environmental and social impact assessment process in Great Whale). Nor did the agreement make sure that our Cree values, practices, and institutions were not put at risk in relation to hydroelectric development. These are all rights provided for in international human-rights instruments.

Moreover, the agreement has not given us access to adequate housing. The 1996 federal estimate of the Cree housing shortfall is 1,500 units: in other words 40 per cent of those of us in need cannot get housing. The agreement has also failed to provide us with employment in development activities. In fact, 30 per cent of Crees are unemployed, although the agreement calls for increased Cree access to jobs.

Unfortunately, the Québec and Canadian governments and the private developers who have come into the region refuse to recognize this. There are just a handful of Crees among the hundreds of people now working for Hydro-Québec in the territory. Likewise, there are very few Crees among the 1,500 people working for the large forestry companies.[36] A few Crees work in mining, thanks to the far-seeing policies of the Troilus mine near Mistissini. All of these improvements were promised by the 1975 agreement, and they have not been delivered. Just as in the past in other parts of Canada, a huge territory has been opened up for development, and millions and millions of dollars are being taken off, without any benefits accruing to the original owners of the land, the Crees.

This is a formidable list of ways in which Canada still does not respect what have become recognized international standards in the treatment of indigenous peoples.

But we could go on: for example, the JBNQA does not yet provide us with adequate control of our own justice system in spite of the fact that in 1991 the Law Reform Commission of Canada strongly recommended separate Aboriginal systems for First Nations.

The Law Reform Commission's report says the current system has "utterly failed" Aboriginal peoples: "The historical disadvantage suffered by Aboriginal persons in the justice system has been too long ignored. . . . From the Aboriginal perspective, the criminal justice system is an alien one, imposed by the dominant white society."[37] Moreover, the findings of five provincial inquiries into treatment of Aboriginal people by the law ". . . reveal serious inequities and evidence of racism," said the Law Reform Commission.[38]

## Promotion of cultural genocide

In describing how the JBNQA has denied Cree self-determination, one last matter must be dealt with, and that is the promotion of cultural genocide. The agreement actually purports to constrain Crees from opposing certain future hydroelectric projects, specifically the Great Whale River, Nottaway, Broadback, and Rupert projects, on sociological grounds. This is an amazing provision forced on the Crees during negotiations and indicates the inhumane, project-oriented, hydro-obsessed thinking of the governments.

The relevant section of the agreement, which was insisted on by the development corporations and largely drafted by them, says that these projects, part of the James Bay hydro project from its first announcement in 1971, should be subject to the environmental regime laid down in the agreement "only in respect to ecological impacts, and that sociological factors or impacts shall not be grounds for the Crees and/or Inuit to oppose or prevent the said developments."[39] As it has turned out, this article in the Hydro Project chapter of the agreement has served to nullify and certainly to contradict protections for the Crees set out elsewhere in the agreement.

We *Eeyouch* believe the above provision is unconstitutional in that it violates Section 7 of the *Canadian Charter of Rights and Freedoms*, which guarantees "life, liberty and security of the person." To deny Crees the right to oppose or prevent any development on sociological grounds is to deny us an effective remedy pertaining to our fundamental human rights and is also in contravention of the *Universal Declaration of Human Rights,* the international covenants, and the other more recent, emerging, human-rights norms. The *Declaration of Human Rights,* for example, says in Article 8 that "everyone has the right to an effective remedy by the competent national tribunals for acts violating the fundamental rights granted him by the Constitution or by law." That would certainly seem to forbid any provision preventing the Crees from opposing a development on sociological grounds.

Furthermore, the Supreme Court of Canada has held that social factors are an integral part of decision-making on environment and development matters. A judge in the case involving the Oldman River in Alberta has commented that it is "unduly myopic" to believe that environmental quality is confined to the biophysical environment only. He said the potential consequences of environmental change for a community's livelihood and social health should be a central concern in all decisions affecting the environment.[40]

The draft *United Nations Declaration on the Rights of Indigenous Peoples* defines "cultural genocide" as "any act which has the aim or effect of depriving [indigenous peoples] of their integrity as distinct peoples, or of their cultural values or ethnic identities . . . or of dispossessing them of their lands, territories or resources. . . ."[41]

The Crees believe that the denial of their right to oppose a development on sociological grounds, written into the JBNQA, promotes their cultural genocide. Many jurists have linked the destruction of indigenous lands to genocide. Two American jurists, for example, write that the removal of indigenous peoples from their lands, or the destruction of their lands, can cause physical and cultural annihilation "because land is an integral part of American Indian religion and cultural cohesiveness."[42]

Once again, the prohibition on Crees from opposing certain developments on sociological grounds was denounced by Clark, when the matter came before the House of Commons, as "an unreasonable imposition to place upon native peoples of that place at that time." He argues,

. . . [the Crees and Inuit] were forced to negotiate under the gun of extraordinary conditions . . . to which a people of a different . . . background would probably not have been subjected. . . . The government of Québec made it clear from the outset that there would be no agreement . . . without the consent of Hydro-Québec. Hydro-Québec indicated that it would agree only if the Inuit people who were affected would accept conditions which denied in advance their right to invoke social impact factors of proposed hydroelectric projects. . . . That was a great deal to ask! It was, in my judgment, an unreasonable imposition to place upon native peoples at that place at that time. . . . [43]

Of course, Québec's efforts to enforce this provision eventually had to be abandoned in relation to the Great Whale hydroelectric project, after we Crees fought our great battle in the courts and in public opinion, resulting in the project's indefinite postponement in 1994.[44]

## Relevance of JBNQA to Québec secession

As we have said, sovereignists argue that the JBNQA is irrelevant to the debate about Québec secession. We, on the other hand, believe it is of central relevance. The sovereignists claim, of course, that the extinguishment clauses forced upon us mean that we have surrendered our right to self-determination under international law. We don't agree. Even the separatist legal advisor Daniel Turp has warned his confrères against this assumption. "International law," he writes, "does not necessarily take domestic law into account if [it] is an obstacle to the exercise of a people's right to self-determination."[45]

We Crees signed the agreement in a federalist context and benefit from obligations involving two levels of government. We would have negotiated very different terms had we been confronted with only one government, representing a unitary Québec State. As the agreement now stands, a continuing

Crown fiduciary responsibility towards Aboriginal peoples has been retained, and the importance of that context has been forcefully underlined by Cree Grand Chief Coon Come:

> ... an independent Québec could not respect the James Bay and Northern Québec Agreement even if it chose to do so. The agreement assumes and functions within a federal regime. Québec as a unitary State would be unable to duplicate this governmental regime, with, for example, all of its inherent checks and balances — the Supreme Court of Canada, the federal Parliament and provincial legislature, and our fiduciary relationship with the federal Crown.[46]

In fact we Crees specifically negotiated a section which reads that "Parliament and the Government of Canada recognize and affirm a special responsibility for the said Crees and Inuit. . . ." Since that was negotiated by the Aboriginal parties as part of the JBNQA, it constitutes a treaty right that Québec and Canada cannot unilaterally demolish.

If the 1898 and 1912 territories were to be included in a sovereign Québec, this would violate the undertakings made to the Aboriginal peoples when the provincial boundaries were extended. Clearly, under the JBNQA, Québec cannot change the status of these territories without consent of the other parties, and the fact that the province of Québec made this federalist arrangement in 1975 could prove to be highly unfavourable to a secessionist Québec's efforts to obtain international recognition of its secession.

The Crees never intended, obviously, that an independent Québec could claim full rights to the northern territory, since the agreement was premised on the perpetual existence of the federal and provincial governments, both maintaining obligations towards the Crees. It can be concluded, therefore, that the Québec government and National Assembly have no right whatsoever to forcibly include Aboriginal peoples and their traditional territories into a new secessionist State. If the sharing arrangements laid out in the agreement were to be repudiated by the Québec government, the agreement would be fundamentally breached: the door would be open to us to claim full rights and jurisdiction over the whole of our traditional territory.

As in many other areas, the Québec secessionist movement is on shaky, indeed, untenable, ground in relation to the JBNQA. In international law there is a basic principle called *pacta sunt servanda* — "treaties must be kept" — which indicates governments have no right to terminate a treaty unilaterally. A treaty normally is intended to be in force in perpetuity, and, in fact, there are treaties (including some British treaties that have lasted for six centuries) that cannot be terminated except by agreement of the parties. An international convention on the law of treaties allows exceptions to this rule, so that treaties do not have to be kept in certain circumstances. This applies only if there has been "a fundamental change of circumstances" that was not foreseen by the parties when they signed the treaty.[47] That is not the case in regard to the JBNQA. The separatist option for Québec was a lively part of the Canadian political scene when the JBNQA was signed in 1975: indeed, only a year later, the PQ was elected to office with a secessionist programme. So the possibility of Québec secession certainly should have been foreseen by those who signed the treaty for Québec.

That Québec and Canada are obliged to obtain Cree (and Inuit) consent to any secession by Québec affecting our traditional territories has been confirmed by one of Canada's foremost constitutional experts, Professor Peter Hogg, who has said as much in language so plain that no one can mistake its meaning: "The secession of a province or region of Canada would require the consent of the Aboriginal people who have Aboriginal or treaty rights in the seceding territory," he said in a paper presented at a Canadian Bar Association law conference in May 1997.

That the JBNQA reinforces the obligations of the two governments towards us was also confirmed by Professor Hogg in the same paper:

> Since Canada's obligations (under the JBNQA) could no longer be fulfilled in an independent Québec and would

have to be assumed by the new State of Québec, a secession would constitute a breach of the agreement. The agreement can be amended . . . only with the consent of the Aboriginal . . . parties to it.

What this all adds up to is that it is imperative for the government of Québec to come to terms with its Aboriginal peoples before the next referendum. Their territories cannot be moved out of Canada without their consent.[48]

From all of this it is crystal clear that the Crees and other Aboriginal peoples in Québec have fundamental rights that could lead to partition within Québec, should separatists proceed with their independence project. Yet, despite all the legal opinion to the contrary, Québec Premier Lucien Bouchard continues to repeat his erroneous mantra to the population in Québec: "The territory of Québec is characterized by its integrity. The territory of Québec is a territory that cannot be divided."[49]

Whether inadvertently or intentionally, Bouchard is profoundly misleading the people of Québec on this central question.

# 9

# Blast from the past: the PQ government invokes colonialism and discrimination

*Wherein a twentieth-century government dredges up a sixteenth-century doctrine to deny the very existence of Aboriginal rights in Québec*

When the government of Québec's lawyers went to the Supreme Court of Canada on 17 June 1996, few of those listening to its lawyers' arguments in the Côté case[1] could have expected to hear the outlandish position being taken. Nearly a quarter-century had passed since other lawyers representing Québec had stood up in Justice Albert Malouf's courtroom in Montréal to enunciate arguments, produced in an almost flippant manner, to the effect that the James Bay Crees had no rights in Québec, and the government had no case to answer. Those lawyers expected to be out of there in a matter of weeks, but they were so far from understanding what was involved that they spent almost six months in court, day after day, answering the Cree and Inuit case.

Yet in the twenty-four years since, it seems the Québec justice department and their masters in the government of Québec either have learned very little, or have decided they don't like what they've learned. Some of their arguments in 1996 were as insensitive and more outrageous than they were even in 1972.

The Côté case is a highly significant Aboriginal and treaty fishing-rights case, where the defendants were Algonquins, members of the Kitigan Zibi Anishinabeg (Desert River Band). The facts of the case were very specific to the defendants and involved historical and legal considerations specific to the territory concerned.

As it had done in the past, the Québec government urged the nine judges of the Supreme Court to turn the Royal Proclamation of 1763 on its head and interpret it so as to preclude, rather than confirm, recognition of Aboriginal rights. The Proclamation is named in the Canadian Constitution in relation to the rights of Aboriginal peoples and had already been characterized by the Supreme Court as an Indian Bill of Rights.

Not content with that, the Québec government lawyers produced a real bombshell: they urged that the Supreme Court declare that the doctrine of *terra nullius* be applied throughout the province so as to deny that Aboriginal peoples in the province of Québec have had any Aboriginal rights at all for centuries. (*Terra nullius* is the doctrine under which European colonizers asserted that continents and territories they had "discovered" henceforth belonged to them, because, they said, these were "lands belonging to no one.")

This extreme argument put forward by Lucien Bouchard's government is remarkably revealing: the Québec government used a case of great importance to the Algonquin Nation where some of its members were charged with infringements of the law as a pretext for obliterating all Aboriginal land rights in the province. Not only was this like taking a club to swat a fly, but it was a breach of human rights and also a violation of the principles of natural justice: the Québec government applied its argument to all Aboriginal peoples, including those who were not present and had nothing to do with the case.

Consider carefully exactly what the Québec government was arguing:

- Section 35 of the *Constitution Act, 1982* (which provides constitutional guarantees for existing Aboriginal and treaty

137

rights), does not apply in the province of Québec, because Aboriginal rights have not existed there for 450 years!

- Aboriginal peoples in Québec in the 1990s do not have Aboriginal rights because such rights were not expressly recognized by French colonial authorities two or more centuries ago!

- Specifically, "no aboriginal right could have survived the assertion of French sovereignty over the territory of New France."

- Because in Québec's opinion neither sixteenth-century international law nor sixteenth-century French civil law recognized that the Aboriginal inhabitants of Québec had any rights, the same view must now be adopted by the Supreme Court of Canada!

This kind of thinking gives a clear indication of what Aboriginal peoples in Québec are up against when we have the temerity to assert our rights with a Québec separatist government in power. To revive the doctrine of *terra nullius* as a weapon against us in Québec is not only absurd, but a violation of our human rights. Moreover, the separatist government attempted to do this only four years after the highest court in Australia had condemned the doctrine of *terra nullius* as racially discriminatory and colonial in the famous Mabo case.[2] As Mr. Justice Brennan said in the Australian judgement: "Whatever the justification advanced in earlier days for refusing to recognize the rights and interests in land of the indigenous inhabitants of settled colonies, *an unjust and discriminatory doctrine of that kind can no longer be accepted.*"[3] Québec, however, argued in the Côté case that the Mabo case lay within a common-law jurisdiction and did not apply in a civil-law jurisdiction such as the province of Québec. The Supreme Court rejected Québec's argument; Chief Justice Lamer ruled that the Québec government's interpretation "risks undermining" the very purpose of the constitutional guarantees provided to Aboriginal peoples in Canada ". . . by perpetuating the historical injustices suffered by Aboriginal peoples at the hands of colonizers who failed to respect the distinctive cultures of preexisting Aboriginal societies."[4] These Australian and Canadian decisions by the highest courts in the land make clear that, under international and domestic law, doctrines of superiority such as *terra nullius* cannot be invoked against territories with indigenous inhabitants.[5] In case there should be any doubt of this, the Australian judgement spells it out precisely:

> A common-law doctrine founded on unjust discrimination in the enjoyment of civil and political rights demands reconsideration. It is contrary to both international standards and to the fundamental values of our common law to entrench a discriminatory rule which, because of the supposed position on the scale of social organization of the indigenous inhabitants of an organized colony, denies them a right to occupy their traditional lands.[6]

This indicates how out of touch with prevailing international opinion the Bouchard government is in relation to the basic rights of Aboriginal peoples. Unfortunately, Quebecers, who are fair-minded people, do not seem to be aware of the discriminatory and colonialist legal arguments being advanced by their government. But we are confident that, if and when they become aware of it, they will be appalled.

Let there be no misunderstanding: the prohibition against discrimination is a universal principle worldwide and certainly applies throughout Canada, including Québec. This being so, how could the Québec government possibly think that it could persuade a senior court to apply an outmoded discriminatory doctrine in Québec simply because it is a civil-law, and not a common-law, jurisdiction?

The Québec argument on *terra nullius* outraged Cree Grand Chief Matthew Coon Come, who asked, in a speech to the Harvard Center for International Affairs in Boston in October 1996,

> Do the Attorney-General of Québec and the Bouchard government really believe it is acceptable to apply a racially discriminatory doctrine within Québec's civil law system, when it is contrary to universal human

rights principles everywhere else? . . . What kind of liberty, equality, and fraternity . . . would permit [them] to state that the legal legacy of a racist and discriminatory doctrine . . . lives on wherever the French civil law once applied?[7]

The Supreme Court confirmed, however, that French law did not explicitly deny the existence of Aboriginal land rights. The Court indicated (as it had done in the past) that in its diplomatic relations the French Crown had treated Aboriginal peoples as sovereign nations rather than subjects of the monarch.

The extraordinary assertions made by the Québec government before the Supreme Court should also be of concern to everyone living in Canada for the light they throw on the separatist interpretation of Québec's "distinct society." It has been an article of faith among the Canadian political establishment, especially since the 1995 referendum, that Québec's "distinct society" should be formally recognized. Part of Québec's distinctiveness, they say, is its adherence to the civil law, as distinct from the common law used in the rest of Canada. To recognize such differences was described as a symbolic act that would have no practical legal consequences. Yet here was the Québec government, only a few months after its status as a distinct society was recognized by resolution of the Canadian Parliament, using its distinctive civil law as a weapon to deny the fundamental rights of Aboriginal peoples.

## Parliamentary assurances prove empty

The James Bay Crees had been concerned about something like this. When the Parliamentary resolution to recognize Québec's distinct society was being considered, the Grand Council of the Crees proposed that a more balanced "distinct society" resolution be drafted, including a nonderogation clause to safeguard the rights of Aboriginal peoples. Such a clause had been included in previous "distinct society" provisions in both the Meech Lake and Charlottetown Accords.

Our efforts fell on deaf ears. In fact, they were specifically rejected by the parliamentarians, who said that to recognize Québec as a "distinct society" would not affect treaty, Aboriginal, or other human rights. The distinct society, our Cree leaders were told, was simply a shield to protect the French language, culture, and civil-law system. The resolution was passed, pushed through by the Liberal majority in the House of Commons, in spite of Aboriginal objections. Now, a few months later, against all assurances to the contrary, the Québec government demonstrated that there is nothing formal and symbolic about the way it interprets the civil law aspect of its "distinct society." The government uses it against Aboriginal rights.

After the Côté case, Bill Namagoose, executive director of the Grand Council of the Crees, commented, "We were told the distinct society was a shield for Québec but it seems the shield has been melted down into a sword. And it is being used against Aboriginal people."


## Aftermath of the Côté decision

Following its severe setback (and implied rebuke) by the Supreme Court in the Côté case, the Québec government has seen no need to apologize or even acknowledge that it had invoked a shameful, discriminatory, and colonial doctrine against all the Aboriginal peoples in the province. Instead, the government responded publicly to the Supreme Court decision by emphasizing that the Aboriginal rights of Aboriginal peoples are not absolute and are subject to regulation by Québec.[8]

From the Aboriginal point of view this behaviour is so outrageous that on 17 October 1996 the Chiefs of the Assembly of First Nations of Québec and Labrador adopted a formal resolution on this whole matter: Discrimination and Colonial Positions Taken before the Supreme Court of Canada: Denial of the Existence of Aboriginal Rights in Québec. The Chiefs indicated that the Québec government was in effect "seeking the complete domination, assimilation, or subjugation of all Aboriginal peoples in Québec." They described the Québec argument as "scandalous ... discriminatory ... outrageous ... colonial," and in violation of the international prohibition against racial discrimination. They held Premier Lucien Bouchard directly accountable for his government's advocacy of the "legally and morally reprehensible doctrines of dispossession and superiority," and they impressed on the federal government the need for specific safeguards for Aboriginal peoples in the context of any recognition of Québec's "distinct society." The Chiefs also asked that Canada should, when next reporting under the *International Convention on the Elimination of All Forms of Racial Discrimination*, include an account of the Québec government's discriminatory position against Aboriginal peoples in the province.[9]

Only a few days later Cree Grand Chief Coon Come outlined his severe conclusions from Québec's arguments in the Côté case in his Harvard speech:

> Let there be no mistake about this: the Bouchard government of Québec has formally advocated the obliteration of the fundamental rights of Aboriginal peoples in Québec, on the basis of the continued application of a discredited, unjust, and discriminatory doctrine. . . . I have drawn a number of conclusions from this. First, the secessionist government of Québec has now moved from policies of ethnic nationalism to those of racial discrimination. Second, the legal positions now being taken by [Québec] appear to be as colonizing as at any time in North American history. Third, the government of Québec is now seeking to place itself in a totally dominant role vis-à-vis Aboriginal peoples in Québec by denying the existence of our . . . constitutional rights. In doing so, it is contravening fundamental principles of human rights under Canadian and international law.[10]

We regret to say that Québec opinion leaders have not expressed outrage against such discriminatory positions as one would expect. Just a year after the Côte case was in Supreme Court, Québec Premier Lucien Bouchard became the second Premier in twenty years to visit a Cree community in northern Québec. The position of his government in the Côte case was not discussed. Rather, he talked about use of natural resources in Cree traditional territory, including the possibility of revenue-sharing with the Crees.[11]

Bouchard's essay into Cree territory was the subject of an extensive editorial in Québec's nationalist newspaper, *Le Devoir*. The editorial's writer, Michel Venne, though approving of Bouchard's initiative, took the opportunity to chastise Matthew Coon Come for his remarks about the Côte case at the Harvard Center for International Affairs.[12]

In particular, Venne objected to Coon Come portraying in the United States an image of a Québec that is racist towards Aboriginal peoples. He wrote that the people of Québec would not happily sign agreements of economic partnership with the Crees, if he used foreign tribunals to denigrate Quebecers. Clearly Venne felt that criticism of the Québec government was equivalent to criticism of the Québec people. He also wrote that Coon Come was going too far when he deduced an attitude of racial discrimination in the legal arguments of the Québec government.

Venne did not bother to mention that it was the highest courts of both Canada and Australia that had characterized the discredited doctrine espoused by the Québec government as racially discriminatory and colonialist. Nor was it explained how the Québec government could argue in 1996 that there had not been any Aboriginal rights within the province for centuries, when (as *Le Devoir* should have known) in 1912 Québec expressly undertook to "recognize the rights of the Indian inhabitants in the territory" in the Québec Boundaries Extension Act.

It is ludicrous for a respected newspaper such as *Le Devoir* to treat criticism of the Québec government as equivalent to denigration of the people of Québec. (Does that apply to criticism made by newspapers as well?) We Cree people know that few Quebecers are even aware of the Côte decision or of the judicial positions taken by the government. In fact, Grand Chief Coon Come expressly dealt with this at Harvard:

> I must emphasize . . . that we have no fundamental quarrel with the people of Québec, with whose aspirations for political and cultural security we can identify. The great majority of Quebecers have shown time and time again that they reject discriminatory double standards, and are not prepared to claim rights for themselves while denying them to others. We respect these Quebecers and wish to work with them. Unfortunately, however, the government of Québec has not met this basic standard of equity and respect for fundamental rights.[13]

The newspaper does not seem to understand the practical consequences of the Québec government's arguments. Had the government been successful, all Aboriginal peoples in Québec would have been in a most vulnerable position. We would have had no territorial rights based on original or historical occupation. Our negotiating positions on a wide range of land issues would have been undermined. If these arguments had been accepted, we might well have been relegated to squatters on our territories subject to the whims of non-Aboriginal governments, in spite of our profound relationship with and dependence on our lands, resources, and environment. The provisions we have negotiated in Canada's Constitution to safeguard our Aboriginal rights would have meant nothing.

In our view, fundamental human-rights issues are more important than the sovereignist preferences of individuals or governments. Had someone argued in the Supreme Court of Canada that all Quebecers had no land rights, we are confident the editors of *Le Devoir* and the Québec government would have expressed their indignation loud and clear against the potential dispossession of Quebecers.

Perhaps if Venne has lingering doubts about the propriety of Grand Chief Coon Come's comments, he may wish to consider what the draft *United Nations Declaration on the Rights of Indi-*

*genous Peoples* says about doctrines of superiority such as *terra nullius*: ". . . all doctrines, policies, and practices based on or advocating superiority of peoples or individuals on the basis of national origin, racial, religious, ethnic, or cultural differences are racist, scientifically false, legally invalid, morally condemnable, and socially unjust."[14] Venne may also wish to reflect on the 1986 Declaration of the Government of Québec on Interethnic and Interracial Relations: "The government of Québec condemns without reserve racism and racial discrimination in all its forms. . . . The government . . . calls on the whole of the Québec population to support its efforts . . . and be constantly vigilant in the face of any manifestation of racism or racial discrimination."[15] Matthew Coon Come impressed on his Boston audience the importance of all this for the future disposition of Cree lands and Québec's borders. "Regardless of any rights in our favour," he said, "the separatist government states it can forcibly include the James Bay Cree people and our territory and resources into a future independent Québec State. This is the threat we face, and we urgently need help . . . to assert our basic rights and freely determine our future and that of our children."[16]

# The simple-majority referendum: democracy or coercion?

*Wherein, not for the first time, secessionists try to impose a phony "democracy" on everyone else in Canada*

Although they will not admit this to the population of Québec, the separatists now realize that they cannot rely on any right

PRITCHARD, *THE OTTAWA CITIZEN*

to self-determination as the basis for their claim to independence, under either Canadian or international law. Therefore, their strategy is to achieve "effective control" after a UDI. This scenario would be triggered from the moment that they obtained a simple majority in a referendum in favour of secession. For them, 50 per cent plus one vote constitutes a democratic expression of the will of the entire population of Québec, sufficient to legitimize their proposed UDI. As their secession proposals have become more frankly illegal, so their claims to "democracy" and "legitimacy" have become more fervent.

The dishonesty of their intentions was revealed to the world during the 1997 federal election, when Jacques Parizeau, Québec Premier at the time of the 1995 referendum, intimated in a new book that he had intended to declare the unilateral independence of Québec within a week or ten days following an affirmative vote.[1]

This was contrary to what the separatists had told the Québec voters. The referendum question had promised that a new partnership would be offered to Canada, and a year would be devoted to negotiating it. Parizeau's revelation had the other separatist leaders scrambling. Lucien Bouchard, who during the referendum campaign had been named by Parizeau as Québec's negotiator with Canada, claimed he had never heard of Parizeau's intention, as did Bouchard's successor in the leadership of the Bloc Québécois, Gilles Duceppe.

It appears that only shades of meaning divided the two leaders: Bouchard himself had said, only five days before the referendum vote in 1995, that Québec would realize its sovereignty first and, then, move on to negotiate partnership with Canada.[2]

Even before Parizeau's revelation, it had become clear that had the separatists won by even one vote they were ready to put into action immediately a carefully conceived plan to break up Canada. Separatist sources told the *Globe and Mail* newspaper a few days after the referendum that had the vote favoured the secessionist option, even by the slimmest of margins, Premier Jacques Parizeau was prepared to reconvene the National

Assembly three days later to adopt formally a resolution requesting negotiations with Canada for a new political and economic partnership.[3]

Within two months, by January 1996, the work of setting up a new State would have been well under way, including preparations for the establishment of a Québec army, for entry of a sovereign Québec into the World Trade Organization, adoption of a new constitution, negotiations with Aboriginal peoples, and so on. Bouchard, then leader of the separatist party in the federal Parliament, would immediately have begun pressing for the opening of negotiations with Canada, and separatists assumed Ottawa would have had no alternative but to at least discuss distribution of the national debt. They also assumed that the United States government, following quick recognition by France, would have pressed the federal government to negotiate the secession of Québec, and when Canada began to negotiate, separatists would have taken it as unofficial sanctioning of Québec sovereignty. The separatists were confident the federal government had no contingency plan to deal with the crisis. Within a year, they believed, whether negotiations with Canada succeeded or not, the secessionist entity would have so far imposed its assumption of sovereignty on the Québec and Canadian populations that the matter would have, in essence, become a fait accompli.

All this would have been in accordance with a plan that had been drawn up in Québec City during the previous few months, a plan so secret that not even members of the Québec Cabinet were permitted to know about it. In the seven months leading up to the referendum, a committee of the highest level Québec civil servants examined every aspect of Québec's economic, customs, and monetary relations with Canada and staked out Québec's negotiating position. Different civil servants worked on different areas of the plan so that no one person could be privy to the whole scheme. Only one copy was made — and that was placed in Parizeau's safe.[4]

That such a plan, which would drastically affect the lives of every person in Canada, most of whom would have had no say in the matter, came within a whisker of being approved and put into operation, illustrates graphically the weakness of the idea of the simple majority vote.

The legitimacy of such a vote for such a momentous decision as breaking up a nation is extremely doubtful. The separatist argument is simplistic. "The Québec people do not have to ask the permission, neither of Prime Minister Jean Chrétien, nor of anyone, to decide its own future," said Bouchard, when leader of the Bloc Québécois in 1995.[5]

Cree Grand Chief Matthew Coon Come, commenting on Bouchard's statement, said, "I find it totally hypocritical that Mr. Bouchard and the separatists can say these things, and at the same time deny the democratic rights of all Aboriginal peoples in Québec to determine their own future."[6]

In fact, before the referendum, separatist leaders ceased even to pretend that they would carry out their secession within the law: "Quebecers want to vote," said Parizeau. "They have the right to vote, they will vote. We cannot submit Quebecers' right to vote to a decision by the court. It would be contrary to our whole democratic system."[7] He failed to mention that no one was opposed to the holding of a consultative referendum. What was being questioned was the self-declared right of Quebecers to impose their will on the Crees and other peoples in Québec and elsewhere in Canada. For Aboriginal peoples, the separatist claims to "legitimacy" and "democracy" translate into an attempt to coerce them into a secessionist Québec.

Contrary to the position the separatists have now apparently adopted, democracy and the rule of law are not wholly separate ideas, but are interrelated. Many others, outside of Québec, realize this. For example, at the beginning of 1995, with the referendum looming, Arctic indigenous leaders from around the world, meeting in Norway, issued a declaration of support for Aboriginal peoples in Québec, saying that, if the Québec government denied the Crees and others the right to determine their own future, then "principles of democracy and legitimacy would be unacceptably compromised."[8]

Many jurists point out that, in the eyes of international law, legitimacy can be achieved only by equitable consideration of all interests. This is especially important when the rights of others, such as Aboriginal peoples, are directly affected. In many situations there are "clashing legitimacies," to use the phrase of now federal minister Stéphane Dion, "whose consequences are unforseeable."[9] Even global impacts have to be taken into account. R. Iglar, a jurist who has written about Yugoslavia, observes that "a people . . . cannot exercise their right (to self-determination) at the expense of the legitimate rights of other peoples living in the parent State."[10]

As Université de Montréal economics professor Kimon Valaskakis and co-author Angéline Fournier have remarked, "the rest of Canada has an immense interest" in a Québec referendum, because if Québec separated, Canada could face a serious economic and financial crisis, the rest of Canada might break up, and some parts might even join the United States. All such questions must be considered in establishing the "legitimacy" of Québec's drive for secession.[11]

It cannot be denied that Québec's referendum process is intended to impose a decision on Aboriginal peoples by ignoring their right to determine their own future. And this could impact severely on the legitimacy of the Québec separatists' actions, as seen by the international community.

## Referendums in Canada are not binding

According to Canadian law, referendums are not legally binding, but are consultative in nature. As we have seen, in the lead-up to the 1995 referendum, Jacques Parizeau produced first a draft bill,[12] and later Bill 1,[13] neither of which was ever passed by the Québec National Assembly. The first, in 1994, would have *required* the National Assembly to declare the independence of Québec within a year following an affirmative referendum vote, thus making the referendum result binding on the National Assembly. When this was challenged, Parizeau did not even table this bill. When he introduced Bill 1 a year later it made no mention of a referendum, but otherwise the major clauses of the earlier bill were transferred into this second draft.

The staggering arrogance of the secessionists' approach to Québec's future is apparent when one considers that Bill 1 purported to empower the National Assembly to undertake at least six unconstitutional and illegal actions, which would have a profound effect on the lives of Aboriginal peoples and everyone who lives in Canada. The National Assembly would hold the power

- to make a unilateral declaration of Québec as a sovereign country (which could include the forcible integration of *Eeyou Astchee* into a sovereign Québec);

- to adopt a new constitution for a sovereign Québec;

- to delimit, unilaterally, the boundaries of an independent Québec;

- to assume, unilaterally, obligations and rights arising out of treaties to which Canada is a party, including treaties with Aboriginal peoples;

- to incorporate all laws passed by the Parliament of Canada as the laws of a sovereign Québec;

- to replace, unilaterally, the Supreme Court of Canada as the court of highest jurisdiction in Québec.

This time the bill did not *oblige* the National Assembly to act on an affirmative referendum vote. Obviously, therefore, since the Québec government was not legally bound by the result, why would other Canadian governments feel so bound? The Canadian government respected the general referendum law in Québec,[14] while, at the same time, making clear that a provincial law cannot bind the federal government. As one jurist has explained, the federal government wanted to retain the right to consult people in other parts of the country and to protect the minority in the seceding province who want to remain in Canada[15] (which, it is worth remarking, it has so far given little indication of doing).

It is hard to understand how a simple majority vote can be either democratic or legitimate when it denies the self-determination rights of Aboriginal peoples who, as established in chapters 1 and 2, quite clearly have such rights. Even if there had been an affirmative vote in the 1995 referendum, most of the important questions would have remained unsettled. No one even yet has a clear idea of the conditions for separation, and no attempt has been made by Québec to address the self-determination of Aboriginal peoples.[16]

# Picking and choosing
# the laws of the land

Québec separatists now make a distinction between democracy and the rule of law in Canada. They claim they prove their democratic pretensions by holding a vote of the citizens on their plan for unilateral secession from Canada. But at the same time they now say that for secession purposes they are not subject to Canadian law, under which they live. For them the ends justify the means, and there is no doubt that this attitude poses an immense danger to Aboriginal peoples in the province (and in the rest of Canada, for that matter).

Democracy and the rule of law, however, are not separate notions: they are inextricably linked. In 1991 the Conference on Security and Cooperation in Europe (including Canada and the United States) issued the *Charter of Paris*, which says that "democracy has its foundations in respect for the human person and the rule of law" and adds, "[Respect for] human rights, fundamental freedoms, democracy, and the rule of law are of international concern" and "constitute one of the foundations of the international order." The conference concluded that such issues are no longer an internal matter for any particular State, but are of concern to "all the participating States."[17] Thus, the Québec government, in its insistence that it can ignore the Canadian Constitution and the rights of Aboriginal peoples, and that this is no one else's business, is way out of step with modern practice.

In 1994 Grand Chief Coon Come protested against the swamping of the Cree vote by the Québec vote in a secession referendum. He noted that the separatists have indignantly rejected a pan-Canadian vote on the issue, because they say they will not be bound by any decision except one taken by themselves. "This isn't an approach Québec would tolerate (for itself), if proposed by Canada," Coon Come said. "So why should we?"[18] The separatist leaders have repeated many times that other Canadians can have no say in Québec's decision, as Bouchard made clear in 1995: "The Québec people do not have to ask the permission . . . of anyone, to decide its own future."[19]

As Professor Peter Russell puts it, "[Aboriginal peoples] are not nations that can be yanked out of Canada against their will by a provincial majority. . . . With few exceptions [they] wish to enjoy their right to self-government within Canada, not within a sovereign Québec."[20] Indeed, international human-rights expert Erica-Irene Daes warns that to deny the right of self-determination to indigenous peoples "will leave the most marginalized and excluded of all the world's peoples without a legal, peaceful weapon to press for genuine democracy. . . ."[21]

The PQ government appears to believe that it can deny Aboriginal self-determination, including the right to choose to remain in Canada, as long as an independent Québec demonstrates to the international community that it will treat Aboriginal peoples well. To ask Aboriginal peoples to embrace Québec's promises would be like justifying kidnapping on the grounds that the kidnappers are treating their victims well. This comparison has been made by Bill Namagoose, executive director of the Grand Council of the Crees: "If the Crees are internationally kidnapped by an independent Québec, we will become Québec's Québec," he told the *Toronto Star* in 1994.[22]

So far the signs are not auspicious. After his election as Premier in 1994, Parizeau failed to attend a single meeting with Aboriginal leaders to discuss secession issues. When a meeting was finally scheduled at the end of May 1995, he refused to show up because his government did not agree with the questions the Aboriginal leaders wanted to discuss and because he could not be assured that the meeting would be a success. The *Gazette* of Montréal commented that the Premier did not want to focus international attention "on the continuing contradictions between his independence plans and the Aboriginal rights claimed by Québec Natives."[23]

The secessionists' coercive approach, a modern form of colonialism for the 1990s, is the antithesis of the democratic process. This is not a far-fetched analogy, as the words of French writer D. Schnapper illustrate: "Colonial society was founded on the inequality of legal and political status of [its] members, while the legitimacy of the modern democracy consists of according equality to everyone"[24] — except, one might suggest, for Aboriginal peoples in Québec.

## Don't do as I do, do as I say . . .

"The Inuit can hold their own referendum if they want to and so can the Cree," said David Cliche, when he was special advisor on Aboriginal affairs to the Québec government in 1995, "but . . . we cannot accept that the territory of Québec be taken apart." In a classic example of eating cake and having it too, he added, "But we do respect the right to Aboriginal self-determination."[25] They respect it so much that, when we Crees and Inuit held our own referendums and voted overwhelmingly against accepting Québec secession, the separatist government refused to acknowledge the validity of our votes.[26]

In fact, one of the most prominent media spokespersons for separation, political scientist Josée Legault, said on a radio talk show that the 90 per cent Cree vote in favour of remaining with Canada was "absolutely ridiculous," and insinuated that the result had been somehow obtained illegitimately because "no one knows how this referendum was carried out."[27] It is illustrative of the arrogant tactics of many separatists that Legault also blamed the solid anti-secessionist vote on what she called the "extremely high" level of Cree illiteracy. But Crees do not have lower literacy rates than other Quebecers, something that Legault conveniently ignored. Indeed, a Statistics Canada study of literacy has shown that some 28 per cent of Quebecers who were given literacy tests could not understand the instructions on a bottle of Aspirin. Other parts of the country did not do especially well either, but Ontario and the western provinces rated about 10 per cent better than Québec, and the Atlantic provinces about the same.[28] A Québec group that works to combat illiteracy has reported that some 900,000 Quebecers could forget about going to vote in an election or a referendum, because "they can't read what is on the ballot."[29] As in so many of her public pronouncements on separation, Legault's statements about Cree illiteracy are entirely without foundation. In fact, Montréal political columnist Don Macpherson used the Statistics Canada study to ask how many of the Québec voters who cannot read an Aspirin label could have understood the complicated question they were asked in the 1995 referendum: "Do you agree that Québec should become sovereign, after having made a formal offer to Canada for a new economic and political partnership, within the scope of the bill respecting the future of Québec and of the agreement signed on 12 June 1995?" Macpherson wondered how many would have realized that "sovereign" in the question meant "a separate country." How many knew that the "agreement" mentioned wasn't with Canada, but between three pro-sovereignty parties in Québec? Would illiteracy explain how up to 30 per cent of those intending to vote for sovereignty mistakenly believed that a sovereign Québec would remain part of Canada? And recall, wrote Macpherson, that the vote was decided by a mere 1.2 per cent of those who voted.[30]

Not everybody in Québec, of course, goes along with this insensitive, modern form of colonialism. "It is necessary to arrive at a fair balance which takes into account at the same time the right of Aboriginal peoples and that of Quebecers to choose their destiny," commented lawyer Carol Hilling, in the French-language nationalist newspaper Le Devoir. "Unfortunately, there seems to be no will on the part of the government of Québec to find a just balance."[31] And of course it has been recognized that the idea of secession will lose legitimacy and support both within Canada and internationally if the separatists fail to deal fairly with Aboriginal peoples.[32]

Paternalistically, Parizeau told a French newspaper in 1995 that Aboriginal peoples could not hold referendums to "detach themselves from Québec," because referendums were "the acts of governments." He added, however, that Aboriginal peoples could consult among themselves, take positions, and negotiate.[33] How generous of him!

This is highly ironic: Parizeau, defending law and order, argued that the right to hold a referendum "flows from the laws of a government" and therefore was not open to Aboriginal peoples; and he made this argument while he himself was pursuing clearly illegal and unconstitutional actions.

We do have the right to hold referendums and have done so in the past, for example, when the Cree people voted to ratify the JBNQA in 1976.[34] This flows from our right to self-determination, which even the National Assembly's five experts appear to regard with favour. In their study they quote favourably the conclusion of a 1986 UN special report on discrimination against indigenous peoples that states that self-determination is "the basic precondition" by which we can determine our own future. This right "in essence constitutes the exercise of free choice by indigenous peoples," says the UN report, whose author, J. Cobo, added that indigenous peoples must themselves to a large extent create the specific content of the principle.[35] Cobo's ground-breaking report gave rise to the UN mechanism that has since been working towards an agreed declaration of indigenous rights.

Parizeau was also incorrect in assuming that only governments can hold referendums.[36] After the Second World War, many plebiscites were held by the United Nations in trusteeship territories to ascertain the wishes of various peoples as to their future. There is even precedence for separate referendums within one territory to determine the wishes of different claimants, as has happened, for example, in the British Cameroons.[37]

# Double standards alive and well among separatists

On the question of referendums, separatist leader Bouchard applies a glaring double standard: on the one hand he insists that the territorial integrity of Canada can be undermined by simply holding a referendum in Québec and then unilaterally forming a new State; on the other hand, he argues that Aboriginal referendums cannot have any weight in determining our future as Aboriginal people or that of our vast territories. To do this he invokes the "territorial integrity" of Québec.

"There is a unitary State in Québec," he told *La Presse* a few months before the 1995 referendum. "We consider that the territory of Québec is characterized by its integrity which makes it a single State. There is a single referendum that will be authoritative, it is that of the whole population. . . ." Aboriginal referendums, said Bouchard, would simply give him an indication of our thinking.[38]

Fortunately this did not go unchallenged. Editorialist Alain Dubuc, of *La Presse*, asked, why this double standard? He recalled that the Québec referendum was being held because of the civilized way Canada was confronting the sovereignist challenge, and added, "In the name of this same fair-play, it would be elementary that the sovereignist leaders, whether or not they are in agreement with the Aboriginal peoples, demonstrate a minimum of respect to [them]. . . ."[39] And Lise Bissonnette, the pro-independence editor of *Le Devoir*, concedes that it is the "most obvious right" of Aboriginal peoples in Québec to hold a separate referendum (although she viewed such an act as a major "provocation").[40]

The Aboriginal referendums in Québec made an impact across the country and raised many questions about the legitimacy of the Québec government's whole strategy. For example, Allan Cairns, professor at the University of Saskatchewan College of Law, has written that the underlying premise for the Aboriginal peoples is clear from the Inuit, Cree, and Innu referendum votes: "neither a Québec majority, nor a Québec government that speaks for the majority on such fundamental issues, speaks for them. . . ."[41]

It is perhaps a comment on the somewhat obsessive nature of secessionists that Quebecers in general take a more democratic view of the rights of Aboriginal peoples than do the separatist leaders. In February 1995 the *Gazette* reported that 54 per cent of Quebecers agreed in an opinion poll that Québec Indians should be allowed to attach their ancestral lands to Canada, even if Québec separates. This suggests that a majority of the Québec population not only supports the right of Aboriginal peoples in Québec to hold our own referendums to determine our future, but also that we have a right to choose to remain with Canada, something the separatists sternly reject. The poll even indicated that 56 per cent of Quebecers agreed that regions of Québec that did not wish to separate should be allowed to stay in Canada.[42] Again, during the 1997 federal election, when an opinion poll asked respondents the question "Suppose the Cree Indians and Inuit of northern Québec decide to stay with Canada. Would they have such a right?" the response was overwhelmingly positive. Seventy-five per cent agreed we have that right, including even 66 per cent of convinced separatist supporters. In the rest of Canada, the response to the same question was reported to be 92 per cent in support of the Crees and Inuit.[43]

That the separatists should insist on their hard-line views when the ordinary people believe otherwise makes a mockery of the separatist professions of democracy and legitimacy and indicates the problems that Aboriginal peoples face vis-à-vis the possibility of Québec secession.

## A multitude of objections

There are a multitude of objections to the referendum process as interpreted by the separatists.

- A simple majority by Quebecers would not suffice for such an important decision as the breakup of a country. Even if most

Quebecers favoured it, separation would still require a constitutional amendment demanding the consent of the federal Parliament, the provincial legislatures, and the Aboriginal peoples concerned. The only alternative to such an amendment is an insurrection by Quebecers, which would be illegal, illegitimate, and would probably have disastrous consequences for everybody who lives in Canada.[44]

- Unilateral secession based on a simple majority vote is particularly unfair to Aboriginal peoples and violates their fundamental human rights. Comments Aboriginal lawyer Mary Ellen Turpel: ". . . Aboriginal peoples' self-determination rights would be overridden, as [they] may simply be outvoted by larger populations in non-Aboriginal regions of Québec. This kind of referendum could not be upheld internationally as supporting accession to sovereignty, because of its implications for Aboriginal peoples."[45]

- In the past, a simple majority vote alone has not been considered sufficient justification for secession from a federal State. Secession movements in Nova Scotia in 1868 and in Western Australia in 1934, though supported by a clear majority of the citizens, were not allowed to succeed because the request did not emanate from the federal government.[46]

- There are many precedents for requiring more than a simple majority. Many democratic countries, including Canada, the United States, and Germany, have modified their constitutions in an effort to find balanced compromises between a simple majority and unanimity. Amendments to the Canadian Constitution require, as a general rule, approval of the federal Parliament along with two-thirds of the provincial legislatures.[47] In other cases unanimity is needed. In corporations, issues of particular importance can call for a two-thirds or three-quarters majority vote. "[T]o dissolve a fish and game club requires a two-thirds vote, according to the Québec Civil Code," remarks *Gazette* columnist William Johnson sardonically. "But to dissolve the country of Canada, according to the Parti Québécois, the Bloc Québécois, and the Reform Party of Canada, a mere fifty per cent plus one will be enough. And they call that democracy."[48]

- Even Québec jurists who favour secession have admitted that "an incontestable consensus . . . a clear and strong mandate from the Québec population" would be required.[49] Daniel Turp, for instance, said soon after being elected to Parliament that there is no international rule that 50 per cent plus one is a sufficient majority to set a secession in motion.[50] Different ideas have been put forward to overcome the inadequacies of the simple majority. Some suggest "an absolute majority," that is, a majority of all registered voters, not merely of those who vote.[51] Others suggest that 60 to 65 per cent of affirmative voters should be required,[52] or that a "double majority" be required, that is an overall majority plus a majority vote in different regions in the province.[53] A Special Joint Committee of the Senate and House of Commons in 1991 recommended such double majorities for approval of constitutional amendments, in a pan-Canadian context.

- There is no set principle or rule dictating that a simple majority vote is sufficient to carry an entity into secession. As Toronto's *Globe and Mail* remarked editorially before the 1995 referendum, "Quebecers [if they vote Yes] will be voting to suspend the basic law under which they have lived for more than a century, to break up an admirable country in two and to rob the minority who vote No of their nationality. Surely that requires more than fifty per cent plus one."[54]

- Since Québec is not oppressed, and enjoys full political freedom and control within Canada, secession on the basis of a simple majority vote would be unprecedented and not a normal application of the rules of either democracy or international law. In summary, there are no "compelling circumstances" to justify Québec's secession under present conditions.

# Many misleading comparisons

The Québec separatists make many comparisons with other parts of the world, most of them entirely invalid or misleading. For example, they often invoke the recent changes in Czechoslovakia, the Soviet Union, and Yugoslavia as justification for their own policies. Even nonseparatists can be heard to argue from time to time that many nation-states are breaking into smaller, more intimate units, based on ethnicity or language, and that, therefore, Québec's urge to go it alone is somehow merely part of a global movement.

A careful analysis of what happened in Europe, however, does not sustain any comparison.

- Yugoslavia was disintegrating and was the site of a destructive civil war.[55] Not only is there no civil war in Canada, there is not even an agreed presumption that Canada will disintegrate should Québec secede.

- Unlike Québec, the secessionist States in Yugoslavia had been self-governing republics before the federation of Yugoslavia was created in 1918.

- Unlike in Canada, the disintegration of the Yugoslav federation was precipitated by unconstitutional actions taken by Serbia. Had Yugloslavia not been disintegrating, it is by no means certain that the seceding republics would have received international recognition as they did (with, as it turned out, rather unfortunate results).

- In those republics, unlike in Québec, there was overwhelming public support for secession in plebiscites (94 per cent in Croatia, 88.5 per cent in Slovenia, 74 per cent in Macedonia, and 99 per cent of votes cast in Bosnia).

- Neither can the separation from the Soviet Union of Latvia, Lithuania, and Estonia be compared with Québec. These States were previously independent and were illegally incorporated into the Soviet Union in 1940.

- Unlike Québec, the Baltic States really were oppressed by the Soviet Union, but in spite of this their independence from the Soviet Union was not recognized by the international community until the Soviet Union agreed, even though support for independence in referendums stood at 77, 79, and 90 per cent.[56]

In contrast to the citizens of all these countries, Quebecers enjoy internal self-determination, and not even separatists dispute that. In addition, these huge majorities in favour of independence compare with the 50 per cent plus one vote that Québec separatists say would be enough to justify their unilateral declaration of independence. Separatist groups in many European countries — Belgium, Brittany, Savoie, Corsica, New Caledonia, Cyprus, to name a few — are no doubt eagerly watching the Québec situation to see if a precedent is established for approval of secession by a 50 per cent plus one vote. We would imagine that the governing States in all of these cases would vociferously oppose the acceptance of such a slim majority as sufficient to justify a claim to secession.

As we have shown in chapter 6, the Parti Québécois government, relying on a conclusion by its five experts, believes the principle of *uti possidetis* would apply in international law to preserve Québec's current boundaries. But many jurists both in Canada and internationally have challenged this conclusion by the five experts,[57] and in particular have severely criticized the application of *uti possidetis* to Yugoslavia, because it conflicted with the right of peoples there to self-determination.

"[It] was an attempt to produce a truce during an armed conflict," wrote one commentator. "It is not plausible to read it as the enunciation of a sweeping norm of international law to cover all secession situations, and certainly not that of Québec."[58] Moreover, it was unsuccessful and, in fact, precipitated an immense and tragic failure. (It is of interest that — as we discuss in more detail in chapter 14 — one of the five experts was a member of an Arbitration Commission that applied *uti possidetis* in Yugoslavia and now, apparently, wants to suggest it for Québec.)

Another comparison separatists like to make is with the European community. Many votes have been held by European countries as to whether they should or should not join, and separatists like to claim that their vote in relation to Canada is analogous. Jacques Parizeau made the comparison on an American television news show, when he said, "Look at the margins by which European countries decide these days whether they're entering the European union or not. One percent, point one of one per cent in certain cases, as to whether they'll go in or not. Now that's how democracy functions."[59]

This comparison ignores an enormous fact: that a decision to secede illegally and without just cause from an independent State is markedly different from a vote to become a member of a supranational body for certain defined purposes. The consequences of Québec secession are more far-reaching and introduce a sense of finality that would be difficult to reverse.[60] As one writer comments, "It is inconceivable that Québec and Canada would reunite. The process of peaceful secession has a momentum that has never been reversed and that will not be reversed in this case."[61] This is to assume that the breakup would be peaceful. How much less likely would a reconciliation be if the break takes place, as is now intended, unilaterally, in an atmosphere of hostility and recrimination?

## Asking for a blank cheque

One last aspect of the secessionists' attitude to referendums is highly objectionable. The 1995 referendum in effect asked for a blank cheque from the Québec people, including the Aboriginal peoples, who were given few details about the proposed constitution of an independent Québec and no clue as to what terms might be negotiated with Canada for the new State. Commenting on the draft bill of 1994 in an article in *Le Devoir*, two political scientists, J. Daigneault and C. Galipeau, compared Parizeau's process unfavourably with that followed by Premier René Lévesque in 1980. Lévesque proposed two referendums, one asking for a mandate to negotiate sovereignty-association with Canada, the second giving the people the prior right to ratify any change resulting from those negotiations.

"It is clear that the referendum process of Mr. Parizeau does not offer any guarantee to Quebecers in regard to the control of their political status," comment Daigneault and Galipeau. ". . . Mr. Parizeau proposes a process where he alone will dictate the final version of the Québec constitution, determine the elements of an economic union with the rest of the country and, moreover, give himself extraordinary powers to realize his sovereignty project."[62] The 1995 Bill 1 proposed by Parizeau did provide that a constituent assembly would draft a new Québec constitution, but nevertheless, Quebecers in 1995 voted on secession without knowing the details of what kind of sovereign Québec was being proposed.

From the point of view of Aboriginal peoples, the situation was even worse: in 1995 the PQ government proposed, in effect, the abandonment by Aboriginal peoples of our historic relationship with the Crown in right of Canada. And this without our approval. Yet this duplicity comes from a government that bases its claims on the principles of democracy and legitimacy.

After the close referendum result, this lack of precision as to the terms on which Québec might separate led to the creation all across Canada of groups demanding that, next time around, Canada should make its terms crystal clear to the voters and government of Québec. Foremost, perhaps, among these terms is the likelihood that the northern Cree and Inuit territories would not remain within the boundaries of an illegal, secessionist Québec. This is just one possibility that has not been fully brought home to Québec voters. Polls before the last referendum indicated that half of Québec voters believed, incorrectly, that sovereignty would be declared only after the rest of Canada had agreed to a partnership deal with Québec; and 28 per cent even thought that "a sovereign Québec would still be a Canadian province."[63]

Many others, even among those who lean towards separation, have commented on the inadequacy of the referendum process. Jacques-Yvan Morin, a former separatist minister, said, for instance, that a draft of a new constitution for an independent Québec should be submitted for popular approval before Quebecers were asked to vote on independence.[64]

International law expert Armand de Mestral of McGill University has written that a referendum held without offering any guarantee of an economic union with Canada is in violation of the most elementary rules of democracy and has raised fears that the voters would not be asked to approve the new Québec constitution before creating the new State.[65] Although provision was made for a "Parliament of Québec" to draft an "interim constitution," it was not to be submitted to the electors either before or after accession to independence.[66]

Political scientist Daniel Latouche, one of the separatists who has been most present in the English-speaking media in other parts of Canada, with, at one time, a regular column in the *Globe and Mail* and frequent appearances on English-language television, scathingly said that the contract offered to the voters before the 1995 referendum "would not pass the test of the Consumer Protection Act" and was nothing more nor less than a blank cheque.[67]

"If the Québec people must embark on the train of the nationalists," wrote a contributor to *Le Devoir*, "the least that [the separatists] could do . . . is reveal to the people the exact destination."[68] Given the vulnerability of the Aboriginal peoples, and their reliance on their ancestral rights, this is of even more concern to them than to most Quebecers.

Still, most people agreed that they should be told the PQ plans. According to an opinion poll, published a month before the 1995 referendum, some 75 per cent wanted the government to make public its offer to Canada before the referendum.[69] Yet in spite of the paucity of details about what was proposed, Quebecers were urged by Cabinet ministers to "vote Yes without all the answers," and — from Monique Simard, the Parti Québécois vice-president, and Serge Turgeon, head of the Union des Artistes — to "vote with their hearts and not expect all the answers on the economic consequences. . . ."[70]

This was the state of vulnerability and ignorance in which the Québec government left the general population. But the rights of Aboriginal peoples were thrust aside in an even more cavalier fashion. We could not estimate the impact of secession on us, except that we knew the government envisaged no role for Aboriginal peoples in any of the proposed new Canada-Québec institutions of the future.

For these and many other reasons, the referendum process as interpreted by the Québec secessionists must be judged unacceptable, undemocratic, and illegitimate.

# II

# Freedom of speech and misinformation in Québec

*Wherein it is shown that, although Québec has political freedom, Crees and others who dissent from separatism are told to shut up*

The complex questions examined in the previous chapters arouse vibrant passions among many people in Québec — more passion, perhaps, than there is understanding of the issues. The political debate is lively, but unfortunately it takes place in a climate, in regard to freedom of speech and information, that is far from ideal. Since Quebecers are not an oppressed or deprived population, the separatists justify their radical option (which scares a lot of people) with a bewildering range of psychological, economic, emotional, and social reasons. So broad a range of factors, in fact, that many people find it hard to come to grips with what the separatists are proposing and why. Here are some of the reasons given:

- Former Québec Premier Jacques Parizeau said Canada is becoming "psychologically unbearable."[1] Moreover, he added, an independent Québec would avoid high federal taxes.

- On another occasion Parizeau told readers of a scholarly American magazine: "Quebecers . . . live in a country that refuses to acknowledge their existence."[2] (He didn't mention

TSITI, *EASTERN DOOR*

that the Canadian Constitution has protected the French language since 1867, and that in 1992 the federal and all provincial and territorial governments, plus the four national Aboriginal organizations, explicitly agreed in the Charlottetown Accord to recognize Québec as a "distinct society." The Accord was subsequently rejected in a referendum by a majority of voters in Québec and other parts of Canada.)

- One of Parizeau's ministers, Louise Beaudoin, has said Quebecers "wish to be a majority in our own country."[3]

- Another minister, Jean Garon, has said they need independence to ensure their "cultural security."[4]

- Deputy-Premier Bernard Landry has said it is "normal" for a people to seek independence[5] (except apparently, an Aboriginal people). He said the idea of "two founding nations" is no longer accepted in the rest of Canada, so Québec must leave.

- Current Québec Premier Lucien Bouchard says there is an inherent right of any province to leave Canada;[6] and in any case, Quebecers will be better administered by a sovereign country.[7] (But only Quebecers, it appears, have inherent rights; Aboriginal peoples do not.)

- Some have it both ways. In May 1992 David Cliche, now a PQ Cabinet minister, said secession is justified on the basis of Quebecers' rights to self-determination.[8] But thirty months later, in October 1994, he categorically denied this: the claim was now based on "the right of [Québec citizens] to request the international community to recognize Québec as a sovereign country."[9]

- A toll-free phone line set up by the Parizeau government to answer questions about separation claimed that Quebecers had not been recognized as a people by the rest of the country.[10]

This is a somewhat incoherent list of reasons, and because of the nationalist mindset of many Québec intellectuals and media, it is difficult for opponents of separation to come to grips with what is being proposed. No sooner is one rationale confronted than it slips away to be replaced by another. The separatist elite in Québec do not appear to accept that in international law the acceptable grounds for a legitimate claim to secession are limited to (a) colonized peoples, (b) denial of political freedom, (c) serious abuses of human rights, or (d) an absence of "internal self-determination." There are almost no other grounds. Separatists erroneously claim that the common will of the people is all that is required: even if that were so, it has not been demonstrated in Québec.

# The political freedoms
# enjoyed by Quebecers

Nor can the separatists argue that the grounds for secession recognized as legitimate by the international community exist in Québec. Québec has its own provincial legislature elected on a full franchise, which exercises full control over its system of civil law, education, and social services. The province receives federal monies at least proportionate to its population and fiscal contribution (indeed, many in Canada are convinced it has received considerably more than its share). Federal laws and policies promote the use of French and the employment of French-speaking Canadians in government. French-speaking Canadians have played a full role in the Canadian democratic process ever since Canada has existed.[11] For thirty-seven of the last forty-eight years, Canada has had a Prime Minister from Québec (and for all but two of the last twenty-eight years). Indeed, until the federal election in June 1997, not only the Prime Minister but also the leader of the opposition in the federal Parliament were from Québec. It is a regular occurrence for the speakers of the Senate and House of Commons to be Quebecers. Many Canadian ambassadors are and have been Quebecers. (Including, oddly enough, Lucien Bouchard, the man who is now attempting to lead Québec out of Canada. He has not only been a federal Cabinet minister, but Canadian ambassador to France.) Three of the nine judges on the Supreme Court are guaranteed by law to come from Québec,[12] and nearly 30 per cent of the federal civil service are francophones, which is a higher percentage than the proportion of francophones in Canada.[13]

Compared with this generous representation of francophone Quebecers within the Canadian federal political system, Québec's own record of including minorities and Aboriginal people in its provincial civil service is unimpressive. Anglophones have been virtually excluded from Québec's public service and Crown corporations. Though those who use English as a first language in the home comprise more than 12 per cent of the Québec population, they account for only 0.7 per cent of the provincial public service.[14] Even at the level of language, which is a primary concern of separatists, Quebecers have been able to ensure that the French language is dominant and thriving. The guarantees for French now are such that they have been described by one of the province's leading political commentators, Lysiane Gagnon, as "a wall-to-wall security blanket . . . as much a guarantee as one can have in a democratic society." She added that "it's difficult to imagine what more could be done. . . ."[15] Québec has only one official language — French.

In a similar vein, François Cloutier, a former minister in Québec provincial governments, wrote in *La Presse* in February 1995:

> If Quebecers were persecuted as are many of the populations on the planet, if they would risk prison for wrongful opinion, if their fundamental freedoms were compromised, if their economic and social development turned out to be impossible, if they were dominated to the detriment of their culture and language, then it would be necessary to achieve independence whatever the price and by any means. This would be a question of survival, honour and dignity. Who can seriously claim that this is the case?[16]

Well, the Québec separatist leaders have come very close to making such absurd claims. Many of Bouchard's speeches during the 1995 referendum were a litany of ancient humiliations. In his interpretation of events, almost everything done by the federal government, every statement made by a Canadian leader worried about the integrity of his country, was twisted into some humiliation for Québec, real or imagined. In his reading of the facts, Québec is confined within a tyrannical federal strait-jacket. The term "strait-jacket" was actually used by Bouchard. "So that's the choice we have," he was reported as saying in the *Gazette*, Montréal's main English-language newspaper, in 1995. "Change ourselves, give up our identity.

The other choice, obviously, is to get out of the strait-jacket and be ourselves."[17]

Of course, even if Quebecers' participation in Canada were inadequate (which it is not), that would not justify the Québec government's denial of the rights of Crees and other Aboriginal peoples in the province. Since Canada is widely recognized to be one of the world's most decentralized countries, it is not surprising that foreigners are amazed at the prospect that Canada has come so close to self-destruction.[18] And it is not easy for outsiders, either, to understand the inflexibility and self-centredness of much separatist reasoning. The shifting sands (and contradictions) of the PQ's basic arguments have drawn notice from American scholars and others who have recently begun to pay more attention to the Québec secessionist issue. In a much-quoted article in the influential American magazine *Foreign Affairs*, Charles F. Doran, professor of international relations at Johns Hopkins University, Baltimore, noted the opposition of Cree and other Aboriginal communities to Québec independence and wondered whether an independent Québec could remain whole: "Only in the twentieth century was the northernmost section of Québec, Rupert's Land, formally granted to the province by British imperial authority," he wrote. "Potentially resource-rich, this territory contains such assets as the James Bay hydroelectric project. Québec categorically denies the claims of others to Statebuilding and separation." He added, ". . . Québec ultimately must confront the paradox of sovereignty. If Canada is divisible, then why is Québec indivisible? If Québec is indivisible, then on what grounds should Canada be obliged to allow Québec's secession?"[19]

## *Misinformation must be countered*

If Quebecers need, as Doran suggests, to face up to such questions and come to a balanced judgement about the future of Québec, there is a desperate need for informed discussion and debate. Informed debate is difficult where information is so often skewed or inaccurate. Senator Jacques Hébert, a long-time activist in Québec, complained of this in a letter to the *Globe and Mail* newspaper in September 1996. He blamed a "doctrinaire gaggle of scribes" in the Québec French-language newspapers who "relentlessly batter Canada and any of its steadfast defenders. . . . With such a distorting mirror in place, it's extremely difficult for the average Quebecer to get all the facts." He said the Québec media was hostile towards federalists such as former Prime Minister Pierre Trudeau, the current Prime Minister Jean Chrétien, and others. In contrast, Progressive Conservative Prime Minister Brian Mulroney had been given "an easy ride" by the Québec media because "he shamelessly cut deals and cavorted with separatists and crypto-separatists to get elected."[20]

At least three of Mulroney's ministers, Lucien Bouchard, Marcel Masse, and Monique Vezina, after spending years in federal politics, worked for the separatist option during the 1995 referendum. With their change of allegiance from Canada towards a sovereign Québec, these ministers appear to have also changed their understanding of the facts of Canadian life. For example, as ministers in Mulroney's Cabinet, they made no public objection to the inclusion of Aboriginal peoples in the negotiations for a renewed constitution. Yet three years later Vezina and Masse accepted the invitation of the separatist Québec government to join a Commission nationale sur l'avenir du Québec, which in its final report referred scornfully to the inclusion of the four national Aboriginal associations as parties to the 1992 negotiations, claiming that the Aboriginal peoples had been included as "a systematic method of isolating and marginalizing the voice of Québec." That commission came to the staggeringly ethnocentric conclusion that "there exist two peoples in Canada."[21]

There is no evidence of any kind that the inclusion of the Aboriginal representatives — which was, after all, not only politically and legally necessary, but was also consistent with principles of democracy and equality — was designed, or indeed served, to isolate or marginalize Québec. The Crees believe that the negative attitude towards Aboriginal peoples revealed by the commission, with its two former federal ministers, was outrageous and was in no way substantiated by the report itself. Nevertheless, the conclusion quoted above is typical of much misinformation that obscures the debate in Québec.

## Attacks on free speech

So fixed is the Parti Québécois government on its independence agenda that it has not hesitated to harass its opponents and try to suppress free debate. The Crees have always taken a stand in defence of their own rights, and as the emotion around the independence issue has risen and fallen, we have often found ourselves the object of separatist hostility. This is probably not unconnected to our successful opposition to the building of the Great Whale hydroelectric project. Cree opposition caused the cancellation of $17 billion worth of contracts between Hydro-Québec and New England power authorities and eventually indefinite postponement of the project.[22]

The Québec government's attitude to our activities at that time is a kind of touchstone of their attitude to freedom of speech. Our Cree activists were supported by a strong movement of New England environmentalists and others, who felt that our position was fully justified. But when, with our allies, we took our arguments into the town halls and legislatures of New England, and even across into the capitals of Europe, the Québec government, under the Liberal Party regime of Robert Bourassa, reacted sharply and paternalistically, even questioning our patriotism.

Some years later the Québec government, by now under the Parti Québécois, adopted the same lofty attitude to Cree efforts to publicize our dilemma in the face of the Québec independence movement. The government objected strenuously in 1994 when Grand Chief Matthew Coon Come had the audacity to travel to Washington, DC, to explain to an American audience his opposition to Québec secession. Discussing the Québec government's attitude to secession, Coon Come said that Parizeau, then the provincial premier, was practising "ethnic nationalism" in the context of Québec secession and accused him of "a double standard, a discrimination we can only assume is based on race."[23] Parizeau did not reply to Coon Come's substantive comments, but accused him of injuring not only Parizeau personally, but through him, "Québec itself."[24]

The separatist party in the House of Commons, the Bloc Québécois, quickly weighed in, asking the Canadian Prime Minister to censure Coon Come for "denigrating unfairly and incorrectly six million Quebecers."[25] (The Prime Minister declined.) The matter was taken to even more absurd levels when Québec Deputy-Premier Landry asked Canada's Minister of Foreign Affairs to condemn Coon Come because of his "concerted attacks against Québec."[26] Landry even suggested to journalists that the chief's statement might amount to criminal action within the Criminal Code.[27] Perhaps there was a competition among separatist leaders as to which could reach the highest level of absurdity because, when Cree spokesmen appeared undeterred before the European Parliament five months later to describe our objections to the separatist process in Québec, their appearance was described by David Cliche as "an act of treason."[28] In contrast to this hysterical atmosphere, it might be noted that when Québec's Minister of Tourism spoke in favour of the dismemberment of Canada at a Washington conference, the Canadian government took no action.[29]

The *Gazette* said in an editorial that Parizeau and Landry had made Coon Come's point for him: "Many supporters of Québec independence . . . claim for themselves freedoms that they refuse to accord others."[30]

As we have noted in the Introduction, opponents of separatism in Québec have to work in an atmosphere of extreme sensitivity to any criticism. We Crees are not the only people affected. In the run-up to the provincial election and following referendum (1993–95), Premier Parizeau did not hesitate to threaten reprisals against businesses that spoke out against the separatist option. The Bank of Montréal, which had produced a devastating analysis of the costs of independence, and the financial house, Wood Gundy, which linked interest rates with the drive for separatism, were threatened with retaliation by the Québec government. Wrote columnist Norman Webster, "Banks and financial houses have been blackmailed outrageously into keeping their mouths shut about the costs of separation. Before the PQ's election, on Parizeau's explicit orders, they were told to shut up or risk being punished by the new government party of Québec."[31] These moves were denounced by newspaper columnists and editorialists, and Michael Mackenzie, Canada's top banking regulator, said Parizeau's remarks were "a direct threat to free speech." Others indicated that the tactic was working: investment dealers said they would be very careful about what they said in future.[32]

Even French-speaking people in other parts of Canada (who might be supposed to have a central interest in the issue) have been told by separatists to butt out when they have expressed an opinion contrary to the secessionist drive. "Don't mix in our affairs," said Bloc Québécois MP Suzanne Tremblay, when the association of francophones outside Québec expressed an opinion.[33] This was described as "intolerance" by Pierre Gravel, a *La Presse* editorialist, who added wryly that he did not hear separatists objecting about interference in Québec affairs when thirty-odd French intellectuals publicly endorsed the sovereignty project.[34]

The effect of this unpleasant atmosphere has been that supporters of sovereignty for Québec appear to have closed their eyes and ears to anything that doesn't feed their option. It certainly cannot be concluded that free and informed debate on Québec secession is being encouraged in the province. Studies suggesting dire consequences for the province of Québec should it separate are simply ignored or dismissed as alarmist. Even a number of regional consultations held in February 1995 in the run-up to the October referendum were said to have been so packed with pro-secessionists that it took an extremely brave person — especially anyone who was francophone — to rise and express an opinion against separatism. "One is almost assured of being booed by the crowd and humiliated intellectually by the commissioners," wrote columnist Gagnon, in *La Presse*.[35]

The Crees have also noted that the one person in a position of authority in separatist circles who had supported the Aboriginal peoples' right to self-determination, Daniel Turp, was silenced for his heresy. "In terms of legitimacy," Turp testified to the National Assembly in 1991, "the Aboriginal peoples, the Aboriginal nations on their territory, are quite ahead of the francophones of Québec, the anglophones of Québec, all the Europeans, and other nationalities on this territory."[36] Three years later, when Turp became a legal adviser to the Bloc Québécois, his first statements were consistent with his long-held academic views: he indicated that he did not share the party's views on the Aboriginal right to self-determination. But he appears to have been quickly and effectively silenced from making further comment on the issue. The Bloc (then under the leadership of Bouchard) put out a press release saying that Turp shared "without ambiguity" Bouchard's position on the rights of Aboriginal peoples.[37] Remarkably, in discussing Turp's position, Bouchard said that he had not read the legal writings of his newly appointed legal adviser. Bouchard, although himself a lawyer, is apparently not an avid reader of the legal writings of his legal advisers: while he continues in 1997 to say that Aboriginal peoples in Québec do not have the right to self-determination, jurist Henri Brun, a major legal adviser to Bouchard's government on constitutional matters, admitted at a colloquium on self-determination that the "indigenous collectivity" in Québec has the right to self-determination and, thus, could be a sovereign people.[38] (He added, of course, that they do not have the size to form a sovereign State.)

Québec secession would have an immense impact on everyone living in Canada, and Premier Bouchard has a responsibility to express reasonable and not simply self-serving views on the subject. Unfortunately, his constitutional views are marked more by ignorance or malintuition than reason; to such a point that a Montréal professor of constitutional and international law, Michel Lebel, in 1996 wrote to the editor of *La Presse* that if Bouchard were a student, "I would not give him a passing mark" for his interpretations of constitutional and international law relating to Québec secession.[39]

Thus, the separatist drive has created a disturbing situation around information and freedom of expression in Québec. This is of great concern to the Crees, because our lands and rights are central to the entire issue of Québec secession. People in Québec are in danger of being pulled into a drastic act that could affect the future of the entire northern part of North America, without a proper debate about the pros and cons of the issue and without access to the honest, unbiased information needed to make a considered judgement.

# 12

---

# What will the international community do?

---

*Wherein are examined the many reasons why*
*the international community will pause before*
*recognizing an independent Québec*

---

If the separatist government of Québec proclaims a UDI, over-riding the objections of Aboriginal peoples (and others) against being forced into an independent Québec, the reaction of the international community will make the difference between life and death for the proposed republic. What will the international community do?

For one thing, the matter will immediately become a matter for international action, because the Aboriginal peoples have already decided that if Québec secession violates their right to self-determination, or their treaty, Aboriginal, or other human rights, they will "actively seek" intervention by the United Nations. This position was asserted as early as July 1991 by an international meeting of indigenous representatives in Geneva. If we Crees, Inuit, and others choose to oppose unilateral secession, we are likely to be supported by Aboriginal peoples across Canada and probably around the world.

This will be a major challenge for both Québec and Canada. Indigenous peoples now have a real presence both on the international political stage and in terms of international law, and our interests can no longer simply be brushed aside as irrelevant by any one State. The international community increasingly recognizes indigenous peoples: for example, late in 1996 the accord to end the Guatemalan civil war made many specific references to indigenous people and to the role of the UN in overseeing and coordinating recognition of their rights. This has created a valuable precedent for UN involvement in redressing issues concerning the rights of indigenous peoples, who are becoming recognized as the world's most disadvantaged, exactly the kind of peoples for whom the international human-rights safeguards developed over the last half century would be of most use.

So, two things have changed in recent decades: international instruments have become more sympathetic and sensitive to the plight of indigenous peoples, and the international community has undertaken obligations towards us which it must fulfil. Yet it has to be admitted: the situation could be clearer, the policies more precisely enunciated, the route to action more positively described. Events in the former Soviet Union and Yugoslavia have shown that attempts to suppress demands for self-determination can generate such a climate of violence that international peace and security are put in jeopardy.[1] Secession is an explosive issue. It is difficult to find an appropriate response to it in the heat of the moment, and it would be beneficial if some definite criteria could be agreed on in advance about how to deal with it.[2]

Montréal analysts Kimon Valaskakis and Angéline Fournier believe that the international community will have learned from Yugoslavia that it is a mistake to grant recognition to a seceding State too hastily and that they are likely to apply this lesson should Québec try to secede from Canada. The two authors even suggest that if Canada refuses to recognize Québec's separation, the international community might decide to consider the situation "an internal Canadian affair."[3] R. Young agrees: "The European Union would be unlikely to grant quick recognition to Québec, partly because of its experience with the former Yugoslavia."[4] In the past, once the UN has determined that a particular action was not in accordance with international law, it has advised member States against recognizing a State that has unilaterally declared its independence.[5]

There could be any number of reasons for this reluctance to recognize a new State. Jeremy Webber, of the McGill Institute for the Study of Canada, warns that Aboriginal self-determination is one of several issues that Canada or other countries might well insist on resolving before accepting Québec's independence.[6] Even separatist legal adviser Daniel Turp has given the same warning. "The satisfaction of certain claims of Aboriginal peoples to self-determination could be, for other members of the international community, a condition for recognition of the sovereign Québec State," he wrote in a Montréal newspaper in 1991.[7] Because of its explosive potential, many commentators in Canada have warned that this issue should already have been given more attention.

## Many violations to be met

The separatist government of Québec appears to believe that the international community will recognize Québec as an independent State if it shows a general willingness to respect the *United Nations Charter*, provides protections for the rights of minorities, and recognizes minimal self-government rights of Aboriginal peoples. For the Crees, these are mere pious hopes and by no means deal with our objections. The separatists are proposing fundamental violations of our rights. As we have seen in chapter 9, even the very existence of Aboriginal rights has been denied by the Québec government, as has our right to remain in Canada if we so wish. As far as the separatists do recognize our rights, they do so in a highly restrictive manner. For example, the Parti Québécois government's bill establishing the route to independence mentions recognition of Aboriginal self-government rights only "on lands over which they have full ownership," but adds that such recognition would be exercised in a manner "consistent with the territorial integrity of Québec." One has to interpret these words: the Québec government does not consider that we Aboriginal peoples own our traditional lands, except, perhaps, for certain small areas. In fact they believe that even many Indian reserves are really owned by the federal or provincial governments. They also ignore that Aboriginal territories often extend well beyond the current provincial boundaries of Québec. Furthermore, their draft act repeatedly uses the word "recognition" in regard to the rights of Aboriginal nations, but "guarantee" in the case of the English-speaking community.

Not surprisingly, then, we Aboriginal nations in Québec are doubtful about even the most favourable intentions that might be placed before the international community by the secessionist government. The violations and problems arising from Québec secession are so serious that they could not be met by any tinkering the secessionist government may do. Remember that, after all, such a government would already have forcibly included Aboriginal peoples and our territories into a new State, would have denied us our choice to remain in Canada, would forcibly have altered Aboriginal nationality, would unilaterally have altered the JBNQA, and would have done all this by a process that was undemocratic, illegal, or illegitimate under international and Canadian law! We are supposed to put our trust in the stated good intentions of such a government?

These are all issues in which it is to be hoped that the international community will take an interest. In particular, violation by a seceding Québec of the Aboriginal right to self-determination would merit more than passive attention, since there is an obligation that this right be applied without discrimination.

## The many international instruments available

In the modern world the instruments available to protect Aboriginal peoples from arbitrary actions by the states in which they live are increasing. Here are some significant instruments which provide relevant standards or guidelines:

**The ILO Convention:** The *Indigenous and Tribal Peoples Convention, 1989,* was approved by consensus in a committee that drafted it and was adopted by the full conference by a vote of 328 in favour (including Canada) to one against, with forty-nine abstentions.[8]

This convention places a wide range of responsibilities on governments to treat indigenous people with respect, fairness, and equality. Many of these international undertakings appear to be relevant to Québec's proposed secession. For example, Article 3 says that indigenous and tribal peoples shall enjoy "the full measure of human rights and fundamental freedoms without hindrance or discrimination" and that "no form of force or coercion shall be used in violation of the human rights and fundamental freedoms of the peoples concerned." Article 2 also suggests that States have fiduciary-type obligations to protect and work with indigenous peoples. It provides that "governments shall have the responsibility for developing, with the participation of the peoples concerned, coordinated and systematic action to protect the rights of these peoples and to guarantee respect for their integrity."

Clearly, in the terms of this convention, all human rights are to be enjoyed by indigenous peoples, without hindrance. An accompanying resolution was adopted by the general conference of the ILO calling for action by States at the national level and urging international bodies such as the UN and the ILO to take specific measures.

**The United Nations:** So far, the ILO convention is the most specific international instrument in defence of indigenous rights, but the draft *United Nations Declaration on the Rights of Indigenous Peoples* is already being cited by legalists and has, even before its formal adoption (which is expected by the end of this decade), already achieved considerable stature among jurists. The draft declaration not only emphasizes fundamental indigenous rights, but requires States, specialized UN agencies, and the United Nations itself "to give full effect" to its provisions in consultation with indigenous peoples.

It is true that the *United Nations Charter* provides for the noninterference by the UN in "matters essentially within the domestic jurisdiction of any State." However, in the constantly evolving world of international law, State sovereignty no longer shields countries from human-rights transgressions. Genocide, for example, does not fall within the ambit of domestic government activity.[9] Nor does the denial of self-determination.

In addition, several other international instruments are relevant to the rights of indigenous peoples. For example, every government that has ratified the UN's international covenants on human rights, which declare the right of all peoples to self-determination, has to submit periodic reports to an international Human Rights Committee that monitors how such matters as the right to self-determination are being observed.

**The European OSCE:** The European States, now grouped in the Organization for Security and Cooperation in Europe (OSCE), have acknowledged the "special problems" faced by indigenous peoples in the exercise of their rights, have distinguished them from minorities, and have agreed that their members' commitments regarding human rights and fundamental freedoms apply "fully and without discrimination" to indigenous peoples. They did this in the Helsinki document, *Challenge of Change*, in 1992.[10] Canada and the United States are members. This is the same group of States that decided in 1991 that human rights, democracy, and the rule of law are of "international concern" and "do not belong exclusively to the internal affairs of the State concerned."[11]

**The European Parliament:** In 1994 the European Parliament adopted a resolution that highlights the right of indigenous peoples to "determine their own destiny by choosing their institutions, their political status, and the status of their territory."[12]

These and other principles acknowledged and agreed on at the international level demonstrate that indigenous peoples are increasingly being treated as subjects of international law and as an important responsibility of the international community.[13] This international duty appears to have elements of a fiduciary, or trusteeship, obligation.

## A wide range of possible measures

Evidently the international community has an important role to play in the debate about Québec secession. In particular, there is a compelling need to ensure full respect of the right of Aboriginal peoples to self-determination.

Arising from all these declarations, covenants, agreements, and resolutions, many actions are open to the international community in face of a unilateral and illegal declaration of Québec independence. They include:

- Any proposed violation of the Aboriginal right to self-determination should be examined by the UN Human Rights Committee in light of the reporting requirements for States laid down in the *International Covenant on Civil and Political Rights*.

- The member countries of the OSCE (including Canada) should apply their agreed-upon guidelines to ensure that the Aboriginal right to self-determination in Québec is fully respected.

- Member states of the European Parliament should, in accordance with their own guidelines, make any future request for international recognition by a secessionist Québec conditional on Aboriginal peoples' freedom to determine their own destiny.

- States should refuse recognition to a secessionist group that obtains territory through armed force or other coercive measures contrary to international law. This obligation is especially addressed in the *Convention on Rights and Duties of States*, which entered into force in 1934. (Canada is not a party.)

- A wide range of nonmilitary interventions by the UN would be appropriate. They include:

  - international supervision of referendums

  - international mediation of disputes

  - possible trade and other economic sanctions

  - refusal to recognize a secessionist Québec

  - refusal of membership in the United Nations and its specialized international agencies.

If the international community were to accept Québec's claim that a unilateral declaration of independence is democratic and legitimate, even though it violated the rights of indigenous peoples, an extremely unfavourable precedent would be created. It would, moreover, make a mockery of the standard-setting process that has been taking place in Geneva over the past decade, and in which, increasingly, Aboriginal peoples are placing great store.

In addition, if Québec is to force Aboriginal peoples and their lands into its newly independent State, and then take measures to establish "effective control," the implied use of force and violence could pose a real threat to international peace and security.

In the current circumstances of the globe, this could be a most destabilizing precedent for the international community. Would it mean that any people, or any region, already exercising internal self-determination within an existing State, could unilaterally declare its independence after receiving a vote of 50 per cent plus one? There are many movements which would welcome such a precedent: for example, the Basques of Spain, the Scottish and Welsh nationalists of Britain, the Corsicans, Bretons, and New Caledonians of France, the Flemish in

Belgium. Could even the Americans be open to State secessions under such a rule, for example in Hawaii, where there is a growing movement of Polynesian protest, or in Puerto Rico? This whole situation is fraught with uncertainties and possible dangers.

We Crees recognize that any international action taken should be appropriate, balanced, and commensurate with the degree of any future violations by a secessionist Québec. But it is now established, following the international campaign to undermine the apartheid regime in South Africa, that "peaceful reprisals" are an acceptable international tool against any State that completely denies the right to self-determination, especially on racial grounds.[14]

# 13

# Canada and Québec: are these trustees trustworthy?

*Wherein Aboriginal peoples look to Canada for respect and protection of their rights, hoping after hundreds of years that there is honour in the Crown*

The Crees and other Aboriginal peoples in Québec believe that, in the face of Québec's secession threat, the federal government should move to safeguard Aboriginal rights and interests.[1] The feds, after all, have a fiduciary[2] or trusteeship duty towards Aboriginal peoples.

Some people think this could be done, if Québec became independent, simply by having Canada hand over its responsibility for Aboriginal peoples to the new Québec government. It has even been suggested that Canada could use us as a bargaining counter: Québec would undertake Canada's trusteeship for Aboriginal peoples, and in return Canada would agree to Québec's entry into the North American Free Trade Agreement (NAFTA).[3]

We *Eeyouch* recoil from such suggestions. We have a right to determine our own future, including the right to choose to remain in Canada. But in addition we do not think a separate Québec State could do the job, could not provide the same range of protections or opportunities for the exercise of our rights and interests. At the moment, the distribution of federal-provincial powers safeguards us against the intrusive actions of provincial governments. In an independent Québec there would no longer be another level of government to act as a check.

Let us consider in more detail, then, the fiduciary or trusteeship obligations that Canada and Québec have towards Aboriginal peoples and how these would be affected by Québec secession.

## *Canada's responsibilities*

"The government of Canada has constitutional responsibility for Aboriginal peoples and cannot renounce that responsibility unilaterally," remarks Kent McNeil, professor at Osgoode Hall Law School, York University, whose study of exactly this problem was commissioned by the Royal Commission on Aboriginal Peoples in 1995. "If Aboriginal peoples do not accept Québec independence," he wrote, "Canada has a constitutional obligation to ensure that their interests are protected in face of a UDI."[4]

GABLE, *THE GLOBE AND MAIL*

This federal responsibility stems from the historical relationship Aboriginal peoples have always had with the Crown. The Supreme Court of Canada has begun in the last decade to pay more attention to this relationship, and two judgements known as the Guerin case (1984)[5] and the Sparrow case (1990)[6] have ushered in a period of greater respect for Aboriginal rights.

Chief Justice Brian Dickson found in the Guerin case that the Crown owed a fiduciary obligation to "the Indians, with respect to the lands." Remember that, only eleven years before, the federal government was still denying that Aboriginal peoples had any inherent territorial rights in Canada.

Six years later, in the 1990 Sparrow case, the Supreme Court said the Guerin decision had become "the general guiding principle" for interpretation of the guarantees entrenched in the Constitution in 1982. "The relationship . . . is trust-like, rather than adversarial," remarked the Court, "and contemporary recognition and affirmation of Aboriginal rights must be defined in light of this historic relationship."[7]

It appears to follow from this trustee relationship that in regard to Québec secession Aboriginal consent would first have to be obtained. This is the opinion of Professor Peter Hogg, of Osgoode Hall Law School, whose authoritative views of the Canadian Constitution we have quoted before. In his May 1997 presentation to a Canadian Bar Association Conference, he outlined reasons why the government of Canada "must not cooperate with a secession by Québec without first obtaining the consent of the James Bay Crees and the Inuit of Nunavik." These include:

> . . . a secession would involve a severance of the fiduciary duty that is owed by the Crown in right of Canada to the Aboriginal people. That fiduciary duty is constitutionally protected by s. 35(1) of the Constitution Act, 1982. In my opinion, that duty cannot be severed, or transferred to a new state, without the consent of the Aboriginal people to whom the duty is owed.[8]

Clearly, under the rules enunciated by the Guerin and Sparrow judgements, the government and Parliament of Canada would have a solemn legal responsibility to protect Aboriginal peoples who insisted on staying in Canada. It would be unacceptable for Canada to evade this constitutional responsibility and instead deal with an entity that had just renounced all Canadian authority. Toronto law professor Patrick Monahan agrees with this interpretation of Canada's duty: "Aboriginal groups in Québec would be able to argue that section 35(1) of the *Constitution Act, 1982*, obliges the Canadian government to oppose and contest a Québec UDI made without their consent," he writes.[9]

At the same time, it should be noted that the federal trusteeship duty was not created in 1982 by the *Constitution Act*. As early as 1763 the Royal Proclamation declared that Aboriginal nations live under the protection of the Crown. In the quaint language of that time, the Royal Proclamation stated that

> . . . whereas it is just and reasonable, and essential to our Interest, and the Security of our Colonies, that the several Nations or Tribes of Indians with whom We are connected, and who live under our Protection, should not be molested or disturbed in the Possession of such Parts of Our Dominions and Territories as, not having been ceded to or purchased by Us, are reserved to them . . . as their Hunting Grounds. . . .[10]

And it then laid out a procedure for dealing with Aboriginal lands.

Brian Slattery, professor at Osgoode Hall Law School, York University, and a leading expert on law pertaining to Aboriginal peoples in Canada, says this "constitutional trust" had already emerged by 1763 as a result of dealings between the Crown and the Aboriginal nations in eastern North America. From that time, fiduciary and other principles underlying historical practices had become "part of the basic constitutional law governing the colonies."[11]

Because of this Crown trust undertaking, the immense transfers of land from Canada to the provinces between 1870 and 1912 were made subject to conditions regarding the protection of Aboriginal peoples. Canada could not and did not hand over its responsibility for Aboriginal peoples along with the land. For example, as we have shown earlier, in 1912 the act extending Québec's boundaries contained a federal undertaking to maintain "the trusteeship of the Indians in the hands of the Government of Canada subject to the control of Parliament." This section was later repealed by the Canadian Parliament in connection with the James Bay and Northern Québec Agreement, and separatists have since argued that this trusteeship duty of the federal government no longer exists in Québec.[12] But although that section was repealed in 1976, the obligation of the federal Crown remains. The repealing law, in fact, specifically mentions that "Parliament and the Government of Canada recognize and affirm a special responsibility for the said Crees and Inuit."[13]

In addition, as we have already pointed out, Canada undertook trusteeship and constitutional obligations towards Aboriginal peoples as part of the conditions for transfer of the Rupert's Land territories from Britain in 1869. Among the "Indian tribes" that were specifically given protection then are the James Bay Crees, and nearly 130 years later this condition remains part of Canada's constitutional duty.

The Supreme Court says that any fiduciary or trustee is expected to behave "according to the highest standards." Justice Dickson, in fact, wrote in the Guerin judgement that "equity will not countenance unconscionable behaviour in a fiduciary, whose duty is that of utmost loyalty to his principal."[14] Since Québec independence would entail far-reaching consequences for the Aboriginal peoples, the federal government has the obligation to intervene actively to protect the fundamental rights of Aboriginal peoples.[15]

In the event of Québec secession, in other words, the usual federal posture of sitting on hands will not serve. In the Crees' view, the federal government should not wait until Québec declares its independence before taking action. We Crees, along with the Inuit and Innu, have already expressed our wishes in our own overwhelming votes in our 1995 referendums, and the Crown should fully respect our right to self-determination, including our right to choose to remain in Canada (if we so desire). Crees believe Canada should respond appropriately to its trusteeship duties as soon as there is a concrete proposal or action by Québec that would impact on Aboriginal peoples.

Nor can the Canadian government transfer this trusteeship responsibility unilaterally to Québec since the terms and conditions of various constitutional instruments explicitly require the Canadian government to carry out its responsibilities.[16] In fact, the federal trusteeship responsibility is so strong that in the event of an infringement of an Aboriginal right by a province, active intervention by the federal government would be required "in keeping with the undertaking of Parliament (in 1870)."[17] We must also recall that, in 1867, jurisdiction over "Indians and the lands reserved for Indians" was given to the federal Parliament and not to provincial legislatures. Therefore, it would seem that, if the Aboriginal people so desire, the federal government and Parliament *must* ensure that we remain in Canada, along with our territories.

Aboriginal peoples have always been extremely vulnerable to the powers exercised by Canada and Québec, and are especially so in the context of Québec secession. This is apparent, whether or not Québec's actions prove to be legal or illegal, legitimate or illegitimate. There is no doubt that fiduciary duties towards Aboriginal peoples do exist and cannot be fulfilled by the Canadian government contrary to the wishes of the Aboriginal peoples concerned.

Such duties reinforce the constitutional requirements that already exist for the consent of the Crees and Inuit in relation to inclusion of their traditional territories in a seceding Québec. As discussed in chapter 8, extensive consent requirements already exist as a result of the constitutionally protected treaty rights in the James Bay and Northern Québec Agreement.

## Québec's fiduciary responsibilities

Although the primary responsibility towards Aboriginal peoples rests with the Canadian government, the provinces also have some trust-like responsibilities that they cannot avoid.

"So long as the Provinces have powers and rights enabling them to affect adversely Aboriginal interests protected by the relationship, they hold attendant fiduciary obligations," remarks Professor Slattery.[18]

This is reinforced by the study by Paul Joffe and Mary Ellen Turpel. "Although the fiduciary obligations of the Crown in right of Canada arose for historical reasons dating back at least to the time of the Royal Proclamation," they write, "this does not mean that the provincial Crowns in Canada do not incur fiduciary obligations."[19]

Such obligations can, for example, arise from specific treaties of the provincial Crown, or from Québec's undertakings towards Indians in the Québec Boundaries Extension Act, 1912. In addition, Québec has incurred treaty obligations to the Crees and Inuit under the James Bay and Northern Québec Agreement (1975), and to the Naskapi under the Northeastern Québec Agreement (1978).

These Québec fiduciary duties are different from those of the federal Crown and do not replace them. But they do require the Québec government and the National Assembly to obey Dickson's stricture that a fiduciary must conduct itself according to the highest standards. Therefore, in the context of Québec's proposed secession, the PQ government and National Assembly must recognize and respect the right of Aboriginal peoples to self-determination. These provincial obligations do not mean that the government of Québec can unilaterally displace the federal government or assume federal obligations without the consent of the Aboriginal peoples and the government of Canada.

In addition to these special Crown responsibilities, the governments of Canada and Québec have both legal and political commitments to respect human rights, and this, too, is a standard by which their behaviour towards Aboriginal peoples may be assessed.[20]

From all of this it seems more than clear that the PQ government has a duty to proceed with the aspirations of Quebecers in a manner that does not infringe or deny the fundamental rights of the James Bay Crees and other Aboriginal peoples in

Québec. The PQ government says it seeks an equal and beneficial "partnership" with Aboriginal peoples, but a reasonable test of that commitment is whether they will observe or ignore the will of the Aboriginal peoples concerned.

Unfortunately the Québec government has not fulfilled its fiduciary obligations towards us since it has not recognized our right to self-determination, in the Québec secession context. As we have seen, the Québec Premier has pointedly denied in the past that we have such a right.

Should the Québec government proceed with its proposed secession from Canada, we *Eeyouch* want everyone to know: we are not prepared to be kidnapped! No way!

# 14

## Time to question Québec's use of the five experts

*Wherein five learned jurists who are asked a trick question produce a most manipulable answer*

In 1992 the Québec National Assembly's Committee on Sovereignty decided to commission a legal study[1] of the borders of a secessionist Québec State by five renowned experts in international law, drawn from four different countries.

The resulting study has formed the basis of the response separatist leaders have given almost every time to the tough questions that are raised about Aboriginal peoples, territory, and the right of the Crees to determine their future in the context of the separation of Québec from Canada. So, every time Premier Lucien Bouchard is asked these days, "What about the Crees?" he replies with grave self-assurance that he has a legal opinion that we Crees have no right to make our own decisions if Québec moves to secede from Canada.

The 1992 Committee on Sovereignty sent identical letters of instruction to the five jurists who agreed to take part in the study. But like almost everything about the separatists' interpretation of the path they are following, the meaning of those instructions was equivocal and has since proven controversial.

Before discussing the study's conclusion in detail, it is necessary to make a few preliminary points about the assumptions

196

on which the experts agreed to base their study and about the information made available to them. The five experts were instructed to take the "accession of Québec to sovereignty" for granted; so the study they produced was based on the premise of *an already sovereign* Québec! From the outset their study assumed that effective control over the present territory of Québec *had already been achieved*; the questions put to them conveniently did not refer to the period immediately following a unilateral declaration of independence.

In addition, from the moment the experts were sent their letters of mandate, the Committee on Sovereignty sought to bias the five experts on one of the key issues of the study, the question of recognition of Aboriginal peoples' right to self-determination. The letter empowering them declared that "neither the government of Canada, nor the government of Québec, nor their Parliaments, have recognized the right of indigenous peoples to self-determination."[2]

Nor were the five experts given all the relevant constitutional documents by the Québec National Assembly Committee's

PRITCHARD, *TORONTO STAR*

secretariat.[3] In particular, they were not given the Imperial *Rupert's Land and North-Western Territory Order* of 1870, which is of critical relevance to Aboriginal peoples in northern Québec. Any analysis that fails to take this important order into account can only be described as incomplete and inconclusive, in relation to the Aboriginal peoples concerned.

As we have shown in chapters 3 and 4, the province of Québec cannot become independent simply by declaring that it is so, in other words, through a unilateral declaration. Short of an agreement with Canada under the Canadian Constitution, it could become independent only by establishing "effective control" over all the territory it claims. In their study, the five experts acknowledge that this is so.

First, they conclude: ". . . the Québec people exercise effectively its right to self-determination within the framework of the Canadian ensemble and there is no legal foundation to invoke this right to justify its eventual accession to independence."[4]

Second: "The accession to sovereignty of a territory is a simple question of fact in regard to international law: the new State is considered as such if its existence is effective."[5] The test of this effectiveness, they add, is international recognition.

There is no doubt about the expertise of the five experts. In international law circles, they are about as authoritative as they come. They hold leading positions in international educational institutions and have all been members of the Human Rights Committee of the United Nations. Yet, perhaps because of the formulation of the questions posed to them, their study has come under increasing criticism in legal circles since it was delivered.

Alain Pellet, professor of Public International Law at the Université de Paris X-Nanterre and at the Institut d'études politiques de Paris, is believed to have been the main author of the report.[6] Before tackling Québec secession, he was a legal advisor to the Badinter Arbitration Commission, whose application of the principle of *uti possidetis* in Yugoslavia (dealt with in chapter 6) produced disastrous results.[7] The four other experts were Rosalyn Higgins, professor of International Law at the London School of Economics; Thomas Franck, director of the Centre for International Studies at the Law School of New York University and previously director of research at the United Nations Institute for Training and Research; Christian Tomuschat, professor of Public Law and director of the Institute of International Law at the University of Bonn, Germany, and currently a member of the UN's International Law Commission; and Malcolm N. Shaw, a professor of law at the University of Leicester, England, and a practising barrister.

So what exactly were the questions posed to these five experts?

Their study was dominated by the seven words of a key assumption they were instructed to make at the beginning of each question: "Assuming the accession of Québec to sovereignty...":

QUESTION 1: *Assuming the accession of Québec to sovereignty,* would the borders of a sovereign Québec be the existing borders, which include the territories attributed to Québec by the 1898 and 1912 federal statutes, or those of the province of Québec at the time the Canadian federation was formed in 1867?

QUESTION 2: *Assuming the accession of Québec to sovereignty,* would the principle of territorial integrity (or *uti possidetis*) prevail under international law over claims for the dismemberment of Québec territory, more specifically:
a) the claims of the Aboriginal peoples in Québec who invoke the right of self-determination of peoples as understood in international law;
b) the claims of the English-speaking minority, particularly concerning the areas in Québec where it is concentrated;
c) the claims of persons, regardless of their ethnic origins, living in certain border regions of Québec?[8]

The five experts reported that indeed, *assuming the accession of Québec to sovereignty*:

1. The borders of a sovereign Québec would remain unchanged and would include the territories annexed to Québec in 1898 and 1912.

2. The principle of legal continuity supports the territorial integrity of Québec, which is guaranteed both by Canadian and international law, over claims for the dismemberment of Québec, whether emanating from Aboriginal peoples, anglophones, or anyone else.

## A far-reaching and risky assumption

The assumption the five experts were asked to make, of course, raises the question of exactly when a seceding Québec would have "acceded to sovereignty."

Would that be the moment when Québec makes its unilateral declaration of independence, or would it be the moment at which the new State achieves "effective control" of its claimed territory and is recognized internationally by other States?

The experts leave no doubt that in their minds "accession to sovereignty" occurs if and when Québec achieves "effective control," and the test of that is international recognition.[9] They make it clear that "effective control" cannot be achieved by simply reinforcing provincial jurisdiction or declaring independence; the new State would actually have to exclude Canadian authority from its claimed territory before it could demonstrate "effective control."[10]

Therefore, a sovereign Québec's borders would be protected under international law *only* after Québec had successfully acceded to sovereignty. Until that moment, the principles of international law which guarantee the borders of a seceding Québec and prevent intervention by other States would not apply.

It is perhaps no wonder that Grand Chief Matthew Coon Come told a meeting of the Canadian Bar Association in Toronto in June 1995 that the question put to the five experts by the National Assembly "was actually a trick question [that] skips over the period, of undetermined length, between the time of a decision to separate and the point [when] Québec is recognized by the international community, and actually becomes independent."[11]

From the time of a unilateral declaration of independence by Québec until that moment of international recognition (if such a time ever came), it cannot be said that the province's present borders would in any sense of the term be legally intact. The five experts actually acknowledge that, in terms of international law, Aboriginal peoples (or any other group that does not want to go along with secession), also have access to the principle of "effective control" on the same terms as Québec, as we have pointed out in chapter 4.[12]

To deny effective control to the secessionists, Aboriginal peoples (or any other group in the province) can choose to maintain their full relationship with Canada, and Canada can maintain its relationships with them; they are not required to establish a new State.

This uncertain and unstable period, during which the "battle" for effective control will occur, is being seriously under-estimated and deliberately downplayed by the separatist government in Québec. Separatists appear to assume that independence will automatically flow from their unilateral declaration. Such a strategy is risky, dangerous, and misleading to the public. Comprehensive public discussion is needed about these perilous, uncertain months or years during which attempts to gain control by Québec will be contested. Full and informed discussion should take place well in advance of any future referendum. Evasions and trick questions cannot replace honest and frank public debate.

A different expert in international law, Professor Richard Falk of Princeton University, comments that the five experts' study is "quite misleading" because it ignores alternative interpretations of the law developed from "diverse, often antagonistic, political and moral perspectives."[13] He points out that to assume that Québec is already a sovereign nation places Aboriginal peoples who claim the right to remain in Canada in the position of appearing to challenge the territorial unity of the new State of Québec. He describes this as "highly artificial." After all, the separatist claims are far from resolved, and Aboriginal peoples have a right to take part in whatever process is established to resolve them. Yet, because of the questions posed to them, it is on this artificial assumption that the five experts have based their entire study.

Nevertheless, some of the five experts' conclusions are positive for Aboriginal peoples. They confirm, for example, that Aboriginal peoples are more than just "minorities." They emphasize the spiritual dimensions of the Aboriginal relationship with the land and recognize that Aboriginals are "peoples" with territorial rights,[14] as well as the right to self-determination.[15]


## Some questionable conclusions

Other conclusions, however, are questionable. The five experts say that, like Quebecers, Aboriginal peoples are not colonized and have no right to independence.[16] Such a conclusion requires a more detailed examination of the history and current circumstances of Aboriginal peoples than the five experts were able to make. (They state clearly in the study that they had neither an adequate mandate nor the competence to analyze the constitutional position of Aboriginal peoples, which, they said, "arouse abundant and often very subtle doctrinal controversies.")[17]

Aboriginal peoples such as the Crees, however, have clearly experienced colonialism, and contemporary legal literature increasingly confirms this.[18] Undeniably, indigenous peoples are among the most vulnerable peoples in the world. It is both ironic and tragic that after their long history as victims of colonialism, the James Bay Crees and other Aboriginal peoples are once again being threatened with an essentially colonialist action, their forcible inclusion in a secessionist Québec.

International jurist Catherine Iorns states that indigenous peoples should be accorded the same legal status as colonized peoples because they have been colonized and subjugated by foreigners, both in the traditional sense (externally) as well as in a not-so-traditional sense (internally, within independent States). "Today we would regard such colonialism as contrary to notions of human dignity and to international law because of the breach of fundamental human rights that it entails."[19]

Again, jurists Richard Falk, S.J. Anaya, and Donat Pharand remark that "the history and experience of Aboriginal peoples resembles that of colonial peoples . . . and international law is moving toward . . . formal acknowledgement of this status. . . ."[20] Peter Russell, of the University of Toronto, says there is a need for "a fundamental reconsideration of [Aboriginal peoples'] colonized status." He adds: "In socio-economic terms . . . the Native component of the population . . . suffers the greatest deprivation of equality, and the continuing imposition of non-Aboriginal rule over the Aboriginal peoples constitutes Canada's most serious constitutional injustice."[21] It can be argued that the situation of indigenous peoples today is analogous to that of peoples in nonself-governing territories, whose well-being the United Nations is supposed to promote to the utmost "as a sacred trust." (This is provided for in Section 73 of the United Nations Charter.) Although no "sacred trust" has been expressly declared in regard to indigenous peoples, in recent years the United Nations has begun to address the same kinds of economic, cultural, social, and political issues in relation to indigenous peoples in independent States (such as Canada) as it always has in relation to peoples in nonself-governing territories.

The colonial experience of Aboriginal peoples in Québec is graphically expressed in a 1994 study for the Québec Mental Health Committee. The study indicates that the predominating mental health problem in eastern James Bay is "the state of religious, economic, social, cultural, and psychological colonization that Aboriginals were locked into for more than a century, the impact of which is still being felt."[22] So the five experts, although they did not make any specific examination of this question, may doubt that the *Eeyouch* and other First Nations in Québec are colonized peoples, but we ourselves know our history and present condition and have no doubt.[23]

The five experts focus too much on whether Aboriginal peoples in Québec have a right to secede. We Crees do not wish to establish an independent State, but reserve our right to secede should we be forcibly included in an independent

Québec, and in those circumstances we claim the right to do so under international law.

A much more pressing question is full recognition of our right to self-determination in the present urgent context of Québec secession. This includes our right to our identity as distinct peoples, our right to hold our own referendums, and our right to choose to remain in Canada. While denying the Aboriginal right to secede, the five experts confirm that the right to self-determination includes the right to one's own identity, to choose one's own future, and to participate in the governance of the State.[24]


## Québec's nonexistent "right" to secede

There is evidence that at least some of the five experts have begun to have second thoughts, or at least to entertain some doubts and a different opinion, about some of the conclusions of their study. Professor Franck, for instance, in 1995, three years after the study, commented in a new book that "the law has almost unlimited tolerance for paradox; but not for blatant unfairness." And the example he used in illustration was the denial of Aboriginal peoples' rights in relation to Québec secession. "For example," he wrote, "what justice would be served if international law were to recognize Québec's right to secede from Canada, but no right for the Ungava native peoples' region to secede from Québec?"[25]

In summary, however, the five experts' study brought the Québec government the opposite message from what they sought: it makes clear that neither Québec nor Quebecers can rely on any right to self-determination in order to claim a right to secede under international law. For that very reason, as we describe in chapter 4, the governing separatists changed their tactics in their drive towards independence. They immediately began to avoid judicial scrutiny, walking out of court hearings that rejected their untenable arguments, proclaiming Québec public opinion above all laws and legal jurisdictions, and instead attempting to base their case for secession on arguments of "legitimacy" and "democracy."

These arguments simply do not wash. As Professor Franck, one of the five experts, has made clear: international recognition of Québec's right to secede without recognition of a similar right for Aboriginal peoples in northern Québec would be "blatant unfairness," and justice would not be served.

The five experts' study was manipulated by the government of Québec to start with and afterwards. First, the experts were asked a tricky question, one that instructed them to take the very shaky process of the creation and recognition of an independent Québec for granted. Then the resulting inconclusive and incomplete study was selectively used to "prove" (among other things) that Aboriginal peoples in Québec do not have valid rights in this context that challenge the sovereignists' claims. Needless to say, the five experts' conclusions that Québec has no right under international law to secede from Canada, and other key conclusions that the separatists do not like, are never mentioned by sovereignist leaders to the public.

Sadly, as is discussed in later chapters of this book, this variety of manipulation, selectivity, and double standards is typical of some separatists' tactics and approach wherever their objective, Québec sovereignty, is at stake.

# 15

# Twenty-one drastic impacts of secession on Aboriginal peoples

*Wherein it is shown that the secessionists really don't respect the rights of the Crees and are ready to press on regardless*

We *Eeyouch* of *Eeyou Astchee* find ourselves in an extremely difficult situation. We have lived in our ancestral home for thousands of years. Our rights within this homeland are now challenged by a nationalist movement whose European forebears never set foot in *Eeyou Astchee* until three and a quarter centuries ago. In spite of this Johnny-come-lately status, separatists are claiming that they have rights within *Eeyou Astchee* which are "sacred" and "sacrosanct," and take precedence over those of the *Eeyouch* people. Can anyone imagine a greater gall than this?

Separatists claim to speak in the name of the whole province of Québec, whose presence as an administrative entity in the vast Aboriginal traditional territories of northern Québec was virtually nil until thirty-four years ago. In fact, it was only in 1993 that the Québec government celebrated the thirty-year anniversary of its presence in the north! Now they are threatening to force Aboriginal peoples and our northern territories into a seceding Québec, in violation of the rights, under domestic and international law, of anyone who does not agree with them.

Further, they are proceeding with their ambitions for independence without considering in any way the drastic impacts their actions would have on the James Bay Crees and other Aboriginal peoples living within Québec.

We have referred to some of these impacts at various places in this book. However, to appreciate how serious and far-reaching these impacts may be, we are listing in this chapter the most prominent of those that can be foreseen:

1. ***Denial of Aboriginal peoples' right to self-determination***
   Should a simple majority of Quebecers opt in a referendum to secede from Canada, the Québec government will seek to deny Aboriginal peoples in Québec our status as "peoples" and our right to choose to remain in Canada. This denial of Aboriginal self-determination could create a negative precedent for indigenous peoples elsewhere, in a wide range of circumstances.

GABLE, *THE GLOBE AND MAIL*

2. *Denial of nationality or citizenship*
Like much else about the Québec secession plan, this subject is mired in confusion. Faced with a unilateral declaration of independence by Québec, Canada might revoke Quebecers' Canadian citizenship, if only to avoid providing social programmes to a massive noncontributing population.[1]

The impact for us Aboriginal peoples, who are often said to be both citizens of our own Aboriginal nations and of the State in which we live, would be even more complex and negative. International and Canadian rules on nationality cannot simply be applied to us without fully taking account of our distinct status and rights. The rights of Aboriginal peoples to self-determination, and the fiduciary obligations owed to us by the federal Crown, run counter to the notion that we can be unilaterally deprived of Canadian nationality or citizenship.[2] Dual citizenship, if offered, could be exceedingly complex and not easy to define, since it would mean that Aboriginal peoples could, in practice, have three citizenships, with the rights and benefits of Canadian citizenship substantially diminished.[3]

3. *Integrity of Aboriginal territories jeopardized*
Provincial boundaries and jurisdictions in Canada often affect the integrity of Aboriginal nations and territories. The traditional territories of Algonquins, Crees, Inuit, Mikmaq, Mohawks, and Innu (Montagnais and Naskapi), among others, extend beyond the administrative boundaries of Québec province. From our perspective, the boundaries being claimed by Québec secessionists are artificially determined, based on Québec self-interest, and make little sense.

4. *Separation and splitting of Aboriginal nations*
In an independent Québec, Aboriginal peoples would be separated from families, relatives, and other members of our nations living in Canada. It has been proposed by one Québec jurist[4] that an agreement between Québec, Canada, and Aboriginal peoples could ensure freedom of Aboriginal movement across borders, but such agreements raise a host

of unresolved issues (as in the Jay Treaty of 1794, still a bone of contention between Canada and many Aboriginal nations, especially the Mohawks). Aboriginal peoples are already the most vulnerable in Canada and our vulnerability could be increased by forcibly including us and our territories in a seceding Québec.

5. *Aboriginal entrapment in an independent Québec*
Should Québec become an independent State, separatists note that their government would not be willing to recognize Aboriginal peoples' right to secede from Québec for any reason. Although refusing to respect Canada's territorial integrity, the secessionists are insisting on Québec's territorial integrity and appear determined to apply an unacceptable double standard that would permanently seal the fate of Aboriginal nations.

6. *Lack of prior knowledge of secessionist terms*
The failure of the secessionists to make known, even for the purposes of a referendum, the terms and conditions on which their proposed independent Québec would be established is especially perilous for Aboriginal peoples, who would be unwillingly thrust into a new State before knowing the precise nature of the Constitution under which we would have to live.

7. *Constitutional rights and obligations would be lost*
Should Québec accede to independence, the constitutional position of Aboriginal peoples would be modified without our consent. This would be especially so if we refused to negotiate our status and rights within a secessionist Québec. Clearly, not all existing rights and obligations in favour of Aboriginal peoples could be included in a new Québec constitution, even if, as is presently promised, certain rights would be transferred from the Canadian Constitution.[5] Our constitutional position in a unitary State would inevitably differ from the present situation.[6] Even if an independent Québec were willing to assume all obligations under the James Bay and Northern Québec Agreement (which Québec

does not consider to be a treaty, already a major denial of the facts), the unilateral elimination of one of the two government parties would fundamentally alter the nature of the treaty and violate the principle of Aboriginal consent. Moreover, what are we to think of such promises when we know that in 1996 the Québec government went to the Supreme Court to argue that Aboriginal peoples have not had any Aboriginal land rights in Québec for the past 450 years?

8. *Future of treaties and treaty-making*
The policy programme of the Parti Québécois says existing treaties of Aboriginal nations will be respected until replaced by new "agreements" between the government of a secessionist Québec and the Aboriginal nations. The programme does not refer to treaty-making by Aboriginal peoples or to an independent Québec government entering into treaties with us. Any erosion of Aboriginal peoples' treaty-making powers would undermine our status and our nation-to-nation relationship with non-Aboriginal governments. Although the Parti Québécois may believe otherwise, treaties and treaty-making continue to be essential to Aboriginal peoples and our status as nations.

9. *Loss of rights for Aboriginal peoples outside Québec*
Some Aboriginal peoples outside the province of Québec have unresolved claims within the province.[7] These and other claims are supposed to be addressed by the Canadian and Québec governments through land-claims negotiations. Current practice is that, if agreements are reached in regard to lands within a given province, the federal government contributes substantially to the financial compensation that is usually involved. Canada would obviously not have the same constitutional authority to act in regard to lands within an independent Québec. Also the Canadian government might not be willing to contribute money towards the resolution of land claims in an independent Québec. It is unclear what recourse, if any, such peoples would have, to satisfy their claims within a new Québec State, or whether any available

recourse would be effective. All of these factors are likely to make satisfactory recognition of land and resource rights exceedingly difficult to attain. Inuit within the Nunavut territory in the Northwest Territories have existing offshore rights that would be affected since the Québec government has indicated that, upon gaining independence, it intends to claim its share of jurisdiction and rights in the offshore around its northern coasts.

10. *Loss of historic fiduciary relationship with federal Crown*

The fiduciary relationship of Aboriginal peoples with the federal Crown would be unilaterally severed if Québec were to establish an independent State. An important aspect of this relationship is to safeguard the rights and interests of Aboriginal peoples against the competing claims, laws, and policies of provincial or local governments. Even if an independent Québec government were to assume a fiduciary relationship with the Aboriginal peoples concerned (which Québec cannot do unilaterally), the consequences of such an arrangement would be substantially different in the context of an independent Québec.

11. *Québec opposes emerging international standards*

A Québec government lawyer has declared in a public address that the Québec government opposes the draft *United Nations Declaration on the Rights of Indigenous Peoples* as contrary to the standards employed by Québec in its dealings with Aboriginal peoples.[8] This suggests that an independent Québec would not favour the newly emerging international standards relating to indigenous peoples (described in previous chapters). The PQ policy programme makes no reference to the UN draft or to the *Indigenous and Tribal Peoples Convention, 1989*. This is wholly unacceptable to Crees, who, with other Aboriginal peoples, have spent more than ten years making oral and written presentations at annual sessions of the United Nations Working Group on Indigenous Populations in Geneva, so that an adequate declaration of rights can be achieved.

12. *What kind of Aboriginal representation?*

Throughout Canada's history, we Aboriginal peoples in Québec have been denied for the most part the right of internal self-determination. Some local and regional powers are recognized for the Crees and Inuit under the JBNQA, but, as established earlier, this was negotiated under unacceptable conditions of duress. Only one Aboriginal person has ever been elected to the Québec National Assembly, and few Aboriginal people are employed in the Québec civil service. In reality the Québec National Assembly is an "alien" institution seeking to impose unilaterally its laws on Aboriginal peoples in Québec. At the federal level there are Aboriginal senators and members of Parliament, as well as a Canadian ambassador of Circumpolar Affairs and a government minister. These federal opportunities for political participation would be forever lost. The shameful lack of any meaningful Aboriginal representation in Québec's political institutions reinforces the right of Aboriginal peoples to secede from any future independent Québec.[9]

13. *Impact of Québec language policies*

As shown in chapter 5, at the very time that Québec was trying to establish itself as a unilingual French State, it was insisting that the Inuit operate key local institutions in French and using riot police to make them conform to these Québec policies. We fear this could happen on a wider scale in an independent Québec. Currently the Charter of the French Language recognizes for Cree, Inuit, and Naskapi the right to use their own Aboriginal languages within the territories outlined in the northern Québec agreements, and to a significant degree exempts them from the requirement to use French. A large number of Aboriginal people in Québec are already bilingual in their Aboriginal language and English. But they are unfamiliar with the French language.

In an independent Québec we would probably be under even more pressure than we are now to, in effect, become trilingual. As matters stand now, even the election of Aboriginal people to the National Assembly in an independent

Québec could prove to be virtually meaningless if the individuals concerned could not function in French. Some separatists have shown a notable lack of tolerance for the use of Aboriginal languages in legislatures.[10] In sum, language problems are likely to become acute for many Aboriginal people in an independent Québec, especially since the bilingual services of the federal government would be permanently eliminated. Also, legislative debates, government publications, communications, and services would generally be in French.

14. *Development pressures in Aboriginal territories*
Resource development in the traditional territories of Aboriginal peoples, without our consent, has been a major and enduring source of conflict with the Québec government. For the Crees these conflicts have been in relation to hydro-electric construction and clear-cut forestry. This is likely to increase in an independent Québec, increasing pressure on already vulnerable Aboriginal communities and cultures. Already, in preparation for an independent Québec, the separatist Bouchard government of the province has significantly lowered environmental regulations, resulting in severe criticism from environmental organizations and others within the province. Even the Parti Québécois' own committee of ecology and the environment recently wrote that the Bouchard government "has one of the worst, if not the worst, ratings on environmental and sustainable development matters over the past 25 years."[11] As compared to the current situation in Canada (with both federal and provincial levels of government), a sovereign Québec would likely offer Aboriginal peoples even fewer means to safeguard their territorial rights and interests.

15. *Fewer safeguards in a unitary State*
Many critical differences exist between a unitary State and a federation, with its many checks and balances, in the protections afforded to the status and rights of Aboriginal peoples. For example, in Canada it is difficult for non-Aboriginal

governments to amend constitutional provisions relating to Aboriginal peoples. Generally, the approval of the federal Parliament and at least two-thirds of the provincial legislatures representing at least 50 per cent of the population is required, in addition to that of Aboriginal peoples. The PQ government in Québec has at times suggested that a constitution for an independent Québec could require the consent of Aboriginal peoples. However, no concrete proposal has ever been tabled by the government.[12]

16. *Loss of constitutional weight*

As Aboriginal peoples we need to have a direct say in constitutional amendments that do not refer directly to us, but which can seriously erode our position. For that reason we insisted on participating directly in the negotiations leading up to the Meech Lake and Charlottetown constitutional accords. It would be much more difficult to maintain such a constitutional balance in a unitary State, which can adopt any amendment it chooses without needing to obtain the consent of other internal powers. This would give an independent Québec an extensive opportunity to shift the weight of constitutional power in its favour, something that could be done without necessarily amending provisions that apply directly to Aboriginal peoples.

17. *Loss of judicial weight and sympathy*

Currently, the Supreme Court of Canada is composed of judges from different regions across Canada, but the equivalent court in a separate Québec State would come only from Québec. For much of Canada's history, the Supreme Court has been made up of judges with little sensitivity to Aboriginal values, perspectives, and systems of law. In recent years, however, Supreme Court judges have shown more insight and understanding. In the absence of adequate checks and balances, a unitary State could provide even greater latitude for appointment of judges willing to act solely in the State's self-interest and to the detriment of Aboriginal peoples.

So far there is no indication that judges in a new Québec

State would be appointed through procedures that would safeguard the rights and interests of Aboriginal peoples. The Québec government has always taken the appointment of judges very seriously within Canada, so it should not be surprised at the deep concern Aboriginal peoples feel about the objectivity of judicial appointments in a secessionist State,[13] especially since many decisions emanating from Québec courts have hardly been reassuring for Aboriginal peoples. For example, Québec courts are noted for giving narrow interpretations of Aboriginal peoples' rights under the Royal Proclamation.[14]

18. *Law of Aboriginal title may be fundamentally altered*
At present, the law of Aboriginal title is determined by federal common law (although it is not the source of inherent Aboriginal rights). It is unclear how Québec courts, applying Québec civil law in a unitary State under a new constitution, would interpret Aboriginal title. A whole new range of arguments might be made against Aboriginal peoples as their constitutional guarantees are interpreted within the context of the legal and political exigencies of the new State. Once again, the omens are not encouraging: the Québec government has already argued in 1996 in the Supreme Court of Canada that because Québec has a civil law system, inherited from France, the discriminatory and colonial doctrine of *terra nullius*, which could totally deny Aboriginal territorial rights, should apply today throughout the province. Would they change their minds if they were independent? Unlikely, to say the least.

19. *Lack of impetus to protect Aboriginal peoples*
Recent polls have shown that francophone Quebecers are less sensitive to the condition of Aboriginal peoples than are the anglophones in the province. A March 1994 poll, for example, found that 52 per cent of francophones in Québec, as compared with 26 per cent of anglophones, believed that the quality of life on Indian reserves was better than that of non-Aboriginal people in Québec. Moreover, 77 per cent

of francophones (compared with 28 per cent of anglophones) believed that federal programmes for Aboriginal peoples should be diminished, or even abolished.[15] Should the majority population of a new Québec State continue in such opinions, the Québec government would have little impetus to act in the interests of Aboriginal peoples when deciding policies.

## 20. *Loss of federal programmes and services*

In an independent Québec, Aboriginal peoples would permanently lose access to federal programmes, services, and other assistance. This would leave us dependent on a single level of government and make us more vulnerable to the policies and competing demands of a new Québec State. Also, in view of the significantly increased burdens, should an independent Québec assume its portion of the national debt, there would no doubt be less capacity to maintain Aboriginal programmes and services. Presently, within the Canadian federation, Aboriginal peoples in Québec have access to two levels of government for our essential needs. In addition, programmes under the James Bay and Northern Québec Agreement are generally guaranteed from two levels of government. Clearly, such federal and provincial obligations provide greater assurance for continuing funding and attention.

## 21. *Uncertainty about Québec attitudes*

Compared with the Canadian federation, an independent Québec State is likely to have less diversity and fewer counterbalancing interests, since that State would be serving mainly a francophone majority with only one official language. This would provide less security to Aboriginal peoples and fewer protections for our rights and interests. These adverse effects could prove to be significant. As things stand now, we are expected to rely on PQ assurances that problems can be worked out later. If equal rights and self-determination are denied to Aboriginal peoples by the present Québec government, on what basis could future negotiations possibly take place? Would a PQ government again resort to the threat or use of force as it did in the language debate in 1977, when riot police were used against the Inuit?

To say the least it would be imprudent — others might say reckless — for the Crees and other Aboriginal peoples in Québec to rely on the airy assurances of the PQ government.

The 1994 version of the Parti Québécois programme restates that a PQ government would not insist upon extinguishment of the rights of Aboriginal peoples when entering into agreements with them. Yet the PQ government still demands "surrender and extinguishment" in land-claims negotiations (most recently in negotiations with the Innu and Atikamekw); still argues that the borders of a seceding Québec would remain intact; and still uses extinguishment arguments to deny Crees and Inuit their right to self-determination in the proposed secessionist Québec. These claims are made even though, as Grand Chief Matthew Coon Come has pointed out, the purported extinguishment of Aboriginal rights in land is a concept that, like "discovery," is increasingly rejected by jurists as racist and incompatible with modern concepts of human rights.[16] This insistence by today's Québec government on an outmoded, colonialist concept does not bode well for promises made should the province secede from Canada.

# 16

# Québec separatists: world-class in double standards, inconsistencies, and discrimination

*Wherein is revealed to an astonished world the amazing range of the secessionists' double standards, lack of fairness, and disrespect for the equality of all peoples*

The Québec secessionist project is a genuine curiosity. Is there any other political movement, claiming to persuade people of its arguments by democratic means, that has chosen to come before the public espousing a programme so riddled with inconsistencies, discriminatory ideas, and plain, blatant double standards? The Québec separatist elites might do well to reflect on the old Assiniboine proverb: "Most of us do not look as handsome to others as we do to ourselves."

The separatists' departures from rigorous political discourse, clung to as they have espoused their dogma over the years, have been described on page after page throughout this book. There are no rationales, other than ethnic nationalism, discrimination, or colonialism, to explain why separatist leaders in Québec are prepared, day after day, to stand up and claim rights for

Quebecers that they choose to deny Aboriginal peoples. We have given some examples of the strong negative impact these strange arguments are having on people in other countries. To quote again Rachel Guglielmo: when the Québec leaders deny the same collective rights to indigenous peoples that they have themselves fought for and won, "the moral strength of their argument is utterly delegitimized, and their quest for equality degraded to nothing more than a bid for political power swathed in self-determination arguments."[1]

In Québec itself the people overall are respectful of human rights and fair-minded. Many francophones reject the inconsistencies and double standards of the separatist leaders and have spoken out against them. "It is immoral to give oneself a right, that of secession, and to refuse it to those who could use it against us," said Stéphane Dion, then a professor of political science at the Université de Montréal, the month before the 1995 referendum. "If the territory of Canada can be divided, so can that of Québec. If the Québécois form a people, it is the same for Canadians and Aboriginal peoples."[2] A few months after the referendum, Dion accepted an appointment to the Canadian Cabinet and was later elected to Parliament. Not surprisingly, his move into federal politics was greeted with derision by secessionist politicians and nationalist journalists, who appear to have blinded themselves to the principles of fairness, equality, and respect for all peoples.

Aboriginal peoples and others who will suffer the consequences of the secessionists' xenophobic ideas, however, have to take them seriously. "So far," said Cree Grand Chief Matthew Coon Come, the day after Dion made his statement, "we have not heard a single argument against our case that is not standing on a foundation of double standards and colonial misconceptions about our rights. We hope that the separatists have the honesty and courage to discuss these issues with us, but we fear they will not."[3] And so far they haven't.

For the benefit of clarity and meaningful debate we gather in this chapter some of the worst of these self-serving inconsistencies, double standards, and discriminatory policies.

- **Legality versus legitimacy**
  Although Quebecers have no legal right to secede from Canada, under Canadian or international law, the PQ government and other separatists argue for Québec secession on the grounds that it is "legitimate." However, they do not extend the same legitimacy to First Nations, denying our status as "peoples," and denying our right to determine our own future. Separatists even go so far as to deny Aboriginal peoples our right to choose to remain in Canada if we so wish. *Double standard.*

- **Skewing of democratic principles**
  Separatists argue that, in the matter of secession, democratic principles override legal and other considerations. Yet they will not recognize the overwhelming majorities in Cree, Inuit, and Innu referendums against the inclusion of their territories and people in a separate Québec State. As shown in chapter 11, separatists have sought to muzzle bankers, business people, jurists, and Aboriginal peoples who express opinions unfavourable to secession. *Discriminatory double standard.*

- **Right to self-identification as a "people"**
  The secessionists (as represented by the PQ government of Québec) claim that the French-Canadian nation can choose to self-identify with other people in Québec to become one "Québec people." In international practice it is accepted that this requires a "common will" of the peoples concerned. The government ignores that this common will does not exist in Québec, and in effect includes Aboriginal peoples as part of a single "Québec people" (for purposes of secession). Separatists thus deny Aboriginal peoples the right to self-identification and self-determination that they claim for themselves. *Discriminatory double standard.*

- **Undermining the functioning of Canada**
  The PQ government seeks to establish that "Quebecers" have a legitimate claim for secession from Canada, because Canada does not work well. But at the same time, the government has refused to participate in federal-provincial meetings, has

provoked endless confrontations with the federal government, and has sought in every way to undermine the functioning of the federation. *Inconsistent and contradictory.*

- **Double standard on the rule of law**
  Former Premier Jacques Parizeau's draft *Act Respecting the Future of Québec* provided for a unilateral declaration of Québec's independence by a process that was declared by the Québec Superior Court to be illegal and unconstitutional. The draft act nevertheless affirmed that the Constitution of an independent Québec "shall affirm the rule of law."[4] Yet in face of the Superior Court judgement, the governments first of Parizeau and later of Lucien Bouchard have walked out of court and have repeatedly refused to change their secession process so as to conform to the rule of law. *Inconsistent, double standard.*

- **Rule of law versus revolution**
  The PQ government insists that Aboriginal peoples must respect the rule of law when we assert our rights and defend our interests. Yet, for purposes of self-determination and secession, the separatists state that they are not bound by the rule of law in Canada. Instead, they will achieve their independence by excluding Canadian jurisdiction and seizing "effective control" over the whole of the territory now within the province of Québec. This is otherwise known as an insurrection or revolution. *Inconsistent, double standard.*

- **Territorial integrity only for Québec**
  The secessionists are willing to rupture the integrity of Aboriginal territories, and those of Canada, by the unilateral secession of Québec. At the same time, they insist that the borders of an independent Québec will be sacrosanct and no derogation will be tolerated from the current provincial boundaries. Thus, their claimed principle of "territorial integrity" applies, in their eyes, only to Québec, but not to Aboriginal territories, Canada, or, it seems, any other entity that might oppose their separatist dreams of independence. It appears to be of little, if any, consequence to the secessionists that we Crees and Inuit

have lived in our traditional territories in northern Québec for thousands of years and have the right to self-determination. *Discriminatory double standard.*

- **Simple majority vote in Québec referendum**
  The secessionists would never accept that a simple majority vote in a pan-Canadian referendum could determine the future of Quebecers. Yet, the PQ government is determined to force Aboriginal peoples to be bound by a simple majority vote in a Québec referendum, denies the validity of Aboriginal referendums, and refuses Aboriginal peoples their right to choose democratically to remain in Canada. *Discriminatory double standard.*

- **Forcible inclusion in an independent Québec**
  The PQ government intends to include Aboriginal peoples and their traditional or historical territories in an independent Québec, even against our express wishes. Yet, the same government insists that the free and democratic expression of Quebecers be respected by other Canadians. *Discriminatory double standard.*

- **Unilateralism**
  The secessionists claim that the adoption of the *Constitution Act, 1982,* without the approval of the Québec National Assembly justifies the accession of Québec to sovereignty. They claim this in spite of the fact that the federal government met the standard of legitimacy set by the Supreme Court of Canada by obtaining the agreement of nine out of ten provinces. Moreover, the governing federal party at the time had more sitting Québec members of Parliament than did the Parti Québécois government in the Québec National Assembly. Nevertheless, although adopting such a holier-than-thou attitude towards the federal government, in 1985 the PQ government and National Assembly did not hesitate to adopt a resolution on the rights of Aboriginal peoples against the express wishes of the peoples concerned.[5] This unilateral resolution is still being used by Bouchard and other separatists to demonstrate to the international community how well

Québec treats Aboriginal peoples. *Double standard and inconsistent.*

- **James Bay and Northern Québec Agreement (JBNQA)**
  The Québec National Assembly approved and gave effect to the JBNQA when a PQ government was in power, fully aware that it created a permanent federal arrangement. From the viewpoints of legality or legitimacy, a secessionist Québec government cannot now unilaterally remove the federal government as a party to that treaty. Nor can it unilaterally assume the obligations of the Canadian government. *Inconsistent and discriminatory.*

- **Lack of flexibility**
  Separatists claim that the lack of flexibility in Canada's constitutional amending formula does not enable Quebecers to fulfil their aspirations within Canada. Yet their proposed solution of a political and economic union with Canada would be far more inflexible than what now exists. In particular, it is being suggested that a joint Council be established made up of equal numbers of ministers from Canada and an independent Québec. As each nation would have a right of veto, this seems a recipe for deadlock and immobility. *Contradictory.*

- **Constitution of an independent Québec**
  The PQ government says a new constitution for an independent Québec will provide for the status and rights of Aboriginal peoples, regardless of whether Aboriginal peoples agree. Quebecers would not, of course, tolerate such unilateral treatment of their own rights in Canada. This is apparently a ploy to appease the concerns of the international community about "fair" treatment of Aboriginal people. *Discriminatory double standard.*

- **Extinguishment of Aboriginal rights**
  The official policy of the Parti Québécois declares that a PQ government will not demand the extinguishment of Aboriginal rights when entering into agreements with us. In spite of this declaration, the government continues to insist on extinguishment of Aboriginal rights as a prerequisite to entering into

land-claims agreements with Aboriginal nations. In addition, secessionists invoke the purported extinguishment of rights to deny that Aboriginal peoples have a right to self-determination in the context of Québec secession. *Inconsistent and discriminatory.*

This extraordinary list of blatantly unjust and discriminatory claims makes rational debate almost impossible. Moreover, it demonstrates the extent to which violation of human rights and discrimination against Aboriginal peoples are integral elements of the positions and policies of the PQ government and other separatists. As long as this continues to be the case, the international community should clearly reject the accession of Québec to independence.

# 17

---

# Summary and conclusions: 110 Cree sound bites about Québec secession

*Wherein a vulnerable but proud people list their many objections to being treated like cattle*

---

I    We *Eeyouch* respect the right of all peoples to self-determination, including the right of Quebecers to seek a better relationship with the rest of Canada.

GABLE, *THE GLOBE AND MAIL*

2   However, the exercise of these rights must not be at the expense of Crees and other Aboriginal peoples.

3   Our right to self-determination as *Eeyouch* is being denied or ignored by both the separatist Québec government and the federal separatist party, the Bloc Québécois.

4   We *Eeyouch* are not seeking to secede from Canada or Québec, but we are asserting our right to choose to remain in Canada, if we so desire.

## Who are "peoples"?

5   In Canada's Constitution, Aboriginal peoples are recognized as "peoples." The Québec National Assembly formally recognizes us as distinct "nations."

6   Nevertheless, the separatist Québec government refuses to acknowledge that Aboriginal peoples are "peoples" with a right to self-determination.

7   The Québec separatists claim for themselves a right as a "people" that they deny to First Nations.

## Not part of the "Québec people"

8   Different "peoples" cannot be compelled against their will to define themselves as a single "people."

9   We *Eeyouch* assert our own distinct identity as a "people."

10  A "people" can include different ethnic, linguistic, or religious groups, but they must have a common will to live together as a "people."

11  There is no such common will among the various "peoples" who inhabit Québec.

12  The Québec government's attempt to compel Aboriginal peoples to be a part of the "Québec people" for secession has no basis in law or democracy.

# The right to self-determination

13 The right to self-determination is a universally accepted human right, which we *Eeyouch* assert in the context of Québec secession.

14 The government of Canada is formally committed to observing the right to self-determination of all collectivities, including indigenous peoples.

15 Québec separatist leaders deny our right to self-determination, because they want to include our traditional territories in an independent Québec.

# Is Québec secession justifiable?

16 A unilateral declaration of independence (UDI) by Québec is illegal under Canadian law and would violate fundamental human rights as confirmed by a recent decision of Québec Superior Court.

17 No "constitutional convention" exists that allows Québec to secede unilaterally. Negotiations with Canada and the Aboriginal peoples are required.

18 The right to self-determination does not automatically confer the right of a people to secede, as Québec secessionists wish to do from Canada.

19 Aside from colonized peoples, continued discrimination, human rights violations, unrepresentative government, and denial of internal self-determination are the only valid reasons for secession from a State — and then only as a last resort.

20 Quebecers are not oppressed within Canada and have no right to secede from Canada on these grounds.

21 Francophone Quebecers are fully represented in Canada's Parliament, civil service, and justice system.

22  Francophone Quebecers play an active role in Canada's academic, business, and artistic worlds.

23  The recent dissolutions of the former Soviet Union, Yugoslavia, or Czechoslovakia do not form a precedent for Québec secession.

## "Effective control" of all territory in Québec

24  After declaring independence unilaterally, the Québec government will try to establish "effective control" over the whole province.

25  Unilateral secession is tantamount to an insurrection or revolution carried out without certainty as to its consequences or success.

26  Before gaining international recognition, a seceding Québec would have to exercise "effective control" over its claimed territory for a sufficiently long period.

27  Even "effective control" may not bring international recognition if the self-determination of Aboriginal peoples has been violated.

28  Secessionist control of Aboriginal territories will not go unchallenged. We *Eeyouch* could peacefully maintain our relationship with Canada, if we so desire.

29  This probable conflict over "effective control" is being seriously underestimated and deliberately played down by the separatist government in Québec.

## Use of force by a secessionist Québec

30  Aboriginal peoples in Québec may want to maintain their relationship with Canada, and this conflict over control of our territories could lead once again to violence being used against us by state authorities.

31 Secessionists have already discussed the use of military or "specialized units" against Aboriginal peoples to enforce Québec's "territorial integrity."

32 Probably only by using force against dissenting peoples could an independent Québec secure "effective control."

33 The Canadian government would be expected to take appropriate action in response to any use of force by a secessionist Québec.

34 The Canadian government need not resort to force. Many nonviolent measures would be open to Canada to counter an illegal secession.

35 We *Eeyouch* abhor the use of force or violence. Disputes should be resolved peacefully, based on recognition and respect for the equal rights of peoples.

## Québec's diminishing borders

36 No Canadian or international law requires that the present boundaries of the province of Québec automatically be those of a sovereign Québec.

37 Canada's Constitution guarantees Québec's provincial boundaries only so long as Québec remains in confederation.

38 From the moment Québec repudiated the Canadian Constitution, a period of vulnerability would apply to Québec's borders.

39 In the event of a UDI by Québec, principles of international law such as *uti possidetis* would not prevail over "effective control."

40 The *uti possidetis* principle was designed to aid peaceful decolonization. Its use in modern noncolonies (as in Yugoslavia) has been disastrous.

41 If Québec renounces its place in Canada, the current provincial boundaries might have to be changed to protect federal and Aboriginal interests.

42 In northern Québec, where we assert our right to self-determination, our claims are more compelling than those of Quebecers.

## The 1898 and 1912 territories in northern Québec

43 Québec has no historical claim to the northern parts of the province, where we have rights based on thousands of years of use and occupancy.

44 Québec has benefitted economically from the 1898/1912 boundary extensions, at the expense of the original indigenous inhabitants.

45 Our northern territories, over which we claim ownership and jurisdiction, were added to the province of Québec without our knowledge or consent.

46 Canada's accepted standard — to transfer territory only if agreed by the inhabitants — was totally violated in the northern extensions of Québec.

47 We *Eeyouch* now insist that any territorial transfers be subject to our free and informed consent, consistent with our right to self-determination.

## Which law prevails after a UDI?

48 Aboriginal and Canadian law are not irrelevant to the Québec secession debate, as some separatist jurists claim, but, rather, are central to it.

49 Aboriginal and Canadian law would continue to apply unless a seceding Québec achieved effective control of

its claimed territory, the test of this being international recognition.

50 Although there would be no legal vacuum, this does not mean that it would be certain which constitutional or legal provisions applied.

51 Inevitably, there would be very many clashes in a secessionist Québec about which laws would apply and which courts would have jurisdiction. Chaos and anarchy would likely result.

## Unilateral imposition of Québec "territorial integrity"

52 Québec separatists claim that the territory of Québec can never be divided, but that the territory of Canada or of Aboriginal peoples can. We *Eeyouch* cannot accept this.

53 We *Eeyouch* have a profound relationship with our territory. Our rights there would override the attempts of a secessionist Québec to establish territorial integrity in a new "State."

54 It is imperative for us that the integrity of Aboriginal lands be safeguarded.

## The James Bay and Northern Québec Agreement

55 The James Bay and Northern Québec Agreement (JBNQA) was negotiated in inequitable, coercive, and unconscionable circumstances.

56 However, the JBNQA provides for federal and Québec obligations in favour of the Crees and Inuit in Québec to continue in perpetuity.

57 Québec cannot unilaterally abrogate or alter the terms of the JBNQA, without repudiating its own signature and dishonouring the National Assembly.

58 The JBNQA cannot be altered without the consent of the Aboriginal parties, the Crees and the Inuit in Québec.

59 The unilateral secession of Québec would abrogate the federalist framework of the JBNQA and would justify *Eeyouch* repudiation of the agreement.

60 Quebecers and the *Eeyouch* are claiming a right to self-determination. But neither can arbitrarily assume the obligations of other parties to JBNQA.

61 The JBNQA does not give Québec the right to include unilaterally the 1898 and 1912 territories in an independent Québec.

62 Once it had proclaimed a UDI, Québec could not selectively invoke certain parts of the JBNQA to its advantage.

63 A seceding Québec could not unilaterally take over federal obligations to Crees and Inuit under the JBNQA.

64 The Québec government claims that we *Eeyouch* surrendered our right to self-determination in the JBNQA. This claim is invalid, illegitimate, and self-serving.

65 A UDI by Québec would destroy a fundamental purpose of the JBNQA, namely the careful allocation of distribution of Canadian and Québec government powers in northern Québec.

## Is Québec's UDI process "legitimate" or "democratic"?

66 Neither legitimacy nor democracy has been adequately demonstrated in the secession plans of the separatist government of Québec.

67 All existing rights, powers, and legitimacies of Aboriginal peoples, and of the rest of Canada, must be fully considered and respected.

68 The Québec secessionists cannot ignore Aboriginal peoples' rights to self-determination, yet claim legitimacy for their referendum process.

69 A majority vote by Quebecers in a single referendum is not sufficient to determine "legitimacy."

70 It is the antithesis of "democracy" to force Aboriginal peoples and others into a secessionist Québec against our freely and overwhelmingly expressed will.

71 It is undemocratic to ask people to approve a UDI without informing them of the precise contents of a new Québec Constitution.

72 It is undemocratic that no role for Aboriginal peoples is contemplated in any of the new Canada-Québec institutions proposed by the secessionists.

73 For Aboriginal peoples, the inequality and forced dominance of the secession project is simply a modern version of colonialism for the 1990s and 2000s.

## Lack of informed discussion in Québec

74 Free, open, and informed debate is lacking in Québec on secession issues. Arguments against secession are often not seriously considered.

75 Consequently, unclear and contradictory secessionist proposals that are riddled with unsubstantiated statements are too often inadequately examined.

76 Thus, Quebecers are apparently expected to leave the Canadian federation without knowing precisely what will replace the existing arrangements.

77 Quebecers have been incited against the *Eeyouch* because we have spoken out internationally about Québec secession.

# Limitations of any Québec referendum

78 In Canadian law, referendums are consultative, not legally binding. This applied to both the 1980 and 1995 referendums in Québec.

79 Even if there were a "Yes" vote in a Québec referendum on sovereignty, it would not settle the matter of Aboriginal self-determination.

80 If a simple majority vote were always definitive, a pan-Canadian referendum could determine the future of Quebecers.

81 Compared with 80 or 90 per cent majorities in past plebiscites of Norway/Sweden, former Yugoslavia, and other countries, 50 per cent plus one is an absolutely insufficient indication of Québec's "popular will to secede."

82 Only the Aboriginal referendums of 1995 with majorities of 96 to 99 per cent against secession have attained such legitimacy.

83 Most Quebecers believe a simple majority vote is insufficient to begin the separation process.

84 Even some sovereignist Québec jurists favour "incontestable," "massive," or "absolute majorities" of all registered voters.

85 The PQ government shows no inclination to shape its policies to reflect these democratic views of the Québec population.

# Aboriginal referendums and their significance

86 The PQ government must recognize the democratic right of Aboriginal peoples to hold our own referendums and must accept their validity.

87 An affirmative Québec-wide vote cannot be used to force dissenting Aboriginal peoples and our territories into an independent Québec.

88 Following rejection of secession in the Aboriginal referendums of 1995, it is a travesty to say that a Québec referendum vote can bind Aboriginal peoples.

## Fiduciary responsibilities of Canada

89 The primary fiduciary duty towards Aboriginal peoples lies with the federal (not provincial) government.

90 Under the Constitution, neither the federal executive nor Parliament can act against the rights and interests of Aboriginal peoples in the context of Québec secession.

91 Not only the *Constitution Act, 1982*, but many other legal instruments, reinforce the federal trusteeship duty towards Aboriginal peoples.

92 In 1976 both Parliament and the federal government confirmed their "special responsibility" to the *Eeyouch* and Inuit under the JBNQA.

93 Canada cannot wait, but must declare now the right of Aboriginal peoples to exercise their self-determination in the context of Québec secession.

94 Following any affirmative Québec vote on secession, Aboriginal peoples must represent themselves in any negotiations with Québec and Canada.

95 Canada's responsibilities towards Aboriginal peoples go beyond fiduciary obligations to include full respect for treaty, Aboriginal, and other human rights.

## Fiduciary responsibilities of Québec

96 Should Québec attempt to secede unilaterally from Canada, it would be violating fiduciary responsibilities to

Aboriginal peoples undertaken in the JBNQA.

97 The PQ government has a duty to pursue the aspirations of Quebecers so as not to infringe on or deny any of the rights of Aboriginal peoples.

98 The PQ government says it seeks an "equal and beneficial partnership" with Aboriginal peoples. The test is whether the government respects our right to self-determination and therefore to decide our own future.

# Responsibilities of the international community

99 The PQ government hopes the international community will recognize Québec independence if it simply promises to treat Aboriginal peoples well.

100 We *Eeyouch* cannot trust such promises. We urge the international community to defend our right to determine our future.

101 If the international community allows violation of our fundamental rights, it would be a mockery of the standard-setting process that is under way in international forums.

102 A Québec UDI, if accepted, would be a destabilizing precedent, encouraging many disaffected minorities to seek the breakup of existing countries.

103 Secession-related problems can generate violence, as in the former Yugoslavia and Soviet Union. This can jeopardize international peace and security.

104 Although the situation in Québec is totally different from that of Europe, the use of force could still emerge as an ominous by-product of Québec secession.

105 The international community has a clear interest and responsibility in ensuring compliance with human rights standards, including the right to self-determination of indigenous peoples.

106 Military intervention by the United Nations should prove neither appropriate nor necessary in the context of Québec secession.

107 Serious violations of our Aboriginal right to self-determination or other rights could be dealt with through a wide range of nonmilitary measures.

108 International action, if taken, should be balanced and commensurate with the degree of persistent violations by a secessionist Québec.

## Potential impacts of secession

109 Potential impacts of Québec secession on Aboriginal peoples would be far-reaching, unforeseeable, and not necessarily susceptible to legal remedy.

110 The Québec government, working with Aboriginal peoples, must inform the public of the full range of potential impacts before any future Québec referendum.

# Notes

## Introduction

1 Bearskin et al., 9.

2 Richardson, 152.

3 Australia, *Royal Commission into Aboriginal Deaths in Custody, National Report* vol. 5 (Australia, 1991), 361.

4 This draft declaration, which will be an indigenous charter of rights analogous to the *Universal Declaration of Human Rights*, adopted by the UN General Assembly in 1948, has been in the process of creation for more than ten years by a UN Working Group on Indigenous Populations in Geneva. The latest text of this draft declaration was reprinted in *International Legal Materials* 34 (1995): 541.

5 Grand Council of the Crees, Nemaska, PQ, *Sovereign Injustice: Forcible Inclusion of the James Bay Crees and Cree Territory into a Sovereign Québec* (Nemaska, PQ: 1995).

6 *Bertrand v. Attorney-Gen. of Québec*, 8 Sept. 1995, RJQ 2500 (Québec Super. Ct. 1995). Decision by Justice Robert Lesage.

7 Speaking notes of Erica-Irene Daes, Chairperson, Working Group on Indigenous Populations, *International Day of the World's Indigenous People*, Palais des Nations, Geneva, 9 Aug. 1995, 2.

## 1. Who and what constitute a "people"?

1 Assemblée Nationale, *Commission d'étude sur toute offre d'un nouveau partenariat de nature constitutionnelle, Journal des débats*, 22 Jan. 1992, No. 15, CEOC-491 (testimony of G. Robertson).

2 Instruments that refer to "peoples" and their right to self-determination include *Charter of the United Nations*, Article 1; *International Covenant on Civil and Political Rights* (1966), Article 1; *International Covenant on Economic, Social and Cultural Rights* (1966), Article 1; *Declaration on Principles of International Law Concerning Friendly Relations and Cooperation Among States in Accordance with the Charter of the United Nations*, rpt. in (1970) 9 ILM 1292, under heading "Principle of equal rights and self-determination"; *Declaration on the Granting*

*of Independence to Colonial Countries and Peoples*, UN General Assembly Resolution 1514 (XV) 15 UN GAOR, Supp. (No. 16) 66, UN Doc. A/4684, adopted 14 Dec. 1960, para. 2; *Final Act of the Conference on Security and Cooperation in Europe* (Helsinki Final Act), signed by 35 States including Canada and the United States, 1 Aug. 1975, rpt. 1975, 14 ILM 1295, Principle VIII; United Nations World Conference on Human Rights, *Vienna Declaration and Programme of Action*, adopted 25 June 1993, rpt. 1993, 32 ILM 1661, para. 2. Also the draft *United Nations Declaration on the Rights of Indigenous Peoples*, and the International Labor Organization's *Indigenous and Tribal Peoples Convention, 1989*, refer specifically to "indigenous peoples" and their rights.

3 Sec. 35 (2).

4 Québec National Assembly resolution *Motion for the recognition of Aboriginal Rights in Québec*, 20 Mar. 1985. Also Parti Québécois government's bill, *An Act Respecting the Future of Québec*, sec. 8, where the term "Aboriginal nations" is used.

5 For example, in *An Act Respecting the Future of Québec* (Bill 1), tabled by Premier Jacques Parizeau on 6 Dec. 1994 (but never passed), the preamble declares: ". . . Canada, far from taking pride in and proclaiming to the world the alliance between its two founding peoples, has instead trivialized it. . . ." The Québec Aboriginal nations, apparently are not included in this highest level, that is, "founding peoples."

6 SQ 1991, c 34, assented to 20 June 1991, by the National Assembly.

7 Assembleé nationale, *Commission d'étude des questions afférentes à l'accession du Québec à la souveraineté, Journal des débats*, 11 Feb. 1992, CEAS-817.

8 L. Balthazar, *Les nombreux visages du nationalisme au Québec, Québec: État et société*, ed. A.G. Gagnon (Montréal: Editions Québec/Amerique, 1994), 23. He wrote, "One will always find some nationalists who insist on the differences between the 'true Quebecers' (francophones by birth) and the others. But, as a whole Québec nationalism is evolving towards a conception of identity that integrates the diverse elements of modern Québec."

9 A. Norris, "600,000 Quebecers have ethnic roots," *The Gazette* [Montréal], 1 Apr. 1995: B1.

10 The Bloc Québécois, which is dedicated to the secession of Québec from Canada, sits in the federal Parliament, a matter of some puzzlement to many non-Canadians.

11 *La Presse*, 27 Feb. 1997: A1, and *Gazette* [Montréal], 27 Feb. 1985: A4. P. Paré recanted his statement the next day.

12 "Hate-mongering won't help Yes side," Editorial, *Gazette* [Montréal], 1 Mar. 1995: B2.

13 J. Brossard, 1995: 185, 362.

14 L. Bouchard, 1993: 55.

15 J. Parizeau, "The Case for a Sovereign Québec," *Foreign Affairs* 99 (1995): 69.

[16] Parti Québécois, Montréal, *Des idées pour mon pays* (Montréal: Parti Québecois, 1994), 1.

[17] E. Thompson, "Quebecers Aren't Canadians, Bouchard," *Gazette* [Montréal], 14 Feb. 1997: A11.

[18] L. Gagnon, "Débat: les mots taboos," *La Presse*, 13 Sept. 1994: B3.

[19] Assemblée nationale, Committee on Sovereignty, Draft Rep. 1991, 10.

[20] The question of common will is examined in various legal writings. See, for example, the testimony of Daniel Turp of the Université de Montréal, before the National Assembly Committee on Sovereignty, *Journal des debats*, 9 Oct. 1991, No. 5 CEAS-136. Also R. Iglar, "The Constitutional Crisis in Yugoslavia and the International Law of Self-Determination: Slovenia's and Croatia's Right to Secede," 15 *Boston College International and Comparative Law Revue* 15.213 (1992): 214. Also J. Brossard, op. cit. n.13.

[21] Dumont, 63.

[22] J.-P. Derriennic, 73-74.

[23] A. Dubuc, "Le triangle infernal," *La Presse*, editorial, 12 Oct. 1994: B2.

[24] D. Makinson, "Rights of Peoples: Point of View of a Logician," J. Crawford, ed., 1988, 69–73.

[25] *Advisory Opinion on Western Sahara* (1975), ICJ Rep. 6, 32, para. 55; see also 37, para. 72, and 68, para. 162; and 122.

[26] Assemblée nationale, *Commission d'étude des questions afférentes à l'accession du Québec à la souveraineté, Journal des débats,* 4 Feb. 1992, No. 24, CEAS-75.

[27] J. Woehrling, in J.-Y. Morin and J. Woehrling, 126.

[28] *Commission d'étude des questions afférentes à l'accession du Québec à la souveraineté, Exposés et études* 1 (1992), 425.

[29] See O. Kimminich, in C. Tomuschat, 16.

[30] Assemblée nationale, Committee on Sovereignty, *Journal des débats* 9 Oct. 1991, No. 5 CEAS-136.

[31] J.-R. Sansfaçon, "Autochtones: Québec prend les devants," *Le Devoir*, editorial, 1 Nov. 1994: A6.

[32] *Indigenous and Tribal Peoples Convention, 1989*, art. 1, para. 2, of the International Labor Organization. Also *United Nations Declaration of the Rights of Indigenous Peoples*, Rep. of the Working Group on Indigenous Populations, 11th sess., E/CN/4/Sub.2/1993/29, 23 Aug. 1993, 50 (Annex 1), Article 8; and the *draft of the Inter-American Declaration on the Rights of Indigenous Peoples*, art. 1, para. 2.

[33] E.-I. Daes, *Explanatory note concerning the draft Declaration on the Rights of Indigenous Peoples*, UN doc. E/CN.4. Sub.2/1993/26/Add. 1, 2, para. 7.

[34] See *Official Statements of War Aims and Peace Proposals, Dec. 1916 to Nov. 1918*, ed. J.B. Scott (1921), 105.

# 2. Does self-determination include the right to secede?

1 United Nations, Art. 1, *Charter of the United Nations*, (1976) Yearbook, UN, 1043. Signed at San Francisco 26 June 1945. Ratified by Canada 9 Nov. 1945.

2 H. Hannum, "Rethinking Self-Determination," *Virginia Journal of International Law* 34 (1993): 40.

3 "Secession" is defined as separation of a part of a territory of a preexisting State, as contrasted with "dissolution" of an existing State when the preexisting State breaks up into several new States. See Nguyen Quoc Dinh et al., 500.

4 United Nations, *Declaration on the Granting of Independence to Colonial Countries and Peoples*, General Assembly Resolution 1514 (XV), 15 UN. GAOR, Supp. (No. 16) UN Document A/4684, adopted 14 Dec. 1960.

5 See *East Timor (Portugal v. Australia)* (International Ct. of Justice Reports 1990) 90, 102, para. 29. See also H. Hannum, op. cit. n.2, 19; A. Rosas, *Internal Self-Determination* in Tomaschat 242; Bucheit, 83–84.

6 "Statements of the Canadian Delegation," Commission on Human Rights, 53rd Sess., Working Group established in accordance with Commission on Human Rights resolution 1995/32 of 3 Mar. 1995, 2nd Sess., Geneva, 21 Oct.–1 Nov. 1996 (31 Oct. 1996 statement on art. 3, right to self-determination).

7 "Statements of the Canadian Delegation," Commission on Human Rights, 53rd sess., Working Group established in accordance with Commission on Human Rights resolution 1995/32 of 3 Mar. 1995, 2nd Sess., Geneva (31 Oct. 1996, statement on art. 3, right to self-determination).

8 *International Convention on the Elimination of All Forms of Racial Discrimination*, adopted by UN General Assembly 21 Dec. 1965, and entered into force 4 Jan. 1969. This convention provides that "the term 'racial discrimination' shall mean any distinction, exclusion, restriction or preference based on race, colour, descent or national or ethnic origin which has the purpose or effect of nullifying or impairing the recognition, enjoyment or exercise on an equal footing, of human rights and fundamental freedoms in the political, economic, social, cultural or any other field of public life."

9 P. Curran and T. Wills, "Québec Has Right to Decide its Own Future: PCs," *Gazette* [Montréal], 10 Aug. 1991: A1; and P. Curran, "Self-Determination Debate Is No Big Deal, PM Says," *Gazette* [Montréal], 8 Aug. 1991: B1.

10 *Declaration on Principles of International Law Concerning Friendly Relations and Cooperation Among States in Accordance with the Charter of the United Nations*, UNGA Res. 2625 (XXV), 25 UN GAOR, Supp. (No. 28) 121, UN Doc. A/8028 (1971). See also C. Tomuschat 9–10, 91.

11 T. Ha, "Québec's borders Are Safe within Canada: Chrétien," *Gazette* [Montréal], 25 May 1994: A1.

12 Testimony in Assemblée nationale, *Commission d'étude des questions afférentes à l'accession du Québec à la souveraineté, Journal des débats* 9 Oct. 1991, No. 5, CEAS-137.

[13] P. Macklem, "Ethnonationalism, Aboriginal identities, and the Law," *Ethnicity and Aboriginality: Case Studies in Ethnonationalism*, ed. M. Levin (Toronto: U of Toronto P, 1993), 9: 31–32.

[14] J. Woodward, 83.

[15] Commission des droits de la personne du Québec, *Mémoire de la Commission des droits de la personne présenté à la Commission royale sur les peuples autochtones* (Montréal, Nov. 1993), 43.

[16] "Québécois-Autochtones: il faut relever le défi de la reconnaissance mutuelle," *La Presse*, 2 Apr. 1994: B3.

[17] For additional authorities, see Grand Council of the Crees, *Sovereign Injustice: Forcible Inclusion of the James Bay Crees and Cree Territory into Sovereign Québec* (Nemaska, PQ, 1995), 46–54.

[18] R. Barsh, "Indigenous Peoples in the 1990s: From Object to Subject of International Law?," *Harvard Human Rights Journal* 7 (1994): 37.

[19] M.C. Lâm, "Making Room for Peoples at the United Nations: Thoughts Provoked by Indigenous Claims to Self-Determination," *Cornell International Law Journal* 25 (1992): 618–19.

[20] R. Guglielmo, "Three Nations Warring in the Bosom of a Single State: An Exploration of Identity and Self-Determination in Québec," *Fletcher Forum of World Affairs* 21 (1997): 197.

[21] J. Gray, "Crees Will Have No Friends, PQ Negotiator Warns," *Globe and Mail*, 19 Oct. 1994: A1.

[22] "The Sovereignty Showdown" (two-hour special broadcast), *Prime Time News*, CBC TV, 16 Feb. 1995.

[23] M. Coon Come, Remarks to the Canadian Club, Toronto, 13 Mar. 1995 (on file with the Grand Council of the Crees of Québec). Grand Chief Matthew Coon Come expresses the same position in his contribution "Consenting Partners: The James Bay Crees, Québec Secession and Canada," *If You Love This Country: 15 Voices for a Unified Country/Pour l'amour de ce pay: Quinze voix pour un Canada uni* (Toronto: Penguin, 1995), 99.

[24] European Parliament, *Resolution on Action Required Internationally to Provide Effective Protection for Indigenous Peoples*, Eur. Parl. Doc. (PV 58) 2 (1994), 3, para. 2.

[25] T. Franck et al., 425.

[26] Québec Cabinet decision No. 97-092, 16 Apr. 1997.

[27] T. Wills, "Lawyers Hail Bloc's 'Opening' to Partition," *Gazette* [Montréal], 23 May 1997: 12.

[28] Z. Nungak, Speech, Washington, DC, 3 Dec. 1966 (on file with the Makivik Corporation).

# 3. Is Québec secession legal?

1 *An Act Respecting the Sovereignty of Québec* (draft bill), Québec National Assembly, First sess., 35th legislature, 1994, made public by Premier Parizeau 6 Dec. 1994, but never tabled as a bill in the National Assembly.

2 *Bertrand* v. *Attorney-Gen. of Québec* (Québec Super. Ct., Québec City, No. 200-05-002117-955). Also under *Bertrand* v. *Bégin* et al., 8 Sept. 1995, RJQ 2500 (Québec Super. Ct. 1995). Decision by Justice Robert Lesage.

3 Québec National Assembly, *An Act Respecting the Future of Québec* (Bill 1), First sess., 35th legislature, tabled by Premier Parizeau 7 Sept. 1995, died on the order paper in December 1995.

4 *Bertrand* v. *Attorney-Gen. of Québec*, 8 Sept. 1995, RJQ 2500 (Québec Super. Ct. 1995). For an English version of the decision, see *Dominion Law Reports* (4th) 127 (1995): 408.

5 Attorney-General of Québec, declinatory motion and motion to dismiss Bertrand action, 12 Apr. 1996 (Québec Super. Ct. 1996 200-05-002117-955).

6 *Bertrand* v. *Bégin*, 1996, RJQ 2393 (Québec Super. Ct. 1996). Decision by Justice Robert Pidgeon.

7 See Brun and Tremblay, 236.

8 See P. Monahan et al., 1996.

9 *Reference by the Governor-in-Council Concerning Certain Questions Relating to the Secession of Québec from Canada, as Set Out in Order-in-Council* PC *1996–1947*, 30 Sept. 1996 (Supreme Court of Canada 1996).

10 For separatist reaction to Rock's announcement see *Globe and Mail*, 27 Sept. 1996: A1, A6, A25.

11 P. Hogg, *Principles Governing the Secession of Québec, Law, Democracy and Self-Determination,* Canadian Bar Association and the University of Ottawa, U of Ottawa, 22–23 May 1997.

12 See D. Turp and A. Vahlas, *Projet de constitution du Québec,* in Turp, Annex 16, 183.

13 Ibid, art. 2, para. 4.

14 On close reading, the "guarantee" is not a clear guarantee at all, but is subject to Québec laws and the territorial integrity of a sovereign Québec: see art. 27 of the draft constitution.

15 D. Turp, op. cit., n.12, art. 23.

16 D. Turp, op. cit., n.12, art. 1, para. 2.

17 G. Normand, "Garon invite Guy Bertrand à se rallier," *La Presse* [Montréal] 17 Jan. 1995: B1.

18 See Bayefsky, 20.

19 See Bucheit, 94.

20 G. Normand, "Garon invite Guy Bertrand à se rallier," *La Presse*, 17 Jan. 1995: B1.

21 M. Shaw, 152.

22 S. Scott, "Autodétermination, sécession, division, légalité: observations," *Commission d'étude des questions afférentes à l'accession du Québec à la souveraineté, Les Attributs d'un Québec souverain* (Québec: Bibliothèque nationale du Québec, 1992), 471, vol. 1 of *Exposés et études*.

23 For a similar conclusion see J. Woehrling, "Les Aspects juridiques d'une éventuelle sécession du Québec," *Canadian Bar Review* 74 (1995): 293.

24 See J.-M. Arbour et al., "Le Droit international admet la sécession du Québec," *Le Devoir*, 18 Aug. 1995: A9. Arbour takes this position along with five other Québec professors, A. Lajoie, P. Mackay, Guy Tremblay, J.-Y. Morin, and F. Crépeau. Their argument is countered and rejected by J.-P. Derriennic, "Le Droit international admet la sécession, il ne la facilite pas," *Le Devoir*, 5 Sept. 1995: A11.

25 *An Act to Establish the Commission on the Political and Constitutional Future of Québec (Bill 90)*, SQ 1990, c. 34, assented to on 4 Sept. 1990.

26 See *An Act Respecting the Process for Determining the Political and Constitutional Future of Québec (Bill 150)*, SQ 1991, c. 34, assented to on 20 June 1991.

27 Resolution 244 of the Progressive Conservative Party of Canada National Convention, 9 Aug. 1991. See also M.-C. Lortie, "Autodétermination: l'oeuvre de l'aile Bouchard," *La Presse*, 10 Aug. 1991: A12.

28 A. Cassese, 252–53.

29 *Re Resolution to Amend the Constitution*, 1981, 1 SCR, 888; see also *Re Objection by Québec to Resolution to Amend the Constitution*, 1982, 2 SCR 815.

30 See S. Scott, Assemblée Nationale, *Commission d'étude des questions afférentes à l'accession du Québec à la souveraineté, Journal des débats*, 26 Nov. 1991, No. 10, CEAS-260.

31 See Brun and Tremblay, 46.

32 See G.-A. Beaudoin, "Quelques mois du référendum: de la rigueur dans les termes," *La Presse*, 24 Mar. 1995: B3. See also M. Lebel, "La Légitimité du projet souverainiste ne peut se fonder sur le droit," *La Presse*, 30 Aug. 1995: A7. Also J. Woehrling, *L'évolution et le réaménagement des rapports entre le Québec et le Canada anglais," J.-Y. Morin and J. Woehrling* (1994), 122, and (1995) vol. 1, 12, 25. Also P. Hogg, vol. 1, 5–32. Also P. Monahan, 9–10. Also Brossard 308.

33 Schwimmer 182.

34 See T. Franck et al., 443.

35 M. Venne, "Le Québec est un pays souverain: Facile à dire, Facile à faire?," *Le Devoir*, 7 Feb. 1995: A1, A8.

## 4. The big sleeper of secession: Québec's explosive strategy of "effective control"

1 Crawford (1979), 45; and de Smith and Brazier, 68.

2 Para. 104 in *Factum of the Intervener Grand Council of the Crees (Eeyou Astchee)* in relation to the federal *Reference* to the Supreme Court of Canada.

3 *Convention on the Rights and Duties of States (Montevideo Convention)*, 49 Stat. 3097, TS 881, 165 LNTS 19. Signed at Montevideo, Uruguay, 26 Dec. 1933; entered into force on 26 Dec. 1934.

4 Crawford (1979), 45–46.

5 G. Marchildon and E. Maxwell, "Québec's Right of Secession Under Canadian and International Law," *Virginia Journal of International Law* 32 (1992): 620.

6 P. Monahan, 1995, 10.

7 K. Gagnon, "Le Gouvernement du Québec ignore la mise en demeure de l'avocat Guy Bertrand," *La Presse*, 10 Aug. 1995: B1.

8 Sec. 18 and 22.

9 P. Hogg, vol. 1, 5-33, 5-34; also B. Pelletier, "La Continuité juridique," *Le Devoir*, 22 Sept. 1995: A11.

10 Gowland-Debbas, 240.

11 It has been said that Québec Aboriginal peoples have not suffered repression comparable to that of black Africans in Rhodesia and therefore cannot invoke the principle of self-determination against a Québec UDI. This opinion was expressed in 1992 by two Toronto lawyers, N. Finkelstein and G. Vegh, in *The Separation of Québec and the Constitution of Canada* (North York: York U Centre for Public Law and Public Policy, 1992), 60–64, but they provide little analysis for this conclusion. However, in a 1995 article, "Does Québec Have a Right to Secede at International Law?" (*Canadian Bar Review* 74), these authors appear to have changed their opinion to a significant degree. They write, ". . . others . . . may equally have a claim to secede from Québec, or remain in Canada, on the basis that they are also a people whose rights to self-determination will not be vindicated in an independent Québec, e.g., natives and anglophones" (252).

12 T. Franck et al., vol. 1, 443.

13 See the paper by lawyer Peter Hutchins, "And Do the Indians Pass With It — Québec Sovereignty, Aboriginal Peoples and the Treaty Order," Canadian Bar Association Seminar on *The Act Respecting the Sovereignty of Québec: Legal Perspectives*, Montréal, 6 May 1995, 18.

14 T. Franck, *Postmodern Tribalism and the Right to Secession*, in Brölmann et al., 12.

15 J.-P. Derriennic, "Le droit international admet la sécession, il ne la facilite pas," *Le Devoir*, 5 Sept. 1995: A11.

[16] J.-P. Derriennic, 70–71.

[17] J. Woehrling, in J.-Y. Morin and J. Woehrling, 131.

## 5. The strong possibility of violence

[1] M. Coon Come, Speaking Notes for address to Centre for Strategic and International Studies, Washington, DC, 19 Sept. 1994 (on file with the Grand Council of the Crees).

[2] R. Séguin, "Parizeau Goes from Pariah to Possible Saviour," *Globe and Mail*, 22 May 1997: A8.

[3] J. Brian, "Let's Face Facts: Separation Could Turn Violent," *Gazette*, 23 Apr. 1997: E1.

[4] C. Turner, "1990 Confrontation Haunts Debate Over Québec," *Los Angeles Times*, 1 Jan. 1995.

[5] P. Monahan, "International Law Isn't on Parizeau's Side," *Globe and Mail*, 19 May 1994.

[6] Project Ploughshares, *Armed Conflicts Report 1993* (Waterloo, ON: Institute of Peace and Conflict Studies, 1994).

[7] Crawford (1979), 247.

[8] C. Tomuschat, 11.

[9] G. Normand, "Parizeau compte sur l'armeé pour la période suivant l'indépendance," *La Presse*, 15 Dec. 1991, A1.

[10] M. Adam, "Le PQ n'exclut pas l'usage de la force pour s'imposer dans un Québec souverain," *La Presse*, 11 June 1994: B2. Also "Sovereign Québec Would Use Police against Dissident Natives, PQ Official Says," *Citizen* [Ottawa], 31 May 1994: A3.

[11] Assemblée Nationale, *Commission d'étude des questions afférentes à l'accession du Québec à la souveraineté, Journal des débats*, 12 Feb. 1992, CEAS-911.

[12] *Réflexions sur la politique de défense du Canada and sur celle d'un éventuel Québec independent*, in Commission d'étude des questions afférentes à l'accession du Québec à la souveraineté, *Les implications de la mise en oeuvre de la souveraineté: les aspects juridiques et les services gouvernmentaux* (Québec: Bibliothèque nationale du Québec, 1992), 333, vol. 2 of *Exposés et études*.

[13] Assemblée Nationale, Commission d'étude des questions afférentes à l'accession du Québec à la souveraineté, *Journal des débats*, 22 Jan. 1992, CEAS-530.

[14] P. Russell, in McRoberts and P. Monahan, 218.

[15] *Rapport d'enquête de coroner Guy Gilbert sur les cas et circonstances du décès de Monsieur Marcel Lemay* (Québec: Government of Québec, 21 July 1995).

[16] "25 policiers de la SQ ont été dépêchés à Fort Chimo," *La Presse*, 25 Aug. 1977: A1; L. Diebel, "More Cops Readied for Inuit Protest," *Montréal Star*, 30 Aug. 1977: A1; "Québec's Show of Force Angers Eskimo Villages," *Globe and Mail*, 26 Aug. 1977: A1.

[17] L. Diebel, "Bill 1 Threatens James Bay Pact," *Montréal Star*, 19 May 1977: A1; S. Oziewicz, "Crees, Eskimos Contend Bill 1 Could Breach James Bay Pact," *Globe and Mail*, 6 May 1977; S. Schwartz, "Inuit Say Québec Violating 1975 Agreement on Rights," *Gazette* [Montréal], 14 June 1977: 5.

[18] "Chimo and Distrust," editorial, *Montréal Star*, 30 Aug. 1977.

[19] D. Burman, D. Proulx, and D. Turp, *Les Droits linguistiques des Amérindiens et Inuit du Québec* (Montréal: Faculté des Études Supérieures, Maîtrise en Droit, Dec. 1977): 76–77.

[20] R. Séguin, "PQ Ready for Army, Brassard Says," *Globe and Mail*, 29 Jan. 1997: A1.

[21] E. Thompson, "Partition Forbidden: Brassard," *Gazette* [Montréal], 20 Jan. 1997: A1.

[22] Ibid.

[23] P. Wells, "Remarks about Use of Force to Back Separation Worry Dion," *Citizen* [Ottawa], 31 Jan. 1997: A4.

[24] P. Wells, "Dion to PQ: Clarify Position on Use of Force," *Gazette* [Montréal], 31 Jan. 1997.

[25] UN General Assembly, *Definition of Aggression Resolution*, General Assembly res. 3314 (XXIX), 14 Dec. 1974. Adopted by the UN General Assembly without a vote.

[26] Ibid, art. 1 provides in part: *Explanatory note: In this Definition the term State: (a) Is used without prejudice to questions of recognition or to whether a State is a Member of the United Nations.* . . .

[27] See J.P. Brodeur, *L'obstacle des troubles intérieurs*, Gagnon and Rocher: 111.

[28] *Legal Consequences for States of the Continued Presence of South Africa in Namibia (South West Africa) notwithstanding Security Council Resolution 276* (1970). Advisory Opinion, 1971, International Court of Justice, 16, 89–90 (separate opinion of Vice-President Ammoun).

[29] *Declaration on the "Guidelines on the Recognition of New States in Eastern Europe and the Soviet Union,"* 16 Dec. 1991, rpt. 1992, 31 ILM 1486.

[30] See M. Bothe, *The Legitimacy of the Use of Force to Protect Peoples and Minorities*, Brölmann et al., 291. Also M. Shaw: 701.

[31] Address to Les Amis de Cité Libre, Montréal, 12 Sept. 1966.

[32] D. Murswiek, *The Issue of a Right of Secession — Reconsidered*, C. Tomuschat: 26.

[33] Commission d'étude des questions afférentes à l'accession du Québec à la souveraineté, *Les Attributs d'un Québec souverain* (Québec: Bibliothèque nationale du Québec, 1992), 474, vol. 1 of *Exposés et études*.

[34] P. Monahan, 29.

[35] J.-Y. Morin and J. Woehrling, 130.

[36] P. Hogg, vol. 1, 5.33–34.

[37] See M. van Walt van Praag, *The position of UNPO in the International Legal Order*, Brölmann et al., 316.

# 6. Borders: what happens following a UDI?

1 Qtd. in R. Moody, *Indigenous Voices: Visions and Realities* (London: Zed, 1988).

2 P. Monahan, 15.

3 M. Lalonde, Address to Les Amis de cité libre, Montréal, 12 Sept. 1966.

4 J. Parizeau, "Frontières d'un Québec souverain: la situation est 'on ne peut plus claire,' " *La Presse*, 25 May 1994: B3. See also J. Parizeau, 293.

5 Commission nationale sur l'avenir du Québec, *Rapport* (Québec: Bibliothèque nationale du Québec, 1995), 60.

6 "Les Autochtones feront partie d'un Québec souverain, quoi qu'il advienne," *Le Devoir*, 22 Sept. 1995: A4.

7 J. Parizeau, "La Stratégie du chef," *Le Devoir*, 8 May 1997: A9; G. Fraser, "Parizeau Details Separation Strategy," *Globe and Mail*, 8 May 1997: A5; C. Hébert, "Coup de massue de Parizeau," *La Presse*, 8 May 1997: A1; "Separatist Lies and More Lies," Editorial, *Gazette* [Montréal], 9 May 1997: B2.

8 E. Thompson, "It's a Lie: Parizeau," *Gazette* [Montréal], 9 May 1997: A1.

9 See R. Lecker, "Québec Map Leads to Trouble," *Citizen* [Ottawa], 7 Oct. 1996: A9.

10 Ibid.

11 Conseil pour l'unité canadienne, *Les Commissions sur l'avenir du Québec: Rapport factuel*, April 1995, 49.

12 Sec. 3, Constitution Act, 1871.

13 *Bertrand v. Attorney-Gen. of Québec*, 8 Sept. 1995, Québec City, No. 200-05-002117-955 (Québec Super. Ct. 1995).

14 Sec. 10 of the draft *Act Respecting the Sovereignty of Québec* provides: "Laws passed by the Parliament of Canada that apply in Québec at the time section 1 comes into force, and the regulations under such laws, shall remain in force until amended or repealed by the National Assembly."

15 J. Woehrling, *Les Aspects juridiques et politiques d'une éventuelle accession du Québec à la souveraineté*, J.-Y. Morin and J. Woehrling, 1995, vol. 1, No. 12, 34.

16 P. Monahan, 15.

17 Z. Nungak, speech, 3 Dec. 1966, Washington, DC (on file with the Makivik Corporation).

18 Remarks made by international law professor Paul Szasz, following his paper *The Fragmentation of Yugoslavia*, Proceedings of the American Society of International Law (1994), 33–47.

19 A.O. Cukwurah, 113. It is said that the principle may be more fully expressed by the words *uti possidetis, ita possideatis*, or "as you possess, so you may possess," but it is usually summarized as *uti possidetis*.

20 Ibid, 112–113.

21 I. Brownlie, 135.

22 *Beagle Channel Arbitration (Argentina v. Chile)*, 52 ILR, 125.

[23] *Frontier Dispute (Burkina Faso/Mali)*, 1986 International Ct. of Justice Rep., 554.

[24] J. Klabbers and R. Lefeber, *Lost Between Self-Determination and Uti Possidetis*, Brölmann et al., 59.

[25] Ibid, 61.

[26] J. Klabbers and R. Lefeber, op. cit. n.22, 38.

[27] Bloomfield, *Egypt, Israel and the Gulf of Aqaba (1957)*, 107–08, qtd. in Whiteman, vol. 2, 1086.

[28] S. Ratner, "Drawing a Better Line: Uti Possidetis and the Borders of New States," *American Journal of International Law* 90 (1996).

[29] P. Hogg, *Principles Governing the Secession of Québec*, Conference on Law, Democracy and Self-Determination (Ottawa: Canadian Bar Association, May 1997), 26.

[30] Op. cit. n.17, 652.

[31] *Québec's Democratic Right to Self-Determination*, Hartt et al., 119.

[32] S.J. Anaya, "A Contemporary Definition of the International Norm on Self-Determination," *Transnational Law and Contemporary Problems* 3 (1993): 143.

# 7. Borders: two-thirds of Québec at issue

[1] Submission to the *Cree Eeyou Astchee Commission*, Québec, 21 Sept. 1995 (on file with the Grand Council of the Crees), 4.

[2] A.C. Hamilton, *Canada and Aboriginal Peoples: A New Partnership* (Ottawa: Minister of Public Works and Government Services, 1995), 6.

[3] Hogg, vol. 1, 2.12–2.13.

[4] *Address to Her Majesty the Queen from the Senate and House of Commons of the Dominion of Canada*, Sched. (A), RSC 1985, App. II, No. 9, 8–9.

[5] Sec. 2(e) of the *Québec Boundaries Extension Act* was repealed by the *James Bay and Northern Québec Native Claims Settlement Act*, SC 1976–77, c. 32. But the preamble of the 1976 act makes clear that the federal fiduciary responsibility for the James Bay Crees and Inuit continues: "And whereas Parliament and the Government of Canada recognize and affirm a special responsibility for the said Crees and Inuit."

[6] *R. v. Sparrow*, 1990, 1 SCR 1103–04.

[7] Dominion of Canada, *Sessional Paper No. 64a*, 1906–07, vol. 13, 43–44.

[8] Ibid, 48.

[9] Dominion of Canada, *Sessional Paper No. 110a*, 1911–12, vol. 24, 39–40, 41–42, 47.

[10] Government of Québec, *Québec-Canada: A New Deal* (Québec: Editeur official, 1979), 89.

[11] Bucheit, 25.

[12] J.-J. Rousseau, *Political Writings*, ed. Vaughan (1915), 340–41.

[13] W. Wilson, Mount Vernon Address, qtd. in G.H. Hackworth, *Digest of International Law* 1 (1940): 425.

[14] *Advisory Opinion on Western Sahara* (1975): International Court of Justice 6, 31–33, 35–36. See also E. Suzuki, "Self-Determination and World Public Order: Community Response to Territorial Separation," *Virginia Journal of International Law* 16 (1976): 827.

[15] L. Chen and W.M. Reisman, "Who Owns Taiwan: A Search for International Title," *Yale Law Journal* 81 (1972): 638, 659–60.

[16] H. Brun, Gagnon, and Rocher, 74–75.

[17] Select Committee on Aborigines, qtd. in R. Barsh and J. Henderson, "Aboriginal Rights, Treaty Rights, and Human Rights: Indian Tribes and 'Constitutional Renewal,'" *Journal of Canadian Studies* 17/55 (1982): 68. See also discussion in P. Joffe and M.E. Turpel, vol. 1, 61 ff.

[18] Dominion of Canada, Sessional Paper No. 64a, 1906–07, vol. 13, 28.

[19] Dominion of Canada, Sessional Paper No. 110a, 1911–12, vol. 24, 23.

[20] S. Scott, *Secession or Reform? Mechanisms and Directions of Constitutional Change in Canada*, North American Studies and Department of Economics, McGill U, 30–31 May 1991, 10. Similar statements by Scott can be found in Assemblée nationale, Commission d'étude des questions afférentes à l'accession du Québec à la souveraineté, *Journal des débats*, 26 Nov. 1991, No. 10, CEAS-257-58.

[21] "All Gall Divided into Three Parts," Editorial, *Globe and Mail*, 7 Aug. 1991: A14.

[22] E. Stewart, "Hands Off Québec's Territory, Bloc Leader Warns Canadians," *Citizen* [Ottawa], 3 May 1994: A3.

[23] B. Came, "The Natives Say No," *Maclean's*, 27 Feb. 1995, 14–15.

[24] Commission d'étude des questions afférentes à l'accession du Québec à la souveraineté, *Les Attributs d'un Québec souverain* (Québec: Bibliothèque nationale du Québec, 1992), 470, vol. 1 of *Exposés et études*.

[25] M. Venne, "Le Concept de l'intégrité territoriale ne passe pas," *Le Devoir*, 14 Oct. 1994: A5.

[26] First Nations in Québec and Labrador, *Declaration*, 13 Oct. 1994 (on file with the Grand Council of the Crees). Also Nunavik Leaders Conference, *Implications of the Québec Sovereignty Process*, Montréal, 8 Dec. 1994 (on file with the Grand Council of the Crees).

[27] J. Aubry, "Québec v. Natives: Who's Sovereign First?" *Ottawa Citizen*, 22 May 1994: A1.

[28] However, see most recently C. Bainbridge and A. Roslin, "Hydro Reviving Great Whale," *Gazette* [Montréal], 7 June 1997: A1.

[29] T. Hall, "Native Land Claims," letter, *Globe and Mail*, 25 Oct. 1994: A18.

[30] Assemblé nationale, *Journal des débats*, 19 Mar. 1991, 28.38, 2493.

[31] B. Came, "The Natives Say No," *Maclean's*, 27 Feb. 1995: 14–15.

32 Presentation to the *Eeyou Astchee* Commission, 30 Aug. 1995 (on file with the Grand Council of the Crees), 17.

33 Made in an Address of the Canadian Parliament to the British Parliament. See n. 4.

34 The James Bay and Northern Québec Native Claims Settlement Act, SC 1976–77, chap. 32, sec. 7.

35 Franck et al., vol. 1, 404.

## 8. The James Bay and Northern Québec Agreement: a treaty denied

1 D. Soyez, "La Baie James: faut-il repatrier ou mondaliser le débat?," *Cahiers de Géographie du Québec* 39.106 (Apr. 1995): 65.

2 M. Coon Come, *Canadian Speeches: Issues of the Day* 5.9: 13–14.

3 Commission on Human Rights, *Report of the Meeting of Experts to Review the Experience of Countries in the Operation of Schemes of Internal Self-government for Indigenous Peoples*, UN ESCOR, Commission on Human Rights, 48th Sess., UN Doc. E/CN.4/1992/42 and Add. 1 (1992) (Nuuk Meeting), Conclusions and Recommendations, para. 15.

4 See H. Aubin, "Ottawa, Cree Putting Squeeze on Québec: Parizeau," *Gazette* [Montréal], 17 Aug. 1991: A4; M. Fontaine, "Parizeau ne prévoit pas d'obstacle à la reconnaissance internationale du Québec," *La Presse* [Montréal], 24 Jan. 1992: B1.

5 B. Diamond, *Eeyou Astchee* Commission, 30 Aug. 1995 (on file with the Grand Council of the Crees), 15, 26. On extinguishment see also P. Joffe and M.E. Turpel; A.C. Hamilton; and Royal Commission on Aboriginal Peoples, *Treaty Making in the Spirit of Co-Existence: An Alternative to Extinguishment* (Ottawa: Minister of Supply and Services, 1995).

6 See, for example, J.-Y. Morin, Assemblée nationale, Commission d'étude des questions afférentes à l'accession du Québec à la souveraineté, *Journal des débats*, 17 Dec. 1991, No. 17, CEAS-456.

7 Assemblée nationale, Commission d'étude des questions afférentes à l'accession du Québec à la souveraineté, *Journal des débats*, 7 Nov. 1991, No. 8, CEAS-203.

8 Ibid.

9 A more detailed account of the court case, the impact of the hydroelectric project on Cree life, and the Cree resistance to the project is given in Richardson, 1991.

10 These quotations are from the frontispiece of Richardson.

11 Ibid, 298.

12 Ibid, 358–61.

13 *Cree Regional Authority et al. v. Attorney-Gen. of Québec*, 1991, 42 FTR 168.

Judge Rouleau's decision was affirmed by the Federal Court of Appeal in 1991, 127 NR 52, 43 FTR 240.

[14] "Villages of the Dammed," *Arctic Circle*, Nov.–Dec. 1990, 27.

[15] *Presentation to the Eeyou Astchee Commission*, 30 Aug. 1995 (on file with the Grand Council of the Crees), 20.

[16] Grand Council of the Crees (of Québec), *Presentation to the Royal Commission on Aboriginal Peoples*, Montréal, 18 Nov. 1993, 8.

[17] House of Commons, *Debates*, 14 Dec. 1976, 1999–2002.

[18] J. Clark, *Native Rights in Canada*, 2nd ed. (Toronto: Indian-Eskimo Association of Canada, with General Publishing, 1972).

[19] P. Cumming, *Canada's North and Native Rights*, Morse 723.

[20] P. Joffe and M.E. Turpel, vol. 3, 633.

[21] Ibid, 612ff.

[22] *Constitution Act, 1982*, s. 35.

[23] *Rapport de la Commission d'étude sur l'intégrité du territoire du Québec* (Québec: Éditeur Officiel, 1971), vol. 4.1 (Dorion Report).

[24] Assemblée nationale, Commission d'étude des questions afférentes à l'accession du Québec à la souveraineté, *Journal des débats*, 26 Nov. 1991, No. 6, CEAS-160, CEAS-167, CEAS-181.

[25] H. Brun, 1974.

[26] Assemblée nationale, Commission d'étude des questions afférentes à l'accession du Québec à la souveraineté, *Journal des débats*, 17 Oct. 1991, No. 6, CEAS-160, CEAS-167, CEAS-181.

[27] *Agreement between the Inuit of the Nunavut Settlement Area and Her Majesty the Queen in Right of Canada* (Ottawa: Indian and Northern Affairs Canada, 1993).

[28] D. Sanders, *Indigenous Participation in National Economic Life*, Background paper, United Nations Seminar on the Effects of Racism and Racial Discrimination on the Social and Economic Relations Between Indigenous Peoples and States, Geneva, 16–20 Jan. 1989, 14 (para. 22). Ref. *Report on the United Nations Seminar on the Effects of Racism and Racial Discrimination on the Social and Economic Relations between Indigenous Peoples and States*, Geneva, 16–20 Jan. 1989, E/CN.4/1989/22, 8 Feb. 1989, para. 22, 51.

[29] Québec's insistence that the rights of third parties be extinguished by Parliament was communicated to the federal government in writing: see House of Commons, *Debates*, 28 Apr. 1977, 5090 (Hon. Warren Allmand, Min. of Indian Affairs and Northern Development).

[30] See House of Commons, *Debates*, 7 Dec. 1976, vol. 120, no. 39, 1759 (J.R. Holmes).

[31] House of Commons, *Debates*, 14 Dec. 1976, 2002.

[32] Hamilton, 11–12.

[33] *Cree-Naskapi (of Québec) Act*, SC 1984, c. 24; proclaimed in force by Order-in-Council 1984-2652, 25 July 1984.

34 *Presentation to the Eeyou Astchee Commission*, 30 Aug. 1995, 9.

35 Stavenhagen, 105.

36 A recent Cree-initiated community sawmill at the Waswanipi First Nation now employs a significant number of Crees from a Cree community perspective, but still only a tiny fraction of the overall number of jobs arising out of forestry activities on Cree traditional lands. The mill is a joint initiative of the Crees' Mishtuk Corporation and Domtar Inc.

37 Law Reform Commission of Canada, *Aboriginal Peoples and Criminal Justice: Equality, Respect and the Search for Justice* (Ottawa: Dec. 1991), Rep. 34. For an account of the range of matters that should be addressed, see also Report of the Aboriginal Justice Inquiry of Manitoba, *The Justice System and Aboriginal People* (Winnipeg: Queen's Printer, 1991), vol. 1.

38 R. Platiel, "Native Justice System Backed by Law Panel," *Globe and Mail*, 12 Dec. 1991: A6.

39 *James Bay and Northern Québec Agreement*, Sec. 8.1.3.

40 *Friends of the Oldman River Society v. Canada*, 1992, 1 Supreme Court Rep. 3.

41 United Nations, Draft United Nations Declaration on the Rights of Indigenous Peoples, art. 7.

42 K. Parker and L. Neglon, "Jus Cogens: The Compelling Law of Human Rights," *Hastings International and Comparative Law Review* 12 (1989): 430.

43 House of Commons, *Debates*, 14 Dec. 1976, 1999.

44 A. Dubuc, "La mort de la grande baleine blanche," Editorial, *La Presse*, 22 Nov. 1994, B2.

45 *Québec's Democratic Right to Self-Determination*, Hartt et al., 119–20.

46 M. Coon Come, Remarks to the Canadian Club, Toronto, 13 Mar. 1995, 5 (on file with the Grand Council of the Crees).

47 For general discussion of treaties see Lord McNair.

48 P. Hogg, *Principles Governing the Secession of Québec*, Conference on Law, Democracy and Self-Determination, Canadian Bar Association, Ottawa, May 1997, 24.

49 E. Thompson, "Partition out of the Question, Bouchard Insists," *Gazette* [Montréal], 21 May 1997, A12.

## 9. *Blast from the past: the* PQ *government invokes colonialism and discrimination*

1 *R. v. Côte*, 17 June 1996 (Supreme Ct. of Can. 1996), 4 CNLR 26.

2 *Mabo et al. v. State of Queensland*, 1992 (High Ct. of Australia 1992), *Australian Law Reports* 107 (1992): 1.

3 Ibid, 29.

4 *R. v. Côté*, 1996, 4 CNLR 26, 48–49.

⁵ *Western Sahara*, Advisory Opinion, International Court of Justice Reports, 1975, 39; and Crawford, 1979, 179–82.

⁶ *Mabo et al. v. State of Queensland*, 1992 (High Ct. of Australia 1992), *Australian Law Review* 107 (1992): 1.

⁷ M. Coon Come, Canada Seminar, Harvard Centre for International Affairs and Kennedy School of Government, 28 Oct. 1996, 9–10.

⁸ L.-G. Francoeur, "Les Droits ancestraux des autochtones ne sont pas absolus, selon Québec," *Le Devoir*, 11 Oct. 1996: A2.

⁹ *Discrimination and Colonial Positions Taken before the Supreme Court of Canada: Denial of the Existence of Aboriginal Rights in Québec*, Resolution No. 11/96, Secretariat of the Assembly of First Nations of Québec and Labrador, 17 Oct. 1996.

¹⁰ See chapter 12 for an account of Canada's international responsibilities under various human-rights instruments.

¹¹ See, for example, E. Thompson, "Bouchard Lauds Benefits of Cree Deals," *Gazette* [Montréal], 14 June 1997: A14; P. Avril, "Fructueux voyage de Bouchard chez les Cris," *La Presse*, 14 June 1997: A18.

¹² M. Venne, "Heureux dialogue," editorial, *Le Devoir*, 14–15 June 1997: A10.

¹³ M. Coon Come, op. cit. n.7.

¹⁴ Draft *United Nations Declaration on the Rights of Indigenous Peoples*, rpt. in *International Legal Materials* 34.541 (1995), 3rd preambular para.

¹⁵ Gouvernement du Québéc, *Déclaration du gouvernement du Québec sur les relations interethniques et interraciales*, 10 Dec. 1986. See, generally, P. Lepage, *Un regard au-delà des chartes: Le racisme et la discrimination envers les peuples autochtones*, Recherches amérindiennes au Québec 25.3 (1995), 29.

¹⁶ M. Coon Come, op. cit. n.7.

## 10. *The simple-majority referendum: democracy or coercion?*

¹ "Parizeau aurait agi tout de suite," *Le Soleil*, 7 May 1997: 1.

² R. Sheppard, "Clear the Track for Jacques," *Globe and Mail*, 8 May 1997: A21. Robert Sheppard quoted Bouchard as having said in a speech in Rivière de Loup, 25 Oct. 1995: "I want to remind you that the mandate being sought by Mr. Parizeau's government and by the sovereignists is that Québec realizes its sovereignty and that, empowered by its sovereignty, Québec will then move on to negotiate a partnership agreement. And that the proposal of a partnership accord is not a condition which will subordinate Québec's accession to sovereignty."

³ R. Séguin, "Separatists Were Poised to Humble Ottawa," *Globe and Mail*, 9 Nov. 1996: A1.

4 J. Chartier, "Le Plan Parizeau: Le comité secret des négotiations, *L'Actualité*, 1 Mar. 1997.

5 J. Dion, "Bouchard accuse Chrétien de bafouer la démocratie," *Le Devoir*, 21 Sept. 1995: A4.

6 *Submission to the Cree Eeyou Astchee Commission*, Montréal, 21 Sept. 1995, 6 (on file with the Grand Council of the Crees).

7 D. Lessard, "Le droit de vote des Québécois est sacré, clame Jacques Parizeau," *La Presse*, 2 Sept. 1995, A1; K. Yakabuski, "Les Québécois veulent voter et vont voter,' " *Le Devoir*, 3 Sept. 1995: A1.

8 Arctic Leaders' Summit, *Indigenous Peoples' Right to Determine Their Own Future in the Context of Québec Secession, Statement of Support*, 27 Jan. 1995, Tromso, Norway, para. 5 (on file with the Grand Council of the Crees).

9 S. Dion, *Antinationalisme et obsession constitutionnelle dans le débat référendaire*, Cité Libre, Montréal, 12 Jan. 1995, and Ottawa, 18 Jan. 1995, 9.

10 R. Iglar, "The Constitutional Crisis in Yugoslavia and the International Law of Self-Determination: Slovenia's and Croatia's Right to Secede," *Boston College International and Comparative Law Review* 15.213 (1992): 229.

11 Valaskakis and Fournier, 161, 195.

12 *An Act Respecting the Sovereignty of Québec* (draft bill), made public by Premier Parizeau on 6 Dec. 1994, but never tabled in the National Assembly.

13 *An Act Respecting the Future of Québec* (Bill 1), tabled by Premier Parizeau on 7 Sept. 1995, died on the order paper in Dec. 1995.

14 *Referendum Act*, Revised Statutes of Québec, chap. 64.1.

15 P. Hogg, vol. 1, 5–30.

16 A. Buchanan, "Québec, Secession and Aboriginal Territorial Rights," *Network* [Newsletter of the Network on the Constitution] 3 (Mar. 1992): 4.

17 Conference on Security and Cooperation in Europe, *Document of the Moscow Meeting on the Human Dimension, Emphasizing Respect for Human Rights, Pluralistic Democracy, the Rule of Law, and Procedures for Fact-Finding*, 3 Oct. 1991, 30 ILM 1672.

18 "Who's Seceding from Whom?" *Nation*, 31 Mar. 1994: 10.

19 J. Dion, "Bouchard accuse Chrétien de bafouer la démocratie," *Le Devoir*, 21 Sept. 1995: A4.

20 P. Russell, 170.

21 E.-I. Daes, "Some Considerations on the Right of Indigenous Peoples to Self-Determination," *Transnational Law and Contemporary Problems* (1993): 10.

22 S. Contenta, "Natives Can Play the Spoilers," *Star* [Toronto], 3 Sept. 1994: B4.

23 "Aboriginal Leaders Furious after Premier Cancels Meeting," *Gazette* [Montréal], 31 May 1995: A5. Also on page B2, under the heading "Hopes for Harmony Fade."

24 D. Schnapper, 152. See also G. Alfred, *L'avenir des relations entre les Autochtones et le Québec Choix: série Québec-Canada, Les Peuples autochtones et*

*l'avenir du Québec* (Montréal: Institute for Research on Public Policy, June 1995) 18, where the author views the secession initiatives by the PQ government as instituting a new colonialism, in the absence of full recognition of Aboriginal peoples' right to self-determination in their own political, geographic, and cultural space.

25 A. Derfel, "We Won't Respect Native Plebiscites Backing Secession, PQ Advisor Says," *Gazette* [Montréal], 7 Feb. 1995: A6.

26 Ibid.

27 *Tommy Schnurmacher Show*, CJAD [Montréal], 15 May 1996.

28 Y. Zacharias, "Quebecers Finish Last in Literacy: No Change in Five Years," *Gazette* [Montréal], 13 Sept. 1996.

29 Y. Zacharias, "Coalition Demands Action to Fight Illiteracy," *Gazette* [Montréal], 9 Sept. 1996; also É. Clément, "Pas de démocratie sans alphabétisation," *La Presse*, 9 Sept. 1996.

30 D. Macpherson, "Counting on Illiteracy: How Many Voters Couldn't Understand the Referendum Question?" *Gazette*, 17 Sept. 1996.

31 C. Hilling, "Autodétermination et sécession confondues," *Le Devoir*, 13 Jan. 1995: A9.

32 See M.-E. Turpel, *Does the Road to Québec Sovereignty Run Through Aboriginal Territory?* Drache and Perrin, 106.

33 S. Tramier, "Jacques Parizeau souhaite que la France appuie le Québec en cas de victoire du 'oui' au référendum sur l'indépendance," *Le Monde* [Paris], 24 Jan. 1995: 6.

34 Indian and Northern Affairs Canada, *Comprehensive Land Claims Policy* (Ottawa: Indian Affairs and Northern Development, 1987), 24.

35 The quotation is T. Franck et al., vol. 1, 442. The UN document quoted is *Study of the Problem of Discrimination against Indigenous Populations*, for the UN Sub-commission on the Prevention of Discrimination and Protection of Minorities, UN Doc. E/CN.4/ Sub.2/1986/7, Add. 4 (J. Cobo special report), paras. 580–81. Cobo's full statement quoted by the five experts with approval was: "It must also be recognized that the right to self-determination exists at various levels and includes economic, social, cultural, and political factors. In essence it constitutes the exercise of free choice by indigenous peoples who must, to a large extent, create the specific content of this principle, in both its internal and external expressions, which do not necessarily include the right to secede from the State in which they live and to set themselves up as sovereign entities."

36 Boyer, 15.

37 Generally, the United Nations will play a role in plebiscites or elections in a particular State or territory, if authorized by the General Assembly or the Security Council: see J. Salmon, in C. Tomuschat, 274.

38 G. Normand, "Bouchard réplique aux Inuit: 'Seul le référendum québécois fera autorité,'" *La Presse*, 23 Aug. 1995: B1.

39 A. Dubuc, "La gaffe," Editorial, *La Presse*, 24 Aug. 1995: B2.

40 L. Bissonnette, "Le référendum cri," Editorial, *Le Devoir*, 25 July 1995: A6.

41 A.C. Cairns, "Why Is It So Difficult to Talk to Each Other?" *McGill Law Journal* 42.63 (1997): 86.

42 P. Authier, "No 60 Per Cent, Yes 40 Percent: Poll," *Gazette* [Montréal], 17 Feb. 1995: A1.

43 P. Wells, "Quebecers Divided on Partition," *Gazette* [Montréal], 15 May 1997: A1. See also M. Venne, "Lacune souverainistes," *Le Devoir*, 3 June 1997: A2, where the writer suggests sovereignists reflect on these results.

44 P. Monahan, 30.

45 M.E. Turpel Drache and Perrin, 105.

46 P. Hogg, vol. 1, 5–31. See also D. Matas, "Can Québec Separate?" *McGill Law Journal* 21 (1975): 392.

47 J.-P. Derriennic, 88.

48 W. Johnson, "Civil Code Is Clear: Separation Should Require a Two-Thirds Vote," *Gazette* [Montréal], 20 Sept. 1995: B3.

49 See J. Woehrling, *Les aspects juridiques de la redéfinition du statut politique et constitutionnel du Québec*, Commission sur l'avenir politique et constitutionnel du Québec, *Éléments d'analyse institutionnelle, juridique et démolinguistique pertinents à la révision du statut politique et constitutionnel du Québec*, Document de travail, no. 2 (Québec: National Assembly, 1991), 38; also in Gagnon and Rocher, 159.

50 P. Wells, "No Rule on 50 Per Cent Plus One: BQ MP," *Gazette* [Montréal], 13 June 1997.

51 J. Brossard, *L'Accession à la souveraineté et le cas du Québec*, 353.

52 G. Bertrand, "L'autre façon de proposer une entente Québec-Canada," *Le Soleil* [Québec City], 16 Jan. 1995: A7.

53 The notion of "double majorities" that would include a majority popular vote, as well as approval in a majority of designated distinct regions, is recommended in a pan-Canadian context for constitutional amendments in Special Joint Committee of the Senate and House of Commons, *The Process for Amending the Constitution of Canada* (Ottawa: House of Commons, 1991), 41–42 (Beaudoin-Edwards Report).

54 "Is 50 Per Cent Plus One Enough to End Canada?," Editorial, *Globe and Mail*, 10 Jan. 1995: A16.

55 For detail on secessionist events in Yugoslavia, readers could consult writings by R. Iglar, *Boston College International and Comparative Law Review*, 15.234; B. Bagwell, *Georgia Journal of Comparative and International Law*, 21, 490, 495, 521–22; P. Szasz, "The Fragmentation of Yugoslavia," *American Society of International Legal Procedure* (1994), 38. A useful description of historical events in the Baltic States is found in S. Himmer, *Emory International Law Revue* 6 (1992): 405ff. For a discussion of self-determination and related

issues in former Czechoslovakia, see C. Saladin, *Michigan Journal of International Law* 13 (1991): 172; and J. Malendusky, *Annuaire français de droit international* 39 (1993): 305.

56 S. Himmer, "The Achievement of Independence in the Baltic States and Its Justifications," *Emory International Law Review* 6 (1992): 405ff.

57 Many jurists have commented unfavourably on the application of *uti possidetis* in Yugoslavia. See N. Finkelstein, G. Vegh, and C. Joly, "Does Québec Have a Right to Secede at International Law?" *Canadian Bar Review* 74 (1995): 259. Also R. Falk [S.J. Anaya, R. Falk and McNeil], *Canada's Fiduciary Obligation to Aboriginal Peoples in the Context of Accession to Sovereignty by Québec* (Ottawa: Minister of Supply and Services, Canada, 1995), 64. vol. 1 of *International Dimensions*. Also J. Frowein, *Self-Determination as a Limit to Obligations Under International Law*, Tomuschat, 217. Also P. Szasz, op. cit. n.16. Also B. Kingsbury, "Claims by Non-State Groups in International Law," *Cornell International Law Journal* 25 (1992): 505–06. Also H. Hannum, "Rethinking Self-Determination," *Virginia Journal of International Law* 34 (1993): 55.

58 A. Buchanan, "A Reply to Grand Chief Matthew Coon Come and Mr. David Cliche," *Network* [Newsletter of the Network on the Constitution], 5 (May 1992): 13.

59 *McNeil/Lehrer News Hour*, New York, 20 Dec. 1994.

60 J.-P. Derriennic 94.

61 R. Young 266.

62 J. Daigneault and C. Galipeau, "René Lévesque dirait-il NON?" *Le Devoir*, 24 Jan. 1995: A7.

63 "PQ's Best Weapon is Mass Confusion," *Gazette* [Montréal], 26 Sept. 1995: B2.

64 J.-Y. Morin and J. Woehrling, 210.

65 A. de Mestral, *La structure de l'association économique Québec-Canada* in *Choix: série Québec-Canada, Un Québec souverain et l'union économique Québec-Canada* 1.6 (Montréal: Institute for Research on Public Policy, 1995), 20.

66 J. Woehrling, "Souveraineté: la loi doit être adoptée par référendum en premier," *La Presse*, 24 Feb. 1995: B3.

67 D. Latouche, "La bonne question," *Le Devoir*, 25–26 Feb. 1995: A12.

68 Ibid; B. Legendre, "Le train référendaire, direction Waterloo," *Le Devoir*, 15 Aug. 1995: A7.

69 M. Fontaine, "L'offre de partenariat doit être connue avant le référendum," *La Presse*, 22 Sept. 1995: B1.

70 A. Riga, "Quebecers Should Vote Yes without All the Answers: Simard," *Gazette* [Montréal], 27 Mar. 1995: A6.

## 11. Freedom of speech and misinformation in Québec

1 P. Wells and P. Authier, "Sovereignty Law Illegal, Rock Says," *Gazette* [Montréal], 16 Dec. 1994: A1.

2 J. Parizeau, "The Case for a Sovereign Québec," *Foreign Policy* 99 (Summer 1995): 69.

3 L. Beaudoin, in "The Sovereignty Showdown" (two-hour special), *Prime Time News*, Toronto, CBC, 16 Feb. 1995.

4 "Les Inuit disent non," *La Presse*, 3 Mar. 1995: B1.

5 M. Venne, "Québec embauche des lobbyistes pour expliquer la souveraineté aux Américains," *Le Devoir*, 23 Mar. 1995: A1.

6 S. Delacourt, "Not Just Separatists See Value of Whip," *Globe and Mail*, 18 Oct. 1994: at A4.

7 "The Sovereignty Pitch: Quebecers Would Be Better Off if They Were in Charge, Bouchard Says," *Gazette* [Montréal], 12 Oct. 1994: B3. (Interview with *Gazette* editorial board.)

8 D. Cliche, "The Sovereignty and Territorial Integrity of Québec," *Network* [Newsletter of the Network on the Constitution], 5 (May 1992): 10.

9 D. Cliche, Ligue des droits et libertés, *Dossier spécial autochtone*, Bulletin 13.3 (Oct. 1994): 33.

10 M. Venne, "La Ligne 1-800 sur l'avenir du Québec coutera $200,000," *Le Devoir*, 3–4 June 1995: A12.

11 G. Marchildon and E. Maxwell, "Québec's Right of Secession Under Canadian and International Law," *Virginia Journal of International Law* 32 (1992): 583.

12 *Supreme Court Act*, RSC 1985, c. S-26, s. 6.

13 K. Valaskakis and A. Fournier, 1995, 179.

14 W. Johnson, 1994, 389.

15 L. Gagnon, "Language Is No Longer the Issue: Control over Immigration Is," *Globe and Mail*, 7 Jan. 1995: D3.

16 F. Cloutier, "Référendum sur la souveraineté: un piège qui risque de se refermer sur le Québec," *La Presse*, 1 Feb. 1995: B3.

17 P. Authier, "Bouchard Arrogant, Johnson Says," *Gazette* [Montréal], 17 Aug. 1995: A1.

18 See K. Valaskakis and A. Fournier, 51; D. Cameron, "Solemn Declarations: American Colonists Had Far More to Complain about than Separatists Do," *Gazette* [Montréal], 22 Dec. 1994: B3; J. Hébert, "Wet Blanket: Claude Castonguay Has a Lot of Nerve to Complain of 'Humiliation,' Hébert Says," *Gazette* [Montréal], 30 July 1994: B5.

19 "Will Canada Unravel?" *Foreign Affairs* 75.5 (Sept.–Oct. 1996): 103–04.

20 J. Hébert, letter, *Globe and Mail*, 26 Sept. 1996: A22.

21 Commission nationale sur l'avenir du Québec, *Rapport* (Québec: Bibliothèque nationale du Québec, 1995), 56.

[22] Richardson 328–61.

[23] M. Coon Come, *The Status and Rights of the James Bay Crees in the Context of Québec Secession from Canada*, Speaking Notes, Centre for Strategic and International Studies, Washington, DC, 19 Sept. 1994, 8 (on file with the Grand Council of the Crees).

[24] M. Venne, "Coon Come a injurié tout le Québec, déplore Parizeau," *Le Devoir*, 20 Nov. 1994: A8.

[25] T. Wills, "Bloc demands PM censure Cree chief," *Gazette* [Montréal], 22 Nov. 1994: A5.

[26] See "On the Record: Coon Come's Speech and Landry's Letter," *Gazette*, 26 Nov. 1994: B5.

[27] P. Authier, "Envoy Should Have Denounced Coon Come: Landry," *Gazette* [Montréal], 25 Nov. 1994: A5.

[28] K. Blacksmith, "Un acte de trahison?" *Le Devoir*, 15 Apr. 1995: A11.

[29] "Free Speech Equals Infamy?" Editorial, *Gazette* [Montréal], 26 Nov. 1994: B4.

[30] Ibid.

[31] N. Webster, "Speaking Out," *Gazette* [Montréal], 7 Jan. 1995: B5.

[32] See A. Dubuc, "Jacques Parizeau est-il en train de perdre les pédales?" and "Banquiers et démocratie," Editorials, *La Presse*, 7 June and 28 June 1994: B2; L. Gagnon, "Le combat des justes," *La Presse*, 11 June 1994: B3; S. Scott, "When Money and Politics Mix: Parizeau Plays Hardball," *Gazette* [Montréal], 11 June 1994: B1.

[33] W. Johnson, "Bloc Wrong to Tell Non-Québec French to Butt Out," *Gazette* [Montréal], 17 Mar. 1995: B3.

[34] P. Gravel, "Silence?" *La Presse*, 17 Mar. 1995: B2.

[35] L. Gagnon, "Les exclus," *La Presse*, 22 Feb. 1995: A1.

[36] Assemblée Nationale, *Commission d'étude des questions afférentes à l'accession du Québec à la souveraineté, Journal des débats*, 9 Oct. 1991, No. 5, CEAS-137.

[37] Bloc Québécois Communiqué, Montréal, 26 May 1994. See also T. Ha, "Bloc Advisor Muzzled after Native Comments," *Gazette* [Montréal], 27 May 1994: B1.

[38] L. Desjardins, "Les lendemains de la souveraineté," *Le Journal du Barreau*, 1 May 1997: 20.

[39] M. Lebel, *La Presse*, 17 Oct. 1996: B2.

## 12. What will the international community do?

[1] Tomuschat, 18.

[2] H. Hannum, "Rethinking Self-Determination," *Virginia Journal of International Law* 34: 48.

[3] K. Valaskakis and A. Fournier, 171.

4 Young, 105.

5 S. Himmer, "The Achievement of Independence in the Baltic States and Its Justifications," *Emory International Law Review* 6 (1992): 272.

6 J. Webber, "Repression Is Not the Solution to Unity Crisis," *Gazette* [Montréal], 4 Dec. 1991: B3.

7 D. Turp, "L'étude des questions afférentes de la souveraineté," *Le Devoir*, 29 Aug. 1991: 15.

8 S.J. Anaya, R. Falk and D. Pharand, vol. 1, 23–4. Note that this convention came into force in 1991, but Canada has yet to ratify it.

9 T. Franck, "The Emerging Right to Democratic Governance," *American Journal of International Law* 86 (1992): 78.

10 Helsinki Document 1992, *The Challenge of Change*, rpt. in UN GAOR, 47th Sess., UN Doc. A/47/361 (1992) 65, para. 6 (29).

11 Conference on Security and Cooperation in Europe, *Document of the Moscow Meeting on the Human Dimension, Emphasizing Respect for Human Rights, Pluralistic Democracy, the Rule of Law, and Procedures for Fact-Finding*, 3 Oct. 1991, (1991) 30 ILM 1670, 1672.

12 European Parliament, *Resolution on Action Required Internationally to Provide Effective Protection for Indigenous Peoples*, European Parliament, Doc. (PV 58) 2, (1994) 3, para. 2.

13 See R. Barsh, "Indigenous Peoples in the 1990s: From Object to Subject of International Law?" *Human Rights Journal* 7 (1994): 33; also P. Joffe and M.E. Turpel, vol. 1, 146ff.

14 See J. Frowein, *Self Determination as a Limit to Obligations under International Law* in C. Tomuschat, 215.

## 13. Canada and Québec: Are these trustees trustworthy?

1 R. Mackie, "Québec Inuit Ask Ottawa to Save Them from PQ Plan," *Globe and Mail*, 9 Dec. 1994: A1; R. Séguin, "Stop Separatists, PM Urged," *Globe and Mail*, 14 Dec. 1994: A6; P. Cantin, "Les autochtones réclament l'intervention d'Ottawa pour contrer le projet péquiste," *La Presse*, 14 Dec. 1994: B1.

2 The customary legal term used is "fiduciary" responsibility, which is defined in the dictionary as "pertaining to a trusteeship." Since "trusteeship" is in more common everyday use, we use that word more often than "fiduciary."

3 D. Pharand, in S.J. Anaya, R. Falk, and D. Pharand, 79.

4 See Dupuis and McNeil, vol. 2, 67–68.

5 *Guerin v. The Queen*, (Supr. Ct. of Canada 1984) 13 DLR (4th) 321.

6 *Sparrow v. The Queen*, (Supr. Ct. of Canada 1990) 1 SCR 1075.

7 Ibid, 1108.

[8] P. Hogg, paper presented at the Conference on Law, Democracy and Self-Determination, Canadian Bar Association, Ottawa, May 1997, 25.

[9] P. Monahan, 1995, 27. Also E.J. Arnett, "The Law Is on Canada's Side, Not the Separatists'," *Globe and Mail*, 3 Jan. 1995: A17.

[10] Royal Proclamation of 1763, RSC 1985, App. 2, No. 1.

[11] B. Slattery, "First Nations and the Constitution: A Question of Trust," *Canadian Bar Review* 71.261 (1992): 271–72.

[12] See, for example, J. Parizeau, *Pour un Québec souverain* (Montréal: VLB Éditeur, 1997), 295, where it is erroneously said that Ottawa abandoned its fiduciary duties in relation to the Crees and Inuit. Parizeau adds that "such things as disagreeable as they might be for certain people, must be said. We live in a State of law."

[13] *James Bay and Northern Québec Native Claims Settlement Act*, SC 1976–77, c. 32, s. 7, preamble.

[14] *Guerin v. The Queen*, op. cit. n.4.

[15] Dupuis and McNeil, op. cit. n.4, 52.

[16] For example, the Rupert's Land and North-Western Territory Order, 1870.

[17] Dupuis and McNeil, op. cit. n.4, 52.

[18] B. Slattery, op. cit., n.11, 274.

[19] P. Joffe and M.E. Turpel, vol. 1, 279–80.

[20] D. McRae, *Report on the Complaints of the Innu of Labrador to the Canadian Human Rights Commission*, Ottawa, 18 Aug. 1993, 5.

## 14. Time to question Québec's use of the five experts

[1] T. Franck, R. Higgins, A. Pellet, M. Shaw, and C. Tomuschat, *Commission d'étude des questions afférentes à l'accession du Québec à la souveraineté, Les Attributs d'un Québec souverain* (Québec: Bibliotheque Nationale de Québec, 1992), vol. 1 of *Exposés et études*. For an English translation of the study see T. Franck et al., "The Territorial Integrity of Québec in the Event of the Attainment of Sovereignty," World Wide Web (Internet), http://www.mri.gouv. qc.ca/etiqeaso.htm.

[2] Annex I, Mandate to the five experts, 4 Mar. 1992. Letter signed by Francois Geoffrion, secretary of the commissions determining the political and constitutional future of Québec.

[3] The official list of documents furnished by the National Assembly secretariat to the five experts is set out in the five-expert study at 453, Annex III.

[4] T. Franck, et al., 425.

[5] Ibid, 444; also 385.

[6] Ibid, 380, where it is said that Professor Pellet drafted the study in close cooperation with the four other signatories.

7 Jurist H. Hannum in an article questions Pellet's opinion that the Badinter decisions provided Yugoslavia with a "second breath"; on the contrary, Hannum wrote, they were more like the "last gasp of the Austro-Hungarian and Ottoman empires." See A. Pellet, "The Opinions of the Badinter Arbitration Committee: A Second Breath for the Self-Determination of Peoples," *European Journal of International Law* 3.178 (1992); and Hannum, "Self-Determination, Yugoslavia and Europe: Old Wine in New Bottles?" *Transnational Law and Contemporary Problems* (1993): 63ff., and "Rethinking Self-Determination," *Virginia Journal of International Law* 34 (1993): 55.

8 T. Franck et al., op. cit. n.4, 379.

9 Ibid, 444.

10 Ibid, 411.

11 M. Coon Come, Canadian Bar Association, 7 June 1995, 13 (speaking notes on file with the Grand Council).

12 T. Franck et al., op. cit. n.4, 443.

13 See R. Falk, in S.J. Anaya, R. Falk, et al., 67–68.

14 T. Franck et al., op. cit. n.4, 389, 438.

15 Ibid, 441–42.

16 Ibid, 422–23.

17 Ibid, 390.

18 For a discussion of Aboriginal peoples and colonialism, see for example P. Joffe and M.E. Turpel, vol. 2, sub-heading 8.1. Also R. Falk, op. cit. n.13, 70.

19 C. Iorns, "Indigenous Peoples and Self-Determination: Challenging State Sovereignty," *Case W. Reserve Journal of International Law* 24 (1992): 296–97.

20 S.J. Anaya et al., vol. 1, 98.

21 P. Russell, *The End of Mega Constitutional Politics in Canada?* McRoberts and Monahan, 219.

22 B. Bella Petawabano et al., *Mental Health and Aboriginal People of Québec/ La Santé mentale et les autochtones du Québec* (Boucherville, Québec: Gaetan Morin Éditeur, 1994; publication of Le Comité de la santé mentale du Québec.

23 On this subject, see also L. Bissonnette, "Une décolonisation intérieure," editorial, *Le Devoir*, 26 Nov. 1996: A8.

24 T. Franck et al., 1992, 424.

25 T. Franck, 1995, 160. See also Cassese, 251–52, where he observes: "It should be added that, strikingly, these commentators [mostly of Québécois origin], while they advocate self-determination for Québec, refuse any similar right for the indigenous populations of the region . . . for whom they are prepared to recognize only 'aboriginal self-government.'"

# 15. Twenty-one drastic impacts of secession on Aboriginal peoples

1 Hartt, 1995.

2 Not all indigenous peoples recognize or choose to accept the citizenship of the State in which we live. Moreover, where State citizenship is accepted by indigenous peoples, it is generally acknowledged that the overall relationship is collective in nature. Nationality or citizenship questions are only one important dimension of a broader context.

3 For legal aspects of this subject see J. Woehrling in J.-Y. Morin and J. Woehrling, 115; D. Turp, Kaplan, 185ff.; D. Johnson, Kaplan, 364; Hartt 1995; the Universal Declaration of Human Rights, United Nations *General Assembly Resolution* 217 A (III), UN Doc. A/810, 71 (1948), adopted 10 Dec. 1948; International Convention for the Elimination of All Forms of Racial Discrimination, 660 UNTS 195, (1966) 5 ILM 352, adopted by UN General Assembly 21 Dec. 1965, opened for signature 7 Mar. 1966, and entered into force 4 Jan. 1969; J. Chan, "The Right to Nationality as a Human Right: The Current Trend Towards Recognition," *Human Rights Law Journal* 12.1 (1991); F. de Castro, *La nationalité, la double nationalité et la supranationalité, Receuil des cours* 102.515 (1961).

4 J.-Y. Morin and J. Woehrling, 1994, 137.

5 Such action is recommended by jurist J. Woehrling, *La Presse*, 24 Feb. 1995: B3. Recognition of Aboriginal rights was also promised in Parizeau's 1994 draft *Act Respecting the Future of Québec*.

6 For example, even if Québec's new constitution were to adopt the same language as Section 35 of the *Constitution Act, 1982*, and recognize existing aboriginal and treaty rights, other instruments which now form part of our rights, such as the Royal Proclamation of 1763, would not be included.

7 These include the Inuit of the Belcher Islands, the Inuit of Labrador, and the Crees of Mocreebec, in north-eastern Ontario. In addition at least seventeen First Nations in Ontario have a direct territorial interest in Québec, arising from history and/or geography, but not all of these will have claims in northern Québec.

8 Christine Cantin, of the Québec energy and resources department, made the statement at a conference in her address, *Rights of Aboriginal Peoples and Exploitation of Resources. Aboriginal Rights and the Law*, Canadian Council on International Law, Ottawa, 1993.

9 It is important to note that the 1970 UN *Declaration on Friendly Relations between States* requires independent States be "possessed of a government representing the whole people belonging to the territory without distinction as to race, creed or colour." This has been interpreted by Erica-Irene Daes, the lawyer and diplomat who has been chairperson of the UN Working Group on the draft *Declaration of the Rights of Indigenous Peoples*, as meaning that

"distinct groups . . . have the right to share power and be included in the running of the State." See, I.-E. Daes, "Some Considerations on the Rights of Indigenous Peoples to Self-Determination," *Transnational Law and Contemporary Problems* 3 (1993): 8.

¹⁰ Specifically, Suzanne Tremblay, separatist Bloc Québécois MP. See "Bloc MP Objects to Use of Inuit Language in Commons," *Gazette* [Montréal], 13 June 1995: A8.

¹¹ L.-G. Francoeur, "Le PQ décote Bouchard," *Le Devoir*, 17 June 1997: A1.

¹² H. Brun, in Gagnon and Rocher, 79, has proposed that the constitution of a sovereign Québec guarantee that no amendments to the constitutional rights of Aboriginal peoples be permitted without Aboriginal consent.

¹³ The Royal Commission on Aboriginal Peoples in 1996 recommended that the Supreme Court of Canada should have at least one Aboriginal member. Vol. 5, c. 5.

¹⁴ See, for example, P. Dionne, *Les postulats de la Commission Dorion et le titre aborigène au Québec: vingt ans après, R. v. B.* 51.127 (1991), where the author describes the often narrow interpretations by Québec courts of Aboriginal peoples' rights in the Royal Proclamation of 1763.

¹⁵ B. Bisson, "Francophones et anglophones ont des vues opposés sur les autochtones," *La Presse*, 11 Mar. 1994: A1.

¹⁶ R. Penner, former Attorney-General of Manitoba, in *British Columbia: Delgamuukw v. The Queen* (Montréal: Institute for Research on Public Policy, 1992), 242–52.

## *16. Québec separatists: world-class in double standards, inconsistencies, and discrimination*

¹ R. Guglielmo, *Three Nations Warring in the Bosom of a Single State: An Exploration of Identity and Self-Determination in Québec,* Fletcher Forum of World Affairs 21 (1997): 217.

² S. Dion, "Au-delà des arguties constitutionnelles, l'identité québécoise se porte bien," *La Presse*, 21 Sept. 1995: B3.

³ J. Gray, "Crees Call PQ Plan . . . a Fraud on Canada's Aboriginal People," *Globe and Mail*, 22 Sept. 1995: A4.

⁴ Sec. 8. Québec National Assembly, 1st Sess., 35th legislature, tabled by Premier Parizeau, 7 Sept. 1995, died on order paper, December 1995.

⁵ *Motion for the Recognition of Aboriginal Rights in Québec,* National Assembly of Québec, adopted 20 Mar. 1985. This resolution violated the commitment given by Premier René Lévesque to table a resolution on this matter only with the consent of the Aboriginal peoples concerned. Although there were no compelling reasons for this breach of faith, the Assembly passed a unilaterally revised version that was to the government's own liking.

# Bibliography

"International Norm on Self-Determination." *Transnational Law and Contemporary Problems* 3 (1993): 131.

___ . "Indigenous Rights Norms in Contemporary International Law." *Arizona Journal of International and Comparative Law* 8 (1991): 1.

___ . "The Native Hawaiian People and International Human Rights Law: Toward a Remedy for Past and Continuing Wrongs." *Georgia Law Review* 28 (1994): 309.

Anaya, S.J., R. Falk, and D. Pharand. *Canada's Fiduciary Obligation to Aboriginal Peoples in the Context of Accession to Sovereignty by Québec.* Ottawa: Minister of Supply and Services, 1995.

Armitage, A. *Comparing the Policy of Aboriginal Assimilation: Australia, Canada, and New Zealand.* Vancouver: U of British Columbia P, 1995.

Balthazar, L. "Les Nombreux visages du nationalisme au Québec." *Québec: État et société.* Ed. A.G. Gagnon. Montréal: Québec/Amérique, 1994. 23.

Barsh, R. "Indigeneous Peoples in the 1990s: From Object to Subject of International Law?" *Harvard Human Rights Journal* 7 (1994): 33.

Bayefsky, A.F. *International Human Rights Law: Use in Canadian Charter of Rights and Freedoms Litigation.* Toronto:

Bearskin, J., G. Lameboy, R. Matthew, Sr., J. Pepabano, A. Pisinaquan, W. Ratt, and D. Rupert. *Cree Trappers Speak.* Chisasibi, PQ: James Bay Cree Cultural Centre, 1989.

Beaudoin, G.-A. *La Constitution du Canada.* Montréal: Wilson and Lafleur, 1990.

Bouchard, L., ed. *Un nouveau parti pour l'étape décisive.* Québec: Fides, 1993.

Boyer, P. *Lawmaking by the People: Referendums and Plebiscites in Canada.* Toronto: Butterworths, 1982.

Brûlmann, C., R. Lefeber, and M. Zieck, eds. *Peoples and Minorities in International Law.* Boston: Kluwer Academic, 1993.

Brossard, J. *L'Accession à la souveraineté et le cas du Québec.* 2nd ed. Montréal: Les Presses de l'Université de Montréal, 1995.

Brownlie I. *Principles of Public International Law.* 4th ed. Oxford: Clarendon, 1990.

Brun, H. *Le Territoire du Québec.* Québec: Les Presses de l'Université Laval, 1974.

Brun, H., and G. Tremblay. *Droit constitutionnel.* 2nd ed. Cowansville, PQ: Blais, 1990.

Bryant, M. "Crown-Aboriginal Relationships in Canada: The Phantom of Fiduciary Law." *University of British Columbia Law Review* 27 (1993): 19.

Buchanan, A. "Québec, Secession and Aboriginal Territorial-Consititution] 3 (Mar. 1992): 2.

———. "A Reply to Grand Chief Matthew Coon Come and Mr. David Cliche." *Network* [Newsletter of the Network on the Constitution] 5 (May 1992): 13.

———. *Secession: The Morality of Political Divorce from Fort Sumpter to Lithuania and Québec.* Boulder, CO: Westview, 1991.

———. "Self-Determination and the Right to Secede." *Journal of International Affairs* 45 (1992): 347.

Bucheit, L. *Secession: The Legitimacy of Self-Determination.* New Haven: Yale UP, 1978.

Cairns, A. "Why Is It So Difficult to Talk to Each Other?" *McGill Law Journal* 42 (1997): 63.

Cassese, A. *Self-Determination of Peoples: A Legal Appraisal.* Cambridge: Cambridge UP, 1995.

Cliche, D. "La Souveraineté du Québec et les nations autochtones." *L'Action nationale* 82.4 (Apr. 1992): 465.

———. "The Sovereignty and Territorial Integrity of Québec." *Network* [Newsletter of the Network on the Constitution] 5 (May 1992): 10.

Coon Come, M. "Consenting Partners: The James Bay Crees, Québec Secession and Canada." *If You Love This Country: Fifteen Voices for a Unified Country/Pour l'amour de ce pays: Quinze voix pour un Canada uni.* Toronto: Penguin, 1995. 93.

———. "The Crees, Self-Determination, Secession and of the Network on the Constitution] 5 (May 1992): 11.

———. "Self-Determination an Inherent Right of Indigenous Peoples." *Canadian Speeches: Issues of the Day* 5.9 (Jan. 1992): 13.

———. Speaking Notes for Grand Chief Matthew Coon Come. Canadian Bar Association, Toronto, 7 June 1995 (on file with the Grand Council of the Crees).

———. Speaking Notes for Submission to the Cree Eeyou Astchee Commisssion, Montréal, 21 Sept. 1995 (on file with the Grand Council of the Crees).

———. Speaking Notes for The Status and Rights of the James Bay Crees in the Contex of Québec Secession from Canada. Centre for Strategic and International Studies, Washington, DC, 19 Sept. 1994 (on file with the Grand Council of the Crees).

Crawford, J., ed. *The Creation of States in International Law.* Oxford: Clarendon, 1979.

———. *The Rights of Peoples.* Oxford: Clarendon, 1988.

Cukwurah, A.O. *The Settlement of Boundary Disputes in International Law.* Manchester: Manchester UP, 1967.

Daes, E.-I. "Some Considerations on the Right of Indigenous Peoples to Self-Determination." *Transnational Law and Contemporary Problems* 3 (1993): 1.

de Smith, S.A., and R. Brazier. *Constitutional and*

Derriennic, J.-P. *Nationalisme et démocratie: Réflexion sur les illusions des indépendantistes québécois.* Montréal: Boréal, 1995.

Diamond, B. Presentation by Chief Billy Diamond to the Eeyou Astchee Commission, 30 Aug. 1995 (on file with the Grand Council of the Crees).

Dion, L. *Le Duel Constitutionel Québec-Canada.* Montréal: Boréal, 1995.

Dion, S. "Antinationalisme et obsession constitutionnelle dans le débat référendaire." Text presented to Cité libre, Montréal, 12 Jan. 1995, and Ottawa, 18 Jan. 1995.

Drache, D., and R. Perrin, eds. *Negotiating with a Sovereign Québec.* Toronto: Lorimer, 1992.

Dumont, F. *Raisons communes.* Montréal: Boréal, 1995.

Dupuis, R., and K. McNeil. *Canada's Fiduciary Obligation to Aboriginal Peoples in the Context of Accession to Sovereignty by Québec.* Ottawa: Minister of Supply and Services, 1995.

Eastwood, Jr., L. "Secession: State Practice and International Law After the Dissolution of the Soviet Union and Yugoslavia." *Duke Journal of Comparative and International Law* 3 (1993): 299.

Fawcett, J.E.S. *The Law of Nations.* Middlesex: Penguin, 1971.

Finkelstein, N., G. Vegh, and C. Joly. "Does Québec Have Review 74 (1995): 225.

Franck, T. *Fairness in International Law and Institutions.* Oxford: Clarendon, 1995.

Franck, T., R. Higgins, A. Pellet, M. Shaw, and C. Tomuschat. Commission d'étude des questions afférentes à l'accession du Québec à la souveraineté. *Les Attributs d'un Québec souverain.* Québec: Bibliothèque Nationale de Québec, 1992.

Frowein, J. "Self-Determination as a Limit to Obligations under International Law." *Modern Law of Self-Determination.* Ed. C. Tomuschat. Boston: Martinus Nijhoff, 1993. 211.

Gagnon, A.-G., and F. Rocher, eds. *Répliques aux détracteurs de la souveraineté du Québec.* Montréal: VLB, 1992.

Gowland-Debbas, V. *Collective Responses to Illegal Acts in International Law: United Nations Action in the Question of Southern Rhodesia.* London: Martinus Nijhoff, 1990.

Grand Council of the Crees (of Québec). Presentation to the Royal Commission on Aboriginal Peoples, Montréal, 28 May 1993.

____ . Presentation to the Royal Commission on Aboriginal Peoples, Montréal, 18 Nov. 1993.

____ . Remarks of Grand Chief Matthew Coon Come to the Canadian Club, Toronto, 13 Mar. 1995 (on file with the Grand Council of the Crees).

____ . *Sovereign Injustice, Forcible Inclusion of Nemaska*, Toronto: 1995.

____ . Submission: Status and Rights of the James Bay Crees in the Context of Québec's Secession from Canada. Submission to the UN Commission on Human Rights, Feb. 1992.

Hamilton, A.C. *Canada and Aboriginal Peoples: A New Partnership*. Ottawa: Minster of Public Works and Government Services, 1995.

Hartt, S. *Divided Loyalties, Dual Citizenship and Reconstituting the Economic Union*. Toronto: C.D. Howe Institute, 1995.

Hartt, S., et al., eds. *Tangled Web: Legal Aspects of Deconfederation*. Toronto: Renouf/C.D. Howe Institute, 1992.

Higgins, R. *Problems and Process: International Law and How We Use It*. Oxford: Clarendon, 1994.

Hogg, P. *Constitutional Law of Canada*. Toronto: Carswell, 1992. 2 vols.

____ . "Principles Governing the Secession of Québec. Law, Democracy, and Self-Determination. Canadian Bar Association and the University of Ottawa, U of Ottawa, 22-23 May 1997.

Howse, R., and A. Malkin. "Canadians Are a Sovereign People: How the Supreme Court Should Approach the Reference on Québec Secession." *Canadian Bar Review* 76 (1997): 186.

Joffe, P., and M.E. Turpel. Royal Commission on Aboriginal Problems and Alternatives. 3 vols. June 1995.

Johnson, W. *A Canadian Myth: Québec, Between Canada and the Illusion of Utopia*. Montréal/Toronto: Robert Davies, 1994.

Kaplan, W., ed. *Belonging: The Meaning and Future of Canadian Citizenship*. Montréal: McGill-Queen's UP, 1993.

Kingsbury, B. "Claims by Non-State Groups in International Law." *Cornell International Law Journal* 25 (1992): 481.

Lalonde, S. "Addendum and the Principle of Effectiveness." *Canadian Bar Review* 76 (1997): 258.

Lâm, M.C. "Making Room for Peoples at the United Nations: Thoughts Provoked by Indigenous Claims to Self-Determination." *Cornell International Law Journal* 25 (1992): 603.

Levin, M., ed. *Ethnicity and Aboriginality: Case Studies in Ethnonationalism*. Toronto: U of Toronto P, 1993.

Ligue des droits et libertés. La Ligue des droits et libertés et le dossier autochtone: Une histoire de persévérence. Mémoire présenté devant la Commission royale sur les peuples autochtones, 17 Nov. 1993.

Macklem, P. "First Nations Self-Government and the Borders of the Canadian Legal Imagination." *McGill Law Review* 36 (1991): 382.

___ . "Ethnonationalism, Aboriginal Identities, and the Law." *Ethnicity and Aboriginality: Case Studies in* 9.

MacLaughlan, H.W. "Accounting for Democracy and the Rule of Law in Québec Secession Reference." *Canadian Bar Review* 76 (1997): 155.

McNair, Lord. *The Law of Treaties.* 1961. Oxford: Clarendon, 1986.

McRoberts, K., and P. Monahan, eds. *The Charlottetown Accord, the Referendum and the Future of Canada.* Toronto: U of Toronto P, 1993.

Marchildon, G., and E. Maxwell. "Québec's Right of Secession under Canadian and International Law." *Virginia Journal of International Law* 32 (1992): 583.

Monahan, P. *Cooler Heads Shall Prevail: Assessing the Costs and Consequences of Québec Separation.* Toronto: C.D. Howe Institute, 1995.

Monahan, P., M. Bryant, and N. Coté. *Coming to Terms with Plan B: Ten Principles Governing Secession.* Toronto: C.D. Howe Institute, 1996.

Morin, J.-Y., and J. Woehrling. *Demain, le Québec: Choix politiques et constitutionnels d'un pays en devenir.* Québec: Septentrion, 1994.

Morse, B., ed. *Aboriginal Peoples and the Law: Indian, Métis and Inuit Rights in Canada.* Ottawa: Carleton UP, 1989.

Nguyen Quoc Dhin, P. Daillier, and A. Pellet. *Droit*

Nicholson, N. *The Boundaries of the Canadian Federation.* Toronto: Macmillan, 1979.

Parizeau, J. "The Case for a Sovereign Québec." *Foreign Policy* 99 (1995): 69.

___ . *Pour un Québec souverain.* Montréal: VLB, 1997.

Ratner, S. "Drawing a Better Line: Uti Possidetis and the Borders of New States." *American Journal of International Law* 90 (1996): 590.

Richardson, B. *Strangers Devour the Land.* 2nd ed. Vancouver: Douglas, 1991.

Rosas, A. "International Self-Determination." *Modern Law of Self-Determination.* Ed. C. Tomuschat. Boston: Martinus Nijhoff, 1993. 225.

Rotman, L.I. *Parallel Paths: Fiduciary Doctrine and the Crown-Native Relationship in Canada.* Toronto: U of Toronto P, 1996.

Royal Commission, Australia. *Royal Commission into Aboriginal Deaths in Custody, National Report.* Australia, 1991.

Royal Commission on Aboriginal Peoples, Canada. *Report of the Royal Commission on Aboriginal Peoples.* Ottawa: Canada Communication Group, 1996. 5 vols.

___ . *Treaty Making in the Spirit of Co-Existence: An Alternative to Extinguishment.* Ottawa: Minster of Supply and Services, 1995. Sovereign People? Toronto: U of Toronto P, 1992.

Sambo, D. "Indigenous Peoples and International Standard-Setting Processes: Are State Governments Listening?" *Transnational Law and Contemporary Problems* 3 (1993): 13.

Savard, R., and J.-R. Proulx. *Canada: Derrière l'épopée, les autochtones.* Montréal: Hexagone, 1982.

Schnapper, D. *La Communauté des citoyens: Sur l'idée moderne de nation.* Paris: Gallimard, 1994.

Schwimmer, É., avec M. Chartier. *Le Syndrome des Plaines d'Abraham.* Montréal: Boréal, 1995.

Scott, C. "Indigenous Self-Determination and Decolonization of the International Imagination: A Plea." *Human Rights Quarterly* 18 (1996): 814.

Shaw, M. *International Law.* 3rd ed. Cambridge: Grotius, 1994.

Slattery, B. "Aboriginal Sovereignty and Imperial Claims." *Osgoode Hall Law Journal* 29 (1991): 681.

Stavenhagen, R. *The Ethnic Question: Conflicts, Development and Human Rights.* Tokyo: United Nations UP, 1990.

Tomuschat, C. "Self-Determination in a Post-Colonial World." *Modern Law of Self-Determination.* Ed. Tomuschat. Boston: Martinus Nijhoff, 1993. 1.

___ , ed. *Modern Law of Self-Determination.* Boston: Martinus Nihjoff, 1993. *Québec: Texte annoté.* Cowansville, PQ: Blais, 1995.

Turpel, M.E. "Does the Road to Québec Sovereignty Run through Aboriginal Territory?" *Negotiating with a Sovereign Québec.* Toronto: Lorimer, 1992. 93.

Valaskakis, K., and A. Fournier. *Le Piège de l'indépendance: Le Québec sera-t-il affaibli par la souveraineté?* Montréal: Étincelle, 1995.

Webber, J. "The Legality of a Unilateral Declaration of Independence under Canadian Law." *McGill Law Journal* 42 (1997): 281.

Whiteman, M. *Digest of International Law.* Washington, DC: US GPO, 1963. 2 vols.

Williams, S. *International Legal Effects of Secession by Québec.* North York, ON: York U Centre for Public Law and Public Policy, 1992.

Woehrling, J. "Les Aspects juridiques d'une éventuelle sécession du Québec." *Canadian Bar Review* 74 (1995): 293.

Woodward, J. *Native Law.* Toronto: Carswell, 1989.

Young, R. *The Secession of Québec and the Future of Canada.* Montréal/Kingston: McGill-Queen's UP, 1995.

# Index